A THEORY
OF EDUCATION

BY **JOSEPH D. NOVAK**

WITH A FOREWORD
BY **RALPH W. TYLER**

CORNELL UNIVERSITY PRESS
ITHACA AND LONDON

For Joan

First published 1977 by Cornell University Press.
Second printing, 1979.
First published Cornell Paperbacks, 1986.

International Standard Book Number 0-8014-1104-1 (cloth)
International Standard Book Number 0-8014-9378-1 (paper)
Library of Congress Catalog Card Number 77-3123
Printed in the United States of America.
Librarians: Library of Congress cataloging information appears on the last page of the book.

Foreword

Many instructors, particularly those teaching science, mathematics, and the social studies, have wished for a comprehensive theory of learning and education that would furnish a consistent basis for explaining their successful efforts and guide their daily work. Joseph Novak has found this in the learning theory developed by David Ausubel, a theory that is much more than behavior modification or conditioning and more clearly relevant to inquiry learning, concept development, and problem solving. This book explicates more concretely the learning theory of Ausubel than Ausubel himself has done. It also reports research studies that show the relevance of the theory to school practice and provides many illustrations of its meaning and usefulness.

Joseph Novak is a major figure in the field of science education. His experience as a student of science and later as a science teacher stimulated his search for a theory of learning that is consistent with modern conceptions of scientific inquiry and his own observations of students in classrooms and laboratories. Ausubel's formulation seemed to answer this need. Novak spent several years testing the relevance and applicability of the major concepts to his observations and teaching activities. He also encouraged his graduate students to test the theory against their teaching practices. The results convinced Novak that the theory was a sound and comprehensive formulation helpful to teachers of various subjects, not only of science.

This book represents a significant and original contribution to the theory of school learning. Such a theory is a very central guide to the development of the curriculum and programs of instruction. Hence, it explicates a major sector of educational activity.

Readers concerned with teaching practices in any field of instruction will find the clarity of presentation and the concrete illustrations helpful in suggesting relevance to the widely varied situations found in schools and colleges. Instructors of educational psychology and of methods courses should find this book useful in clarifying and illustrating David Ausubel's writings. It is a volume deserving a place in one's own professional collection as well as a book for classroom and library use.

RALPH W. TYLER

Chicago, Illinois

Preface to the Paperback Edition

After the excitement in education generated by the Soviet launching of Sputnik in 1957 wore off in the late 1960s, much of schooling was essentially "business as usual." Concern centered on teaching the vast numbers of students and dealing with problems of minority education, inflation, and gradually tightening budgets. Despite substantial increases in federal funding of school programs and educational research and development, the flow of reports on the schools from the Silberman report (1970) to the flurry of recent reports showed no substantive change in schooling. In some respects our schools were less adequate than in the 1950s, at least when measured by the standards necessary for preparing students to compete in a technological society and in an economy under pressure from Far Eastern and European democracies. In the 1980s, economic competition with friendly countries, not competition with political adversaries, has led to concern with the quality of schooling. From 1956 to 1984 more money was spent on school, with a threefold increase in per-pupil expenditure in constant dollars; but for most schools no improvement in yield was evident (Goodlad, 1984). In the first edition of this book I contended that improvement in education was unlikely without changes generated from a viable, evolving theory of education. This continues to be my conviction.

Much work that is relevant to the thesis of this book has been done since 1977. In philosophy, a consensus emerges that positivism is neither a valid nor a productive view of epistemology, though positivism remains alive and well in most schools of education, psychology departments, and science texts and lectures. Popper (1982) claims that he "killed" positivism; and whether or not other philosophers agree, they subscribe to the obituary. What is emerging is a *constructivist* view of epistemology, building on ideas of Kuhn (1962), Toulmin (1972), and others and contending that humans construct knowledge using the concepts, principles, and theories they have, and change their *knowledge claims* as new ideas and associated methodologies lead to new constructions of how people and the universe operate. Articles in recent issues of the *Educational Researcher* and in books and other journals are recognizing the significance of this shifting epistemology. Brown (1979), Bernstein (1983), and others contribute to our understanding of constructivist epistemology, and recent books, such as Lincoln and Guba's (1985), show new ways to do educational research.

A similar situation prevails with regard to the psychology of learning. As early as 1967, Mandler declared that the promissory note of the behavioral psychologists turned out to be a "rubber check," at least with respect to learning of the type that takes place in schools. But behaviorism and derivative practices (such as rigid adherence to the use of "behavioral objectives) continue to be rampant in schools, and in military and industrial training programs. Resnick (1983), Pribram (1985), and many others observe that behavioral psychology, since it does not deal with the *meaning* behind the behavior, has little value in interpreting human learning, and they argue for the emerging "cognitive science" that focuses on how humans construct and use conceptual frameworks. But what is commonly ignored is that much of the methodology of popular cognitive science and artificial intelligence brands of psychology continues to be rooted in positivistic epistemologies. Increasingly our work shows the central importance of constructivist views of epistemology in guiding both educational research and practice. In my view, all courses in psychology dealing with human learning should explicate constructivist epistemology and discuss the constraints placed on methodologies (and research reporting) by positivist dogma. Any attempt to advance a theory of education must also be based firmly on constructivist views.

Has *A Theory of Education* made any difference? Although it is still early to expect a verdict, I believe there is evidence that the answer is yes. It has helped to make our research work more coherent and programmatic, leading in part to the refinement of an important research and teaching tool, the *concept map*. More than 100 able graduate students and visiting professors have been attracted to work with, and to extend, our research program since 1977. *A Theory* helped to stimulate Gowin (1981) to pursue his analysis of the structure of knowledge and to apply his ideas to the improvement of laboratory instruction, thus leading to his invention of the Vee heuristic. The Vee facilitates understanding the process of knowledge construction and the important role that theory and values play in that process. In working with the theory, concept maps, and Vee diagrams, our students observed that they were "learning how to learn," and in time we saw the value of using our research-based ideas and tools explicitly to help students learn how to learn. Ausubel's assimilation theory of learning has continued to be used and refined (Ausubel et al., 1978) in our research. This work and Gowin's contributed to my recent book with Gowin, *Learning How to Learn* (1984), which is also finding a place in teacher education and in instructional design for preschool to postgraduate students. Tentative evidence suggests that theory-based educational tools can help students learn how to learn in every field from chemistry and mathematics to linguistics and sports. The theory continues to evolve and to provide a basis for what Gowin and I describe as *theory-driven* research (Chap. 8) in contrast to *method-driven* research characterized by adherence to statistical procedures (such as meta-analysis) or evaluation measures (such as SAT tests, Likert scales), so often characteristic of positivistic research programs. This paperback edition provides a perspective to our current research in instructional practices that I hope will lead to substantive improvement of education and the criteria by which we judge excellence in education.

The concept map is proving to be increasingly useful in our work and is being adopted by students and teachers in many other countries. Its value inheres in part in its simplicity and yet in the profound meaning that can be conveyed on a single page. The key concepts and concept relationships necessary for understanding a course of study or a single lesson can be shown simply. Both teacher and learner can use the tool to show what valid and invalid concepts and propositions the learner already has, and teacher and student can use the maps to negotiate new meanings and to correct misconceptions.

The core of my beliefs is that "concepts are what we think with." As we change our concepts and conceptual frameworks in positive ways, we may or may not change our *behavior*, but the *meaning* of our experience changes and we act and feel able to do better. The goal of education is to empower humans to take charge of their own learning and acting and to choose courses of action that will help others to become empowered. I believe that *A Theory of Education* can continue to be of value. I thank the many graduate students and visiting professors who have challenged my thinking and helped me to learn, as well as made direct contributions to our research programs. I am especially grateful to David Ausubel and Bob Gowin, who continue as close friends and valued colleagues. I welcome criticisms and new insights from those who choose to employ the theory.

J.N.

Ithaca, New York

References

Ausubel, David P., Joseph D. Novak, and Helen Hanesian. 1978. *Educational Psychology: A Cognitive View*, 2d ed. New York: Holt, Rinehart, and Winston.

Bernstein, Richard J. 1983. *Beyond Objectivism and Relationism: Science, Hermaneutics and Praxis*. Philadelphia, Pa.: University of Pennsylvania Press.

Brown, H. I. 1979. *Perception, Theory and Commitment: The New Philosophy of Science*. Phoenix ed. Chicago: University of Chicago Press.

Goodlad, John I. 1984. *A Place Called School*. New York: McGraw-Hill.

Gowin, D. Bob. 1981. *Educating*. Ithaca: Cornell University Press.

Kuhn, Thomas S. 1962. *International Encyclopedia of Unified Science*, 2d ed. Enlarged vol. 2: *Foundations of the Unity of Science*, No. 2. Chicago: University of Chicago Press.

Lincoln, Yvonna S., and Egon G. Guba. 1985. *Naturalistic Inquiry*. Beverly Hills, Calif.: Sage.

Mandler, G. 1967. "Verbal Learning: Introduction," in *New Directions in Psychology III* by G. Mandler, P. Mussen, K. Kogan, and M. A. Wallach. New York: Holt, Rinehart and Winston.

Novak, Joseph, and D. Bob Gowin. 1984. *Learning How to Learn*. New York: Cambridge University Press.

Popper, Karl. 1982. *Unending Quest: An Intellectual Autobiography*. London: Open Court.

Pribram, Karl A. 1985. "'Holism' Could Close Cognitive Era," *Monitor* 16(9), 5.

Resnick, Lauren B. 1983. "Mathematics and Science Learning: A New Conception. *Science, 220*, 477–478.

Silberman, Charles. 1970. *Crisis in the Classroom: The Remaking of American Education*. New York: Random House.

Toulmin, Stephen. 1972. *Human Understanding*. Vol. 1: *The Collective Use and Evolution of Concepts*. Princeton, N.J.: Princeton University Press.

Preface

This book addresses some educational questions that troubled me when I was a student in the Minneapolis public schools and during much of my adult life. Why do so many students learn so little? Why do schools seem to be so ineffective in helping people learn? The simplistic answers, that some students don't try to learn and some teachers don't try to teach, were not acceptable to me. Why do students have little motivation to learn and why are some teachers so ineffective? Two decades of work in educational research, teaching, teacher training, and curriculum development have led me to believe that the most important element for the improvement of education is the application of our growing understanding of the way people learn to curriculum, teaching, and the learning environment, including all forms of learning materials. This concern for the process of human learning, and especially concept learning, motivates my commitment to the theory of education presented here.

I believe that concepts are at the center of all human behavior, and we now have a powerful cognitive learning theory to guide our research and teaching efforts to improve concept learning. At present, schools fall far short of their potential for helping students to acquire useful concepts and, consequently, more positive attitudes toward themselves and other people. We can take positive and specific steps to improve concept learning, for now sufficient theory is available to us to guide our work. We do not have at this time an equally viable theory for affective growth, so we must rely on the judgments of sensitive educators to guide our practices. Unfortunately, such judgments often conflict, and there are few good empirical tests to guide our decisions.

Most of my new ideas over the past twenty years have come from lively dialogue with my colleagues, especially my graduate students. Only a few of those who have contributed to my thinking can be cited in this book. The theory of education presented here is not the product of a single person's work, but rather is drawn from the creative minds of many people. The theory is not complete, but only obsolete theories cease to grow and evolve. This book represents a status report on the theory of education that guides my work.

We are all forced to think with the concepts that are familiar to us, for we think with concepts and we cannot use those we do not know. The theory of education presented here grows out of my work in science education and from occasional experiences with other disciplines. Students from other areas, however, have contributed to the theory and have found it valuable. I believe the theory is viable for the sciences, mathematics, and the social sciences, and has some validity in the humanities. It is offered in its present form—as is any theory—to be used, expanded, and modified as experience warrants. In time, this theory will be discarded—as are all theories.

It is my hope that the theory will contribute to the improvement of education, and thus to the improvement of the human condition. As populations continue to grow and as food and other resources become increasingly scarce, peoples of the world face challenges that our present educational efforts cannot meet. We must improve the quality of education if the human race is to survive. I believe we can.

Many people have contributed to my work and to the ideas presented in this book. Some of my coworkers are mentioned in the text, but there are many others to whom I am indebted, including some who have given strong emotional support when it was needed. Dr. Nyle Brady encouraged me to use a 1973/74 sabbatical and study leave to write the first draft, and Cornell University has been a good intellectual home for my work. Funds from Shell Companies Foundation and from Hatch Act grants have been helpful, together with support from the Department of Education and the Physics Department of Cornell and from the Ithaca City School District.

Permission to use materials has been granted as indicated in the text. Typing and other tasks associated with preparation of the several revisions of this manuscript have been competently done by Maureen Mitchell, Nina Smith, Patti Farrell, Lois Yennie, and Sid Doan. The staff of Cornell University Press has been helpful and generous with its support. Finally, I very much appreciate Dr. Tyler's taking time from a busy schedule to prepare the Foreword.

JOSEPH D. NOVAK

Ithaca, New York

Contents

PART I

THE THEORY AND ITS IMPLICATIONS FOR SCHOOLING

The first part of this book presents a coherent theory of education and shows briefly how this theory has implications for the improvement of school programs. The theory draws together concepts from philosophy relevant to education, the psychology of human learning, curriculum theory, and instructional theory. Although some research evidence is cited, most discussion of empirical studies is reserved for Part II.

CHAPTER 1

An Overview

Almost every parent, student, teacher, school administrator, teacher educator, and educational researcher has at least on some occasions felt hopeless about the future of education. We have witnessed innovation after innovation, and yet the basic problems in teaching and learning persist. By the criterion of technological advancement, our schools have been enormously successful, but nagging questions remain concerning the quality of our educational efforts and the quality of life in such "developed" societies as our own. Substantial improvement in educational practices and attendant improvement in the lives of educated people are not likely to occur without a workable theory of education and without the new educational practices that can be derived from such a theory. This theory of education must have at its center a model of human learning.

Every culture has a framework of concepts and practices. The task of education is to transmit to the children in that culture the concepts and practices they will need as adults. Concepts and practices change over time, however, so education not only must include careful selection of those that are of most lasting value, but also must assist children in acquiring the capacity to generate and use new ones. Theories are based on the concepts and practices that exist at one point in time, so inevitably theories will also change. We have witnessed most dramatic changes in scientific theory over the past four centuries, and we shall certainly witness changes in educational theory in the future. The value of theories derives less from their permanence than from their contribution to the generation of new and better concepts and practices.

I must define a few terms that will be used throughout this book: facts, concepts, and theories.[1] Facts are records of events. An event can be a lightning bolt, the movement of a dial on an instrument, a student's response to a question, or the writing of a line of poetry. Facts are the records of events that occur in the world, but we should recognize that facts are no better than the persons or instruments that record events. Concepts describe some regularity or relationship within a group of facts and are designated by some sign or symbol. Thus, red is a concept describing the regularity of color, but the label "red" is also used to describe a regularity in the political stance of an individual or group. In the former case the concept red is comparatively simple, but it may take years of study to understand the political connotations of red. Theories serve to link concepts or to suggest ways in which concepts may be related. Theories are like higher order concepts in that they may suggest order or relationships between less inclusive concepts. For example, we can speak of the *concept* of organic evolution or the *theory* of organic evolution, referring in either case to the concepts of mutation, species, change, and time that together comprise this concept or theory.

In the past century we have generated many concepts relevant to education: I.Q., underachiever, curriculum, creativity, motivation, problem solving, and more. We lack a coherent theory to relate these concepts to each other and help us to modify or discard some of them and invent others. Books on educational theory have been published, but they have failed to accommodate many of the concepts that should be most influential in educational planning. And in education, as in any endeavor, *concepts are what we think with.* If we cannot get our concepts clarified and organized, our thinking remains muddled and we are successful neither in solving problems nor in generating new concepts that would help us solve them.

Education is an area of work through which one can hope to improve the quality of life. We have become the dominant form

---

[1] I am indebted to D. Bob Gowin for much counsel and assistance in clarifying my understanding of these terms.

of life on earth through the capabilities of our brains. The vast store of knowledge accumulated in human cultures and transmitted to our youth allows us to live comfortably under a variety of climatic conditions. But physical comfort does not necessarily imply personal happiness. "Advanced" societies have often achieved physical comforts through dire assault on natural resources and/or through subjugation of other people. The growth of science and technology has led to remarkable achievements—as evidenced by the air-conditioned automobile cruising on a superhighway—but what problems these "advances" have brought to our society! When critics label our technocracy as a "wasteland," they refer to a system bankrupt in its efforts to improve the *quality* of human life. They do not deny that science is important in our culture. As Theodore Roszak (1972) says, "Science is not, in my view, merely *another* subject for discussion. It is *the* subject. It is the prime expression of the West's cultural uniqueness, the secret of our extraordinary dynamism, the keystone of technocratic politics, the curse and the gift we bring to history" (p. xxiv).

Roszak and others who lead the counterculture movement against scientific objectivity and its product technology correctly identify many limitations of rational or objective methods of knowing. Roszak recognizes that knowledge gained through so-called objective methods is of limited validity, for as our models of the world and our instrumentation change, old "objective truths" are often discarded. He argues that the experience of the individual provides another kind of validity; it may not possess the "objectivity" of scientific or technological knowledge, yet it can be valuable in guiding actions. Roszak (1969) states:

This would mean that our appraisal of any course of personal or social action would not be determined simply by the degree to which the proposal before us squares with objectively demonstrable knowledge, but by the degree to which it enlarges our capacity to experience: to know ourselves and others more deeply, to feel more fully the awesomeness of our environment. This, in turn, means that we must be prepared to trust that the expanded personality becomes more beautiful, more creative, more humane than the search for objective correctness can make it. [pp. 236–237]

Too many people have been led to believe that science can solve all of our problems. The notion that it can was derived in part from a misunderstanding of the nature and limitations of science both by spokesmen for science and technology and by scientists themselves. When science is recognized as a framework of evolving concepts and contingent methods for gaining new knowledge, we see the very human character of science, for it is creative individuals operating from the totality of their experiences who enlarge and modify the conceptual framework of science.

So my position is that theory development, experimentation, and the development of interpretive models are needed and can be valuable to the advance of educational practice, provided we recognize the tentative and evolutionary character of the concepts we derive from them. The injection of scientific methods into education has been counterproductive not because "objective" approaches to educational problems have been inappropriate but because our views of the nature of "objective truth" and the methods of gaining new knowledge have been distorted.

Behaviorist psychologists have also argued that the study of education should be more "scientific." Their methodology, however, is rooted in a kind of experimentalism that was promoted by Francis Bacon 350 years ago and fails to recognize the complexity of the interactions among the experimenters' variables and the changes those interactions produce in the variables and in the concepts that govern their interpretations. This misunderstanding of the nature of scientific inquiry is so important to educational inquiry that I have devoted a chapter to it.

In summary, this book was written to encourage a more scientific study of educational problems—not a scientific study as methods of science are described in elementary textbooks, but rather a conceptual approach to understanding, which is now being recognized by leading philosophers as the essential basis for any human understanding. I shall present some empirical evidence in support of the concepts and theories advanced here, as well as the basic epistemological premises on which this work was founded.

The Need for a "Wholistic" Approach

The principal objective of this book is to show methods by which we can gain insight into human learning, particularly in the schools; so some of the theories of learning that are directed toward human subjects must be examined. Furthermore, empirically based arguments in support of a philosophical position or a learning theory require data from learning in schools if they are to be valid for school instruction. But schools are complex settings, and school instruction is governed by numerous antecedent conditions.

It thus becomes necessary to use some framework of analysis, and a model for curriculum and instruction will be discussed. Too, the use of experimental approaches to instruction raises social and political issues; an analysis of some major educational trends and issues in schools is required. Finally, the role of teachers, while it may take varying forms, will always be important. Throughout the book I have tried to provide commentary on implications for teacher roles or on issues being considered.

In recent years some of the best minds in education have been engaged in *policy studies*. The complex problems of school administration, local, state, and federal tax support for schools, the social settings of schools in our society, and the relationship of schooling to economic growth are indeed a fascinating challenge. We see one major defect in most of the writings on educational policy—they fail to recognize that our *primary* concern is with *learning*, and hence, every policy issue must take cognizance of the best that we now know about human learning. The intelligent people who are working to improve education through advocacy of new educational policies rightly recognize the bankruptcy of much previous educational research and curriculum development; we contend that the problem inheres in the theoretical bankruptcy of previous approaches and not in the lack of power that can derive from appropriate theory-based practices.

I fully recognize the audacity of attempting to describe and synthesize philosophical, psychological, sociological, pedagogical, curriculum, and teacher education issues in a single effort. I continue to see educational theory and practice as disjointed, and I view consequent educational innovations as a kind of "Brownian movement" (to borrow a phrase from Alvin Toffler's *Future Shock,* 1970)—changing, yes, but going nowhere. It appears to me that students of education, teachers, administrators, and lay people have been seriously searching for some coherent view of education. Crude though this synthesis may be, it may help to bring the subject into focus.

Philosophers Thomas Kuhn, Yehuda Elkana, and Stephen Toulmin

Every lawyer and judge has learned that the truthful statement "I saw it with my own eyes" does not necessarily indicate the truth of a witness's report; it indicates only the kind of cues to which the observer was sensitive at the time and suggests some of the biases of the witness' view of reality. Recent work in perceptual psychology has shown that what people recognize and observe in an experimental setting depends very much on their emotional and conceptual frameworks. All of us have had the experience of observing a familiar object or reading a familiar passage and seeing some element that we have never recognized before. As our conceptual· and emotional frameworks change, we see different things in the same material.

As Thomas Kuhn (1962, 1970) has pointed out, the history of science shows the changes that have occurred in the conceptual spectacles through which scientists have viewed reality. An Aristotelian sees rocks as falling to the earth because that is where rocks seek to go, whereas a contemporary physicist views the earth and rock moving together at a rate determined by their masses and velocities and by the distance between them. Both views are interpretations or "conceptual goggles," but, unlike the Aristotelian view, the modern view explains why a rock (or satellite) can stay in orbit around the earth. Kuhn has described the role of conceptual goggles—or, as he calls them, paradigms—in guiding the work of scientists. Kuhn shows how over the past millennium new paradigms have been developed by creative scientists when old paradigms failed to explain apparent inconsistencies in what scientists were observing and what they expected to see. Viewed with Aristotelian goggles, the sun is pulled around the earth in an invisible chariot, but through Copernican goggles the earth revolves around the sun, and through Einsteinian goggles the sun and earth are in motion relative to one another and to all other masses in the universe. That old goggles (paradigms) are not always joyfully discarded is evident in the travails of Galileo, threatened with death, and from the continuing resistance to evolution as a concept helpful in understanding the origins of human beings.

Yehuda Elkana (1972) agrees in general with Kuhn's stress on the importance of paradigms in the work of scientists, but he sees changes in paradigms as more gradual, more evolutionary than does Kuhn. Instead of conceiving of a "scientific revolution" in which an old paradigm is discarded and a new paradigm invented, Elkana contends that a kind of social evolution occurs, in which increasing numbers of scientists begin to see that more and more phenomena in a given field of inquiry are better explained by a new paradigm.

The differences between the thinking of Kuhn and Elkana are minor compared with the differences between their views and those of philosophers who place central emphasis on the research methodology used by scientists. For example, Karl Popper, in his widely cited *Logic of Scientific Discovery* (1934, 1959), describes the role of instrumentation, research protocols, and logical processes of scientific inference as one proceeds from observations to conclusions. Popper minimizes the conceptual framework of the scientist and stresses instead the scientist's methods of analysis, as if they were independent of the goggles he is wearing. The differences between the views of Popper and those of Kuhn and Elkana might be of only esoteric interest were it not for the fact that much federally supported curriculum development in this country has been carried out as if Popper were right and Kuhn were wrong. New math, science, and social science curricula developed in the 1960s have placed emphasis on "inquiry methods" and most have disregarded, disavowed, or been oblivious of the role of conceptual frameworks in the observation of phenomena and the acquisition of understanding. The money and prestige behind the curriculum projects in science and mathematics have attracted educators in other fields, and the current euphoria associated with "process methods" in social studies, language arts, and even humanities is partly the consequence of the 1960s "curriculum revolution" in science and mathematics.

Illuminating as the writings of Kuhn (1962, 1970) and others have been, a recent book by Stephen Toulmin (1972), the first in a three-volume series, gives added dimension to the nature of concepts and their role in human thought. Toulmin's views have exceedingly important implications for education. His description of the evolutionary character of concepts in society and the fundamental role that these concepts play in human understanding stand in contrast to the Kantian views of the human search for "absolute" truths expressed in the writings of Francis Bacon (1620, 1952), Karl Pearson (1900, 2d ed.) and Karl Popper (1934, 1959). Various forms of associationist or stimulus-response psychology are rooted in these obsolete epistemologies, but Skinnerian and other associationist psychologies continue to dominate educational psychology. Fortunately, an alternative exists in the work of David Ausubel.

David Ausubel: The Psychology of Learning

Most graduate students in my classes and seminars are surprised when they learn that we will study in depth the psychological theory of David Ausubel. "Who is he?" "Why Ausubel?" These are the questions raised by almost everyone, and no doubt by many readers of this book. I shall attempt to answer these questions fully in Chapter 3. At this point a brief overview of Ausubel's theory will suffice.

In the Preface of his *Educational Psychology: A Cognitive View* (1968), Ausubel states: "The most important single factor influencing learning is what the learner already knows. Ascertain this and teach him accordingly" (p. vi).

Simple as this statement appears, some profound issues are to be found in it. To ascertain what the learner already knows means to identify those elements in the learner's existing knowledge store that are relevant to what we hope to teach, or, in Ausubel's terms, to identify the relevant subsuming concepts that are available in the learner's cognitive structure.

Even the term *cognitive structure* has special meaning for Ausubel. He views the storage of information in the brain as highly organized, with linkages formed between various older and newer elements leading to a conceptual hierarchy in which minor elements of knowledge are linked with (subsumed under) larger, more general, more inclusive concepts. Thus cognitive structure represents a framework of hierarchically organized concepts, which are the individual's representations of sensory experience. (See Ausubel, 1968, p. 506.)

Since every individual has had a unique history of sensory experiences, we should expect that any specific element in an individual's cognitive structure is idiosyncratic; that is, the concepts of one individual are to some degree different from the concepts of another. These differences are usually not great enough to prevent communication; your concept of learning is close enough to mine that this "concept label" (learning) means to you approximately what I want to convey when I use the term. Another important idea in Ausubel's theory is the process of concept differentiation. As new experience is acquired and new knowledge is related to concepts already in a person's mind, these concepts become elaborated or altered, and hence they can be related to a wider array of new information in subsequent learning.

We see, then, that to "ascertain what a learner already knows" in an area of study requires that we determine the relevant concepts the learner possesses and the extent to which they are differentiated. This is no simple task.

What does Ausubel mean by "teach him accordingly?" Individuals can learn information that has little or no association with existing elements in cognitive structure; for example, they can learn to associate such nonsense syllables as LEU and JEX. In *rote* learning one acquires new information without specific association with existing elements (concepts) in cognitive structure. *Meaningful* learning occurs when new information is

linked with existing concepts (subsuming concepts or subsumers, in Ausubel's terms). According to Ausubel's view, new
information acquired in meaningful learning is stored in a
somewhat altered form (as a product of assimilation with the
subsuming concept[s]) and modifies (differentiates further)
the subsumers to which it is linked. Since subsuming concepts
can be substantially more differentiated in one individual than
in another, the same new material can be learned very meaningfully by one person and almost by rote by another. News
reports that a high-protein sorghum plant has been found may
have little meaning to the average citizen, but to a plant special-
ist this news connects with a whole panoply of concepts, from
selective breeding and hybridization to production of commer-
cial seed and resulting increases in production of plant protein.

Sometimes rote learning is desirable. If I give a person my
phone number, I don't want him to remember that it is a Murray Hill number in the upper five thousands. Anything other
than the precise number will not suffice to call my home. Most
of the things we consider important to transmit to students,
however, do not require subsequent recall in a form identical to
that in which they are presented, even though much of school
teaching and testing appears to contradict this view. If we teach
students that photosynthesis is the process by which plants convert light energy into food, it should be quite acceptable if they
define photosynthesis as "a food-making process in plants that
utilizes light energy." If the concept of photosynthesis is to be
learned *meaningfully,* however, the student must have some
available concept of plant, food, light, energy, and making or
converting. If we do not want a definition of photosynthesis to
be learned by rote, we must ascertain to what degree the associated subsuming concepts are present and developed or differentiated.

Not all information received by the brain derives from external stimuli. Some information is received from sources internal
to our bodies, as from our muscles, which signal positions or
stresses. Some internally derived information is categorized as
pleasure or pain. Storage and assimilation of information from
our muscles, together with externally derived information, are

important in *skill learning*—learning to swim, for example, or play golf, or pipette a solution. Internally derived signals of pleasure or pain are categorized as *affective* stimuli that are recognized as emotions or *affective learning*. Affective learning is associated with skill learning and cognitive learning. Thus we can learn to "love" golf or "hate" mathematics because we have acquired a positive affective store (positive attitude) with respect to golf and a negative affective store with respect to math.

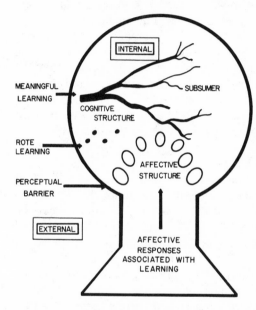

Figure 1.1. Schema of cognitive learning (rote and meaningful) derived from external sources through perceptual barriers, and affective learning derived from internal sources. Affective structure cannot be defined theoretically at this time, but it is postulated that some form of information from internal (emotional) signals is stored in the brain.

Figure 1.1 shows rote, meaningful, and affective learning in schematic form. This book will deal primarily with methods for understanding and facilitating cognitive learning, but some consideration will be given to motor or skill learning and especially to affective learning, for they have much significance for education.

Robert Gagné, Jean Piaget, Jerome Bruner, B. F. Skinner, and others who have studied cognitive learning are much better known in the United States than David Ausubel. In Chapter 4, I shall try to show how important elements from other psychologies fit into an Ausubelian theoretical framework and how this framework can be used to design better educational experiences and better educational research. Just as research in science leads to clarification and elaboration of theory and improved technology, research in education too should clarify, extend, and modify theory and suggest improvements in instructional practices. In time, of course, all theories become overburdened and fail to explain important observations; then the ground is prepared for what Kuhn calls a paradigm shift or "scientific revolution." The creative genius needs only to formulate a new theory or paradigm that explains the discrepant observations as well as the phenomena that are explained by the old theory. The history of education, unlike the history of science, does not reveal a succession of creative minds devising new and increasingly powerful theories. Is it that education cannot be like science or is it that education, like biology up to the nineteenth century, has been a field of inquiry without paradigms?

Current Issues in Education

Should compulsory education be required only to the age of twelve or fourteen? Should students have more freedom to determine how their time is spent in school? Should schools be abolished? These questions are at the core of many educational issues, and in my view they signal the substantive failure of our educational system to provide enough successful cognitive, affective, and motor learning experiences to our young people. Despite the growth of school costs—from $253 per pupil in 1930 to $1,188 per pupil in 1970, in 1970 constant dollars—the value of schooling is increasingly questioned. More money spent on education may be helpful but statistics argue against this proposition; what is needed is better use of our fiscal, human, and physical resources. We cannot continue to jump from one administrative scheme to another (from the traditional class structure of the 1930s and 1940s to team teaching in the 1950s to bussing of school children to achieve racial balance in the 1960s and 1970s), from one curriculum emphasis to another (from "life adjustment" education in the 1930s to academic excellence to beat the Russians in the 1950s and 1960s) or from one pedagogical panacea to another (from the pressure for all teachers to have at least a B.S. degree in the 1950s to present concerns for sensitivity training and encounter sessions for teachers). Nor can big technology step in to solve problems that educators have failed to solve, as General Electric, Xerox, International Telephone and Telegraph, Westinghouse, and many other companies have learned to their economic misfortune. All these efforts have missed what should have been the focus of attention—children and how they learn.

When the immense universe of educational issues is observed even casually, one can be overcome by a sense of futility. Jonathan Kozol's *Death at an Early Age* (1967), John Holt's *How Children Fail* (1964), and Ivan Illich's *Deschooling Society* (1970) convey a sense of hopelessness about existing schools in a way that captures the sympathy of any open-minded observer. These and other writers have tried to offer solutions for our educational problems; I find unpersuasive Holt's *How Children Learn* (1967), Kozol's *Free Schools* (1972), and Everett Reimer's *School Is Dead* (1971). These writings, while showing insight and sensitivity toward children, provide no theoretical framework for learning with consequent implications for education. Collectively, the authors can only hope that their seat-of-the-pants intuition is better and more convincing than that of other educational leaders. I applaud their insights and commend their writings, but we need more than good personal intuition to make substantial advances in the quality of education.

With dozens of books directed at such issues as racial discrimination in schools, with dozens more concerned with the merits of tracking versus homogeneous classes, with hundreds of books promulgating television, media-equipped learning centers, and the value of computer-assisted instruction, to say nothing of the hundreds promoting one form or another of teacher education and certification, it is obvious that this one book cannot speak specifically to all educational issues. I repeat, many educational issues have a better chance of resolution if we can understand in a *basic* way how children learn. Societal and political attempts to solve school problems will have a greater chance of success if they grow from consideration of alternatives that are reasonably consonant with what we know about the process of learning. Throughout this book I shall be referring to educational issues that are particularly relevant to the discussion of the learning process and instructional design.

Evolution in School Programs

Schools are a reflection of society. They are in general no better and no worse than the society that supports them. The plush suburban community has plush schools; students in these schools may value good grades over experience, so that they can go to college and emulate their parents, who value two cars and a large home more than family vacations together or day-to-day associations that take time away from television or golf. If a society is prejudiced and bigoted, we see prejudice and bigotry in the schools. How, then, do school programs advance to improve the quality of life? It is in part a chicken-and-egg problem; do we improve society to improve schools, or do we improve schools so that the graduates move out to improve society? Where do we break into the cycle?

In one area, racial discrimination, the impetus for the visible change that has occurred has come not from educators but from politicians and judges. The politician appears to have the best lever to effect positive social change; but although political action can affect access to education and the fiscal support of education, ultimate improvement in the quality of education per se is principally the domain of the educator.

Without question the greatest influence on societal change has been technological advance. So, too, most visible changes we see in schools are the results of technological innovation. This does not mean that people are happier in present-day society or that students are happier. (The third-ranking cause of death among teenagers in New York State is suicide.) As Roszak and others argue, big technology may have caused big social change, but this change has not brought overflowing happiness to our citizenry. Toffler maintains that technologically induced social change has brought a kind of general psychosis of apprehension toward change, a condition he calls "future shock." The 1972 elections returned a Democratic Congress and a Republican president and vice-president in a kind of voter attempt to stop the world, much to the chagrin of many concerned citizens in 1973. Apprehension regarding "unknown" Jimmy Carter as an alternative to known but "uninspiring" President Ford led to a narrow plurality for Carter when other Democratic candidates were returned to the House and Senate with overwhelming pluralities.

The planet Earth is finite; it is our home; its resources, except for solar energy, are limited. For the past fifty years, technological advance, exploitation of resources, and growth in gross national product (the value of all goods and services sold) have dominated societal change. For many reasons, we are witnessing the decline of the "growth" ethic as a principal value in society. Not all countries who want power can burn twenty million barrels of oil each day, as we do in the United States. Rather than the past exponential increase, we may see a reduction in the use of oil in the United States during the 1970s. More and more families may ask if they need two big cars, or even two "economy" cars. With more societies demanding access to the limited resources of the world, the present high rate of inflation is not likely to decline, and will bring crushing economic problems to nations, cities, and many families. While I share reservations that have been expressed about the dire predictions in Meadows et al., *The Limits to Growth* (1972), it appears possible that in the future social change may be governed more by scarcities than by technological growth. This issue must be considered as we examine patterns of past and possible future educational changes.

If society moves increasingly from a growth or consumption ethic to a conservation ethic, we shall see decline in public support for more and fancier schools, smaller classes (that is, more teachers), college education for the majority of high school graduates, and expensive administrative and technological gimmicks. Already this trend is evident in the readiness of voters to turn down new school bond issues, in the halt in the decline of mean class size, and in the decline in the percentage of high school graduates who enroll in college. These changes do not mean that public concern for education is declining; they signal a more critical posture in which students, voters, and professionals are asking how available resources for education can be used to better advantage.

The most powerful and most broadly applicable concept in biology is that of evolution. In the history of life on earth we see patterns in changes that have occurred in plants and animals. To survive, any species must acquire sufficient energy to grow to maturity and must produce enough progeny so that the number of new reproducing individuals is at least equal to the number of dying individuals. The mechanisms that have evolved in plants and animals for capturing energy and for reproduction are diverse, but all of them work; the two and a half million species we see continue to survive (with a few exceptions). Birds have wings to move about, whereas fish have flat tails and fins. The fossil record shows that the bird has been with us for only about 100 million of the 4,500 million years of our planet's existence, and the bony fish for only about 400 million. Human types have been around for less than five million years. We see that the need for energy and reproduction for survival has been solved by varying structural forms.

Unlike patterns in life forms, the patterns of social and school structures are changing on a time scale of decades rather than millennia. Another important difference is that human beings can create social and school organizations. But our evolutionary spectacles should show that a variety of forms can survive provided each form meets certain minimum requirements and newer forms have some additional potentials for multiplication. Thus we should see that the one-room schoolhouse pattern is still viable, and that when it is combined with new learning resources available today, it is not much different from large "open classroom" schools where heterogeneous age grouping, pupil-pupil tutoring, and individualized programming are practiced. It is crucial for every pattern of schooling that opportunity be provided for cognitive learning and affective learning, including those behaviors needed to "socialize" a child. I shall examine in Chapter 7 elements in selected patterns of school organization that are consistent or inconsistent with what we now know about cognitive and affective learning, considering also that resources needed for education are limited. I shall try to show that some emerging patterns of individualized instruction, technological support for learning, school-building designs, and enhanced opportunities for affective experience are consistent with theories of cognitive and affective learning.

Empirical Studies and Their Implications

Historically, biology was a field of conjecture and speculation long after physics had moved to base most of its assertions on data open to interpretation by all members of the discipline. By 1930, however, most fields of biology also based assertions on evidence that had "intersubjective testability"; that is, any knowledgeable biologist examining the same data would arrive at the same conclusions. Differences in interpretation and speculation continue in valuable ways in all sciences, but these variances are found in "frontier" studies where clarification of principles is proceeding, or where major theoretical frameworks are in need of overhaul preceding what Kuhn calls a scientific revolution or paradigm shift.

Empirical evidence to support assertions in education has been lacking. There is some hope now that education can increasingly become a field where data may be brought to bear on many issues and where we can demand in many areas that assertions be accompanied by empirical evidence. We must not demand too much too soon. If education can become more like science (and many would contest that it should not), it will take time. Louis Pasteur had to demonstrate many times that wine was turned sour by microbes, not by evil spirits or some harmful "essence," before he was believed. The mass of evidence assembled by Charles Darwin in 1859 and thousands of studies since then still have not convinced some skeptics of the plausibility of evolutionary mechanisms. Although we can show only a few examples of empirical studies that clearly support some principle or theory of learning bearing on an educational problem, we should not discount the value of such achievement simply because enormously greater questions remain unresolved. If we take a lesson from science, we know that it is best to solve easy problems first. The more difficult questions may take more time. Darwin observed that species appeared to change, but he did not know why. Now that we know natural radiation can cause rearrangement of chemical coding elements in deoxyribonucleic acid (DNA), the hereditary material of all cells, we can answer questions on which Darwin could only speculate. The riddle of cell mutation and regulation of cell metabolism is not completely solved, for we would certainly have a cure for cancer if these data were in. Therefore, I need make no apologies for the fact that the research reported in this book, and other selected studies as well, leave whole groups of educational problems unanswered. We have comparatively hard data on some questions, and the set of reasonable answers narrows to a few alternatives on others. Donald Ring and I conducted a study that showed that achievement of college students in an introductory chemistry course appeared to bear a linear relationship to the knowledge of chemistry they had at the beginning of the course. This relationship is shown in Figure 1.2. Many questions remain to be answered: Was achievement proportional to "entry" knowledge because the college course was poorly taught? Was the apparent linear relationship an artifact of the way in which achievement was measured in the college course? (Numbers on the ordinate in Figure 1.2 represent total points earned in laboratory and lecture evaluations.) Could students with little initial knowledge of chemistry have demonstrated high achievement if they had had more time to study? These and other questions remain, but the data bear on some issues; for example, college professors frequently assert that college chemistry students who have not studied chemistry in high school are better off than those who have. I have seen no data to support such an assertion except the occasional observation that students may misjudge their adequacy in a subject, limit their study efforts and hence fail the course. Every chemist knows that individual cases do not produce the general rule. When water is boiling, molecules are escaping into the atmosphere, but some molecules are also entering the boiling water from the atmosphere. Pronouncements by professors that a student is better off if he starts a course knowing nothing make provocative rhetoric but do not square with the facts.

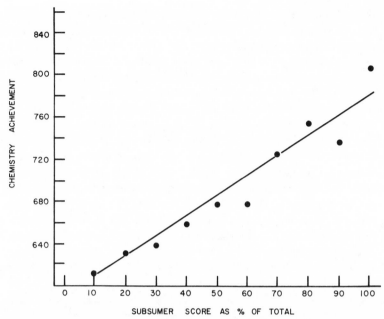

Figure 1.2. Achievement in college chemistry (indicated by total points earned during a semester on exams and quizzes) shown as strongly related to scores on a test to measure subsuming concepts of chemistry held by students at the start of the course. (n = 770)

I shall try to show in Chapter 2 that progress in science derives from answering questions in some kind of sequence, developing explanatory concepts as we proceed. If we gather more and more evidence indicating that achievement is proportional to the amount of relevant knowledge that students have as they commence an area of study, not only do we support Ausubel's theoretical structure, but we then can move profitably to other questions. What questions should be next? There is no ready answer; creative genius in science asks the *right* next questions, and in rare instances creates a new paradigm that leads to a whole new set of questions and answers. One thing is certain: we cannot continue to allow doctoral students to reach into the grab bag of educational research issues and pull out any project that meets their fancy. Most research in education is done by doctoral students and most of these studies lead us nowhere. We need long-term, carefully organized research programs led by committed scholars in education. We need substantially increased support for scholarly research in education. We must insist that the research support be rooted in sound educational theory and that it have some potential for modifying and improving this theory.

It is impossible to explicate in one book a philosophy of education, a psychology of learning, patterns of curriculum development and school organization, and empirical evidence that renders some alternatives more tenable than others; this book can be only a beginning. Although any discussion in these areas must necessarily be abridged, too many books on education have fragmented the field, and thoughtful lay people, students, and educators have been searching for some organic synthesis. The discussions of philosophy will omit much of value; the exposition of learning will skip over large bodies of relevant material; and considerations of curriculum will be heavy on the sciences and light in other areas. My only defense is that I believe we need an organic, integrative view of education to serve as a basis for better analysis of individual elements which can be expanded coherently in the future. Before my colleagues in education throw this intellectual baby out with the bath water, I beg them to ponder the potential of this theory of education.

CHAPTER 2

The Philosophical Basis for Education

The Problem of Knowledge

To say that we have been living in a period of knowledge explosion is to echo a truism. Measured by the number of professional journals published and scholarly papers written in almost any field, the growth in human knowledge has been explosive. If we could measure the growth of knowledge by its effect on human suffering, however, we would have to conclude that we have lost ground. While it is true that millions of people now enjoy comforts beyond those of kings and emperors of the past, more than a billion people are experiencing starvation or near starvation. Our knowledge explosion has permitted us to free slaves and serfs, but improved medical practice and lowered mortality rates have led to regional population growth vastly beyond the resources available to meet minimum human needs. Paul Ehrlich's *Population Bomb* (1968), Barry Commoner's *Closing Circle* (1971), and many other books warn that the use of new knowledge to reduce mortality and to exploit natural resources is heading us down the path to worldwide disaster.

The environmentalists, such as Ehrlich and Commoner, and the counterculture spokesmen, such as Roszak, are not alone in asking where our knowledge explosion is taking us. Many thoughtful scholars are concerned that new knowledge can lead to new tyranny. Increasing numbers of scholars and laymen are recognizing that the resources of the world are finite. To transport Western values and technology to underdeveloped nations will lead not only to destruction of their present cultural values but also to an impossible demand for the world's limited natural resources.

In his essay "The Problem of Knowledge" (1971), Elkana asserts that every culture has its own science. To export Western science and technology wholesale to other countries is to ignore the unique values of their conceptions of reality, and their indigenous problems. Western culture has changed over the past three hundred years and Western science has changed with it. We can supply Western science and technology to an underdeveloped country over a short span of time, but we cannot transform the values of these peoples in the same span of time. Moreover, we lose the knowledge that could be gained if Western science were allowed to interact with the indigenous science in a dialogue of competing systems.

Some of us who have been raised on textbook explanations of the "seven steps of the scientific method" may be shocked by Elkana's assertion that every culture has its own science, or even by the notion that the nature of Western science is changing, evolving with Western culture. Schools have been impressively successful in spreading the myth that science has a special method of arriving at truth, that scientific truth is free from value judgments, transcends all cultures, and holds for all time. Any discipline that cannot use the method of science, the myth holds, cannot establish "objective" knowledge; in short, the discipline cannot establish immutable truths. Given the historical fact that scientific "truth" has changed from the times of Copernicus, Galileo, Kepler, Newton, and Dalton, it seems incredible that the myth of immutable and culture-free science is so persistent. In the past decade a forceful assault has been made against this myth by leading historians and philosophers of science. The consequence is an emerging view of science as a human enterprise, evolving methods and conceptions as the sociology of the scientific community evolves. This view of science has highly significant implications for education, and especially for educational research. Not only have the history and philosophy of science been largely ignored in the field of educational philosophy, but what little has been taught often has been a liability to creative thinking (see Gowin, 1972).

We must pause briefly to trace the origins of the myth of scientific method, still so prevalent in society and in the field of education. It is important to know precisely which beliefs need to be discarded.

For almost two millennia, discourse on nature was limited largely to what had been written by Plato, Aristotle, Democritus, and Pliny. With the work of Copernicus in the sixteenth century and Galileo in the seventeenth, systematic observation of natural phenomena and development of explanations based on these observations led to the gradual abandonment of Greek and Roman writings as the sources of all knowledge. Heretical as these early observers were (recall that Galileo escaped burning at the stake for heresy by recanting his views), they laid the groundwork for a new approach in the search for explanations of natural phenomena. As the Renaissance progressed, the origins of modern science took shape from systematic observation and venturesome new interpretations in the fields of astronomy, human physiology, and physics, and in some areas of biology. Central to this development was the emphasis on careful observation and on what came to be known as the "experimental method." Galileo's famed demonstration that large stones fell just as quickly as small stones when dropped from the top of the Tower of Pisa nicely demonstrated how variation of a single factor (size of stones) could provide new information from observations.

Experimental science was first dogmatized by Francis Bacon in 1620. Here are two passages from his *Novum Organum* (1620, 1952):

The subtility of nature is far beyond that of sense or of the understanding; so that the specious meditations, speculations and theories of mankind are but a kind of insanity. [p. 107]

. . . But our hope of further progress in sciences will then only be well founded, when numerous experiments shall be received and collected into natural history, which, though of no use in themselves, assist materially in the discovery of causes and axioms; which experiments we have termed enlightening, to distinguish them from those which are profitable. They possess this wonderful property and nature, that they never deceive or fail you; for being used only to discover the natural cause of some object, whatever be the result, they equally satisfy your aim by deciding the question. [p. 127]

Bacon's writings help to move "natural philosophy" from discourse on the meanings of early Greek and Roman writings to emphasis on observation of nature and discourse on the meaning of these observations. He helped to accelerate the development of modern science, for systematic observation will probably always be of basic importance in science. Darwin himself took heed of Bacon's teachings, as illustrated in this description of his work: ". . . by collecting all facts which bore in any way on the variation of animals and plants under domestication and nature, some light might be thrown on the whole subject. My first notebook was opened in July 1837. I worked on true Baconian principles, and without any theory, collected facts on a wholesale scale . . ." (1897, pp. 67–68).

From 1620 on, the *Novum Organum* was probably the most influential writing on scientific method; that is, until 1892, when the first edition of Karl Pearson's *Grammar of Science* was published. Pearson was even more adamant than Bacon on the fundamental importance of observation. Here are a few passages from his *Grammar* (1900):

The unity of all science consists alone in its method, not in its material. The man who classifies facts of any kind whatever, who sees their mutual relation and describes their sequences, is applying the scientific method and is a man of science. [p. 12; italics in original]

. . . The civil law is valid only for a *special* community at a *special* time; the scientific law is valid for *all* normal human beings, and is unchanging. [p. 87]

. . . The right of science to deal with the beyond of sense-impressions is not the subject of contest, for science confessedly claims no such right. [p. 110]

. . . Science, as I have so often reiterated, takes the universe of perceptions as it finds it, and endeavors briefly to describe it. It asserts no perceptual reality for its own shorthand. [p. 181]

We see in the writings of Bacon and Pearson that the pursuit of science is primarily the dispassionate observation of nature. Moreover, it is assumed that all persons see the same events when they observe a phenomenon; personal experience, frames of reference, past conceptual development, emotional responses to a phenomenon—none of these should influence what the "scientific" observer sees. This is the myth that has been sold as *the* scientific method for generations.

Some very important developments occurred after the publication of Pearson's book. Albert Einstein published his theory of relativity (1905); Gregor Mendel's original (1859) papers were rediscovered early in the twentieth century and the science of genetics was born; in the same period the cell theory was elaborated, connecting the structures and functions of cells with those of organisms, and the science of psychology was developed; in 1930 the quantum theory was advanced. All of these developments put considerable strain on the Baconian view that science consists mainly of careful observation. It began to appear that much remained to be said about hypothesis and theory building, and about the testing of theories.

Continuing in the Baconian tradition, Karl Popper published *The Logic of Scientific Discovery* (1934, English translation 1959), in which he analyzed the methods by which science advances through the "falsification" of untenable hypotheses. Popper recognized that the stress on inductive reasoning from observed facts which characterized the philosophy of the positivists or logical positivists, as they were called, led to a trap, since one must finally deal with the question of what is a fact. To Popper, the positivists' view, common in the 1920s and 1930s, must lead to an infinite regress, in which the quest for the irreducible facts must at some point lead to a priori assumptions. The problem of what constitutes observable facts becomes inextricably confounded with the psychological problem of what it is we perceive.

As to his philosophical objective, Popper was explicit: "The central problem of epistemology has always been and still is the problem of the growth of knowledge. *And the growth of knowledge can be studied best by studying the growth of scientific knowledge*" (p. 15; Popper's italics). His proposal was to "make clear the distinction between the *psychology of knowledge* which deals with empirical facts, and the *logic of knowledge* which is concerned only with logical relations" (p. 30; Popper's italics).

To Popper, "the results of an inquiry into the rules of science—that is of scientific discovery—may be entitled 'The Logic of Scientific Discovery' " (p. 53). He states further:

> We say that a theory is falsified only if we have accepted basic state-ments which contradict it. . . . This condition is necessary, but not sufficient; for we have seen that non-reproducible single occurrences are of no significance to science. Thus a few stray basic statements contradicting a theory will hardly induce us to reject it as falsified. We shall take it as falsified only if we discover a *reproducible effect* which refutes the theory. In other words, we only accept the falsification if a low-level empirical hypothesis which describes such an effect is pro-posed and corroborated. This kind of hypothesis may be called a *falsify-ing* hypothesis. The requirement that the falsifying hypothesis must be empirical, and so falsifiable, only means that it must stand in a certain logical relationship to possible basic statements; thus this requirement only concerns the logical form of the hypothesis. The rider that the hypothesis should be corroborated refers to tests which it ought to have passed—tests which confront it with accepted basic statements. [p. 86–87]

Popper's emphasis on the refutation of theories through the falsification of hypotheses derived from theories that took cog-nizance of the changing nature of scientific truth. His conten-tion that a theory can be regarded as true until it is falsified, however, continued to place emphasis on science as a search for "truth," rather than as a means of developing functional con-ceptual models, in the knowledge that in time they will be modi-fied or discarded. Popper's work did give recognition to the evo-lutionary character of scientific knowledge even though his attention was focused on the methodology of science and not on the changing theories or scientific conceptual frameworks. Thus his work represented a transitional stage from Baconian and Pearsonian views of science to more contemporary ones.

By 1950 another view of science was being popularized by persons whose attention was focused on the history of scientific discoveries rather than on analysis of scientific method. Perhaps the most distinguished in this group was James Conant, chemist, historian of science, and later president of Harvard University. Conant published a popular account of his view that methods of science could be understood best by the study of case histories selected to illustrate ways in which scientists have worked in the past. His book *On Understanding Science* (1947) influenced my thinking, and the course he instituted at Harvard influenced the thinking of many students. One person whose association with Conant led to a change in careers was Thomas Kuhn. As a member of Conant's case history experimental course, Kuhn was impressed by the views of science suggested by the case histories, views that were radically different from those he had come to know as a student of physics. As a result, Kuhn shifted to the study of the history and philosophy of science.

Kuhn's analysis led him to see that science was characterized more by the paradigms employed by scientists than by their methods of inquiry. In his *Structure of Scientific Revolutions* (1962), Kuhn describes paradigms in a variety of ways (for which he has been criticized); his primary notion, however, is that a paradigm is a conceptual scheme or a pair of perceptual goggles through which scientists in a given discipline view problems in that field. In Kuhn's view, a researchable problem and the methods to be used to solve that problem are primarily determined by the relevant paradigm used by scientists. A scientist who believes that chemicals are composed of molecular units consisting of specific elements combined in specific proportions studies the behavior of chemicals in a very different way than the alchemist, who held that the behavior of chemicals was determined by "inflammability," "incombustibility," and other "principles." The biologist who views the condition of a living cell as the product of its intricate organization and chemical processes pursues the study of cells differently than one who views the living condition as the result of a "vital force" that is inherent only in living things and disappears at death.

The history of science shows, of course, that paradigms used by scientists have changed over time. Kuhn's central thesis is that this change is comparatively abrupt. He describes two kinds of scientific activity, one of which is characteristic of most of the work scientists do when they conduct experiments and make observations, and which he calls "puzzle solving." The other kind of scientific work is much less common and most scientists never contribute to it, since only rare creative scientific genius can invent a new paradigm—Kuhn's requirement for revolutionary science. In contrast to puzzle solving, which constitutes much of normal science, in which research is guided by an accepted paradigm, revolutionary science arises when conflicting results are obtained or a paradigm fails to apply to an important group of problems; in this case a new paradigm must be invented and a scientific revolution ensues. In normal science, instrumentation may be refined—as microscopes were, after the "cell theory" paradigm was accepted—and a wider array of examples may be studied (everywhere microscopists looked, they found that living things were made of cells). In revolutionary science, a new paradigm is created and new kinds of problems can be attacked; for example, after Einstein proposed that mass can be converted into energy ($E = mc^2$), new experiments in nuclear physics and new observations in astronomy could be undertaken in ways that were not possible earlier.

Kuhn stresses the abruptness of the change in thinking during a scientific revolution and views the competition of the old and the new paradigm as a contest in which proponents of the new eventually win:

At the start a new candidate for paradigm may have few supporters, and on occasions the supporters' motives may be suspect. Nevertheless, if they are competent, they will improve it [the paradigm], explore its possibilities, and show what it would be like to belong to the community guided by it. And as that goes on, if the paradigm is one destined to win its fight, the number and strength of the persuasive arguments in its favor will increase. More scientists will then be converted, and the exploration of the new paradigm will go on. Gradually the number of experiments, instruments, articles, and books based upon the paradigm will multiply. Still more men, convinced of the new view's fruitfulness, will adopt the new mode of practicing normal science, until at last only a few elderly hold-outs remain. And even they, we cannot say, are wrong. Though the historian can always find men—Priestley, for instance—who were unreasonable to resist for as long as they did, he will not find a point at which resistance becomes illogical or unscientific. At most he may wish to say that the man who continues to resist after his whole profession has been converted has *ipso facto* ceased to be a scientist. [p. 159]

A problem with Kuhn's thesis is that sometimes competing paradigms coexist and both continue to function for years, as the wave and particle theories of light did. When one paradigm eventually becomes dominant, it may prevail as a result of the gradual accumulation of information rather than through a sudden gestalt shift in the minds of practicing scientists. Kuhn has done us an important service in stressing the role of the conceptions held by a community of scientists as fundamental to scientific inquiry. Like Joseph Schwab (1962), who contrasts stable inquiry with fluid inquiry, Kuhn has directed the attention of those interested in the problem of knowledge from the methods or logic of scientific discovery to the social and conceptual frameworks that guide scientific inquiry and, I shall argue, all human inquiry.

As I began to use Ausubel's theory in my work, it became evident that the functioning of concepts in the cognitive structure of an individual is somewhat analogous to the role of Kuhnian paradigms in the scientific fields. Paradigms help the scientist to see new meanings in old data or to seek specific new information for puzzle solving. Concepts in cognitive structure (or Ausubel's subsuming concepts) facilitate meaningful learning and hence allow development of these concepts and increased potential for problem solving in the specified area. Barbara Bowen, who worked with our group from 1968 through 1972, became interested in this analogy and has described the implications of Kuhnian philosophy for interpretation of Ausubelian psychology (Bowen, 1972). She also has argued that Lev Vygotsky's (1962) views on the role of language in concept learning can be linked to Kuhn's perception of the role of paradigms in the advance of science, whereas Piaget's views on developmental psychology minimize the importance of language and instruction. Ausubel's theory emphasizes concepts as components of cognitive organization and their role in the assimilation of new knowledge.

In Chapter 1 it was noted that the contrasting views of El-kana, Kuhn, and Popper might be of only esoteric interest if most of the federally supported curriculum projects of the 1960s had not proceeded as though Popper were right and Elkana and Kuhn were wrong. Commenting on the new science curriculum programs, Elkana (1970) writes:

> They are based mainly on one conclusion . . . : after the Einsteinian revolution and the new attitude of relativism with respect to the value of scientific theories, there is only one thing which remains certain and unchanging—the scientific method. While the value of theories is transitory and they serve only as instruments of prediction, it is implied by the positivistic-instrumentalist philosophy of science that we at least know how science is being done, that we finally discovered 'the language of science' and thus know the 'method of science.' This one and only true method of science is the method of empiricism, of mathematical positivism, and again, the elimination of all metaphysics. According to this view, science develops by empirical refutation of old theories, by objective formulation of 'critical experiments' and by empirical decision as to which of the alternatives is the better predicting instrument. [p. 22]

> In the last twenty years, a new philosophy of science has been taking shape, which has left behind the ahistorical, or even anti-historical positivism. As we are still in the period of its being formulated, I shall only be able to point out some of the characteristics of this new philosophy. According to it, the attempt of the older tradition to describe the language or method of science is no more than an exercise in logic, valuable as such, but which *has nothing to do with science in reality.* [p. 24]

> It is only to tactics of science that the 'method of science' applies. And it is only the tactics of science which the usual textbooks, or even the recent science teaching programs emphasize. In my view, science teaching has to give as prominent a place to the strategy of science as to its tactics. Such an approach would show how the experimental results can be interpreted in view of different metaphysical attitudes, and would show that there are no theory-independent facts; all facts are interpreted in the light of some theory, and thus the status of rival theories would be more clearly explained. [p. 33]

So we see in Elkana an appeal that the teaching of science encompass the role of theories or conceptualizations that scientists devise, that interpretation be based not solely on the "logic of scientific method." We will find this view elaborated and documented in the important recent work of Toulmin (1972).

Human Understanding: The Philosophy of Stephen Toulmin

Occasionally in the history of a discipline a new leader emerges and his works alter the course of that discipline. This is as true in the arts as in sciences and humanities. Stephen Toulmin's three-volume *Human Understanding* may alter the course of philosophy for generations to come. Although only the first volume, *The Collective Use and Evolution of Concepts* (1972), has been completed at this writing, the ideas Toulmin has developed should lay the foundations for a reshaping of much of philosophy. If we can judge from references to ideas to be included in the two succeeding volumes, *The Individual Grasp and Development of Concepts* and *The Rational Adequacy and Appraisal of Concepts,* Toulmin also may significantly influence future thinking in education and in the social sciences.

Toulmin borrowed one of the most powerful concepts in biology—evolution—and used it to achieve a description of human understanding. This description can be summarized in Toulmin's words (1972, p. x): "A man demonstrates his rationality, not by a commitment to fixed ideas, stereotyped procedures, or immutable concepts, but by the manner in which, and the occasions on which, he changes those ideas, procedures and concepts." And he quotes Kierkegaard: "Concepts, like individuals, have their histories, and are just as incapable of withstanding the ravages of time as are individuals."

Although Toulmin was not the first to propose that the concept of evolution applies to interpretation of the history of ideas as well as to the history of organisms, he has benefited from recent advances in the field of biology and the interpretive power of the contemporary concept of evolution. In fact, the history of the concept of evolution, from Lamarck to Darwin to Herbert Muller to contemporary views, is an excellent example of the evolution of human understanding, and of the interrelation of concepts in seemingly distinct disciplines. From 1820 to 1850, the *uniformitarian* and the *catastrophist* concepts were much debated among geologists. Uniformitarians argued that geological features are the products of gradual erosion, deposition, and so on, whereas the catastrophists argued that they were produced by such sudden dramatic events as the flood of Noah's time. The catastrophists' view was consistent with the scriptures, and they frequently used theological writings to support their position, especially the view that ordinary geological processes could not produce the enormous variety of geomorphic features in the 5,800 years since the beginning of the earth, as proclaimed by the Bishop of Ulster, who reckoned that the creation had occurred in 4004 b.c. Gradually evidence accumulated that the earth was much older, perhaps hundreds of millions of years old, and the main prop of the catastrophist concept crumbled. By 1860 even such diehard catastrophists as Louis Agassiz at Harvard found it necessary to introduce so many catastrophes to explain all of the geological irregularities that the innumerable small catastrophes began to look like ordinary observable geological changes, less dramatic by far than "ordinary" earthquakes and volcanic eruptions. Charles Darwin, who published *The Voyage of the Beagle* in 1839 and who held uniformitarian views, began to see that gradual changes in organisms too could lead to new forms, thus accounting for both the variety and the similarity of the animal and plant life he observed during his world tour on the *Beagle*. His *Origin of Species by Means of Natural Selection,* published in 1859 but conceived twenty years earlier, lucidly explained how the wide variety of life forms could be accounted for by gradual changes in existing forms and by "natural selection" resulting from ordinary exigencies facing organisms in a variable environment.[1]

---

[1] It is interesting to note that while Darwin was applying his creative imagination to the development of the theory of natural selection, he thought he was adhering to strict Baconian principles and doing nothing more than impartially recording observations.

Darwin did not know of Mendel's work with inheritance in peas, published in an obscure journal in 1859, and the mechanisms of change in organisms were not explained until the development of genetic concepts in the twentieth century. As the science of genetics progressed and its concepts evolved to our present views of the structure and function of DNA in all kinds of organisms, and to our understanding of the redistribution of genetic material in populations of organisms, the mechanisms of the changes in organisms postulated by Darwin were amply explained.

Another concept that is related to concepts of organismal evolution is that of *ecological niche*. Darwin recognized that certain organisms always occupied similar ecological settings, suggesting that survival of that organism depended on the continued existence of this type of niche. As climatic and geologic changes occurred, it was reasonable to assume that some organisms would lose the old niches, fail to compete successfully with organisms in other niches, and hence become extinct. Most organisms, of course, can survive under a wide variety of conditions; cactus plants can do well in a tropical greenhouse. When survival depends on successful competition with other species better adapted to the environment, however, the less well adapted species die out. We shall see this idea operate with respect to the survival of concepts as well; some concepts (catastrophism, for example) flourish until a new competing concept is introduced (uniformitarianism), and then they die. Toulmin (pp. 414–415) points out that some niches have existed for incredibly long periods; some years ago a coelacanth, a member of a marine species previously known only in the fossil state, was found living off the coast of Madagascar. The paleospecies have survived enormous spans of geologic time because their specific ecological niches have continued to exist throughout millions of years. Sometimes a concept may find a cultural niche where it may survive long after it has become extinct in the culture that originated it. The point here is that concepts of science, based on observation, are considered to be "truths" that have universal, continuing relevance. Unfortunately, this mythologized view of science has been widely disseminated in science courses. With the help of new studies of the history of science and such books as James Watson's *Double Helix* (1968), it becomes increasingly evident that science does not exhibit the culture-free objectivity ascribed to it for generations. Studies of the history of science have been so damaging to the popularly disseminated view of objectivity in science that Stephen Brush (1974) asked, "Should the history of science be rated X?" Should we deliberately hide from our students new interpretations of the methods by which the sciences advance, lest they lose faith in the long-promulgated myth that science is coldly objective? Michael Polanyi (1956) asserted that passion plays an important role in the advance of science, and the notion has been echoed in many recent writings; the *human* aspect of science is here to stay. Toulmin's analysis (1972) clarifies the situation:

In particular, so as to focus on the central element in human understanding, we must ask:

What are the skills or traditions, the activities, procedures, or instruments of Man's intellectual life and imagination—in a word, the *concepts*—through which that human understanding is achieved and expressed? [p. 11]

Until men became accustomed to a time-scale millions of years in length, the functional patterns in the present state of Nature remained unanswerable evidence of a Fixed Order. In turn, this Order was interpreted as displaying the Rationality and Forethought of its Creator, since how should it be understood, except as an outcome of deliberate Design? So the first duty of the devout scientist (or 'Christian Virtuoso') was to master its Fixed Laws. In this way, four distinct conceptions were compressed into a single article of scientific faith: the moral legitimacy of scientific enquiry rested on the discovery of rational Laws of Nature, and the Divine Creation of the World was a standing argument for its historical stability. [pp. 13–14]

Given this immutable Order of Nature—including the human body and brain along with the rest of the material world—it was a short step to assuming that Human Nature was similarly fixed and permanent. So the fundamental epistemological question was simple:

By what principles or processes does the Human Mind acquire intellectual mastery over the Order of Nature?

Since both terms in this relationship—the Intelligence of Man, and Intelligible Nature—presumably operated on stable, unchanging principles, the relationship between them was presumably stable and unchanging also. The philosopher's task was then to analyse and explain the fixed and universal principles of Human Understanding by which ideas were formed and rational thought directed. Once again, there might be disagreements over matters of detail, but over the basic point all philosophers were united. Fixed Mind masters Fixed Nature according to Fixed Principles. The operative question was, 'What Fixed Principles?' [pp. 15–16]

Toulmin goes on to describe the view that matter is essentially inert, hence it possesses fixed order established at creation. Faith in Euclidean geometry confirms the fixed certainty of natural order. But during the past 250 years, so-called laws of nature no longer imply the fixed laws of a Creator, and other "invariants" of the seventeenth-century world have crumbled as well.

From the ultimate unchanging particles of matter, through the planetary system and animal species, to the timeless imperatives of morality and social life: every aspect of Nature is considered today as historically developing, or 'evolving'. . . . Instead of Fixed Mind gaining command over Fixed Nature by applying Fixed Principles, we should expect to find variable epistemic relationships between a variable Man and a variable Nature. [p. 21]

. . . we can understand the intellectual authority of our concepts clearly, only if we bear in mind the socio-historical processes by which they develop within the life of a culture or community; yet, in turn, a clearer analysis of that intellectual authority gives us the means of developing more exact ideas about those very processes. [p. 26]

The remainder of Toulmin's book explains how human understanding evolves, how we broke with the tradition of search for fixed truths and moved to a view of evolving concepts as the basis of human understanding. Toulmin describes the goals and problems of disciplines, using science as a model but referring also to other disciplines. He concludes with a section on the variety of rational enterprises, in which rationality is based on our conceptual framework and not on logical analysis, which, he contends, must always regress to a set of a priori assumptions or fixed principles. Toulmin analyzes what he regards as the neo-Kantian views of Robin G. Collingwood (1940) and Kuhn (1962). Kuhn has fallen into the "invariants" trap by insisting on the revolutionary nature of paradigm changes, with the old swept out and the new dominating. But striking conceptual advances occur in "normal" science as well as in "revolutionary" science. In Toulmin's view, Kuhn's revolutions must be seen as the products of many minor conceptual shifts, and hence must go the way of Agassiz' catastrophies.

After chasing the revolutionary hare as far as it can lead us, we are therefore back where we started. An adequate theory of conceptual change must answer the questions left over by Collingwood: viz., 'On what occasions, and by what processes and procedures, does one basic set of collective concepts—in science or elsewhere—come to displace another?' It must answer these questions in a way that explains, in one and the same set of terms, both why our ways of thinking in some fields remain effectively unchanged over long periods, and also why in other fields they sometimes change rapidly and drastically. And it must answer them, finally, in a way that makes clear the respective roles, in this historical development, of 'rational procedures' on the one hand, and 'causal processes' on the other. What we need, therefore, is an account of conceptual development which can accommodate changes of any profundity, but which explains gradual and drastic change alike as alternative outcomes of the same factors working together in different ways. Instead of a *revolutionary* account of intellectual change, which sets out to show how entire 'conceptual systems' succeed one another, we therefore need to construct an *evolutionary* account, which explains how 'conceptual populations' come to be progressively transformed. [pp. 121–122]

In the evolution of concepts as in biological evolution, Toulmin argues, changes occur in *populations*. Novel concepts come and go, but they influence thinking in a given discipline only when conditions are favorable; only when the new concepts have "advantages" can they displace others. Toulmin sees that Karl Popper's capsule description of scientific method, as a dialectical succession of 'conjectures' and 'refutations', can at once be reinterpreted in evolutionary terms: it lays down the ecological conditions on which alone variation and selection can lead to effective scientific change. [p. 140]

Approaching our present problems from this populational point of view, we may distinguish six main groups of questions:

(i)   What defines the limits of an intellectual discipline, and why are there distinct disciplines at all?

(ii) What is the nature of conceptual variation, and how does the current pool of conceptual variants provide the material for disciplinary change?

(iii) To what processes and procedures of intellectual selection is such a pool of variants exposed?

(iv) By what channels of transmission and perpetuation are selected variants incorporated into a discipline, so as to modify its established content?

(v)   How do differences in the degree of isolation and competition affect the influence of intellectual selection, and so react on the unity, character, and development of intellectual disciplines themselves?

(vi) Within what sorts of environment do intellectual disciplines operate, and how do the standing demands of those environments affect the processes and procedures by which conceptual variants are judged? [pp. 143–144]

Toulmin's answers to these questions, while pertinent to our thesis, go beyond the scope of this book. A few additional conclusions from Toulmin's work, however, merit at least passing attention.

In describing the way in which new recruits into a discipline are enculturated, Toulmin shows that they come to know and to apply the concepts and methods popular at the time, and gradually to inject their own concepts.

In the quasi-political power plays which professional scientists quite rightly undertake 'in the name of' their respective disciplines, institutional victories can never be more than temporary. Each new generation of apprentices, while developing its own intellectual perspectives, is also sharpening up the weapons for an eventual professional take-over. Five, ten, or twenty years hence, their word will carry weight in the profession, their authority will guide and reshape the discipline; and meanwhile, at their heels, still other younger men are coming along, who will in due course form the generation of their own successors. [p. 287]

And so new people and new ideas replace older ones in a continuous succession. This fact provides some comfort to novices who are struggling to get funds and recognition for their scholarly efforts, but there is an unhappy ecological analogue: new ideas must find a niche in order to survive.

Failing suitable niches, the genetic potential of a given organic population will remain unexploited; while, in the absence of suitable populations, the ecological demands of a given niche will go unmet. Yet it would be equally unprofitable to ask, 'Do ecological niches exist only in virtue of the current organic populations; or do those populations exist only in virtue of the available niches?', and to ask the corresponding question about scientific ideas and institutions. In either case, the question itself involves a false antithesis. Rather, we must say that niches exist partly (though not solely) in virtue of populations, and that populations exist partly (but not solely) in virtue of niches. [p. 315]

One lesson is that, when federal or private foundation money is poured into an area of research exclusively for those who adhere to a specific conceptual framework and/or research methodology (Skinnerian operant conditioning in its various forms, for example), many professional niches are closed to less favored innovators. Fortunately, although selective funding may close off conceptual niches, most renegades who persist can find some professional route to nourish their ideas, and in time some of them will flourish.

Funding policies of the U.S. Office of Education and some other federal agencies have had a negative effect on conceptual evolution in education precisely because they have sustained outmoded views in comfortable professional niches.

Toulmin's analysis of the work of Noam Chomsky and Jean Piaget also has special relevance to education. Toulmin sees Chomsky's views on the "native" or "innate" character of human language capacity as reverting to a Kantian a priorism and as casting a century of Darwinian insights out the window.

In a similar way, Piaget's views of universal developmental stages in children derive from a Kantian scheme in which all rational thought develops toward its inescapable and unique destination. As we shall see in Chapter 8, some important data do not support this view. The first volume of Toulmin's *Human Understanding* should be required reading in any serious study of educational philosophy. The second and third volumes may also prove to be highly instructive to educators who seek to understand the philosophical roots of human rationality.

The Use of Knowledge
The Principle of Parsimony

The history of the human search for understanding is long—as long as human history. The organization of observations and systematic efforts to interpret these observations, however, has been with us only a few centuries. The importance of Bacon's contributions, at least to the development of Western science, have already been discussed. One other major influence on Western scientific thought was William of Occam. Writing in 1340, Occam stressed that explanations should be economical and simple, with no more constructions than are needed to explain an event or phenomenon; all unnecessary causes and explanations should be scrupulously removed. This principle of excising unnecessary causes became known as "Occam's razor." Sir William Hamilton (1853) stressed again the importance of Occam's canon and termed it the "law of parsimony." Hamilton rephrased the law this way: "Neither more, nor more onerous causes are to be assumed, than are necessary to account for the phenomena."

The history of physics and biology illustrates the power of parsimonious thinking. In biology, a half dozen or so major principles serve to give meaning to an almost infinite variety of observations. Evolution, gene theory, and complementarity of structure and function are a few of the constructions that meet Occam's criteria and which have served to advance our understanding of living systems. In contrast to physics and biology, psychology and education have been characterized by innumerable "principles," each of which has at best dubious interpretive value over a very narrow range of phenomena. The field of education has been strikingly devoid of parsimonious explanations; psychology has fared only a little better. Despite the millions of dollars spent on "research" in these fields, probably the only major principle on which all would agree is that experience does influence behavior. The extent to which heredity influences learning remains a subject of lively debate, and the extent of interaction between hereditary potential and environment is also debated by people whose convictions range over a wide spectrum, from belief in profound interaction effects to belief in virtually no interaction at all. Faced with the lack of parsimonious explanatory schema in education, what can we do? One answer is to borrow some powerful principles from other fields and apply them to education. This, of course, is exactly what Toulmin has done, and perhaps is one reason why I find his analysis so eminently sensible.

The Principle of Evolution

Three principles developed in the sciences appear to have particular importance for education. First, and most valuable, is the principle of evolution. This idea has already been discussed with reference to Toulmin's theory, but a few additional comments are in order. For one thing, I am well aware that many educators do not "believe" in evolution; that is, they do not believe that new species (especially *Homo sapiens*) have evolved from pre-existing species through random mutation and natural selection. They are in effect creationists. Part of this misfortune results from the popular mythology that scientific methods lead to *truth,* and they must deny the "truth" of evolution if it conflicts with the "truth" of scriptures. The *laws* developed by scientists, however, are not absolute truths but rather explanatory models to be used, modified, and in time perhaps replaced by more parsimonious ones. Absolute truth can be established only by faith, not by the methods of science. But even the history of religions shows that these "absolute truths" have an evolutionary character.

With regard to learning theory, the principle of evolution, if accepted, requires that we view human capacities for learning as part of the continuum observed in other life forms. It is also to be expected that neural mechanisms involved in learning and the basic physiology of human brain cells are in no significant way different from those of other animals. We know, with as much certainty as we know anything in science, that the way DNA controls the synthesis of new substances in cells differs in no significant way from species to species. We do *not* know at this time how a neuron changes or what synthesis results in the storage of information. We must proceed on *faith* that the principle of evolution will hold and that neural mechanisms for storing information are biochemically similar in a variety of animal forms. This is the parsimonious view. Moreover, it is to be expected that the *biological* mechanisms for the coding, storage, and retrieval of information are essentially identical in all humans, if not in all mammals. How, then, can we account for individual differences in learning? We need a learning theory that explains the manifest differences in people's ability to learn without invoking differences in neural mechanisms.

Here, then, is one reason that Ausubel's theory has been attractive to me. Ausubel (1968) states that "the most important single factor influencing learning is what the learner already knows" (p. vi). We must therefore search for an explanation of variation in human learning capacities primarily in the cognitive and affective experiences that an individual has had. In the absence of organic brain damage and such occasional biochemical hereditary defects as phenylketonuria, most differences in human learning capabilities at any point in one's life up to old age should be predominantly the product of prior learning experiences. We will return to this issue in later chapters.

The Principle of Conservation

The second principle, in its simplest form, is that "you can never get something from nothing." For many years students learned that matter can be changed in form, but the total amount of matter remains always the same. The whole science of chemistry is based on this principle; we have learned that hydrogen combined with oxygen may form a new substance (H_2O), but if we add electric energy to a tube of water, we can again obtain pure hydrogen and pure oxygen in the proportion of two parts of hydrogen to one of oxygen. In 1905 Einstein suggested that matter could be destroyed, but in turn one would get extra energy (it takes energy to "destroy" matter). He modified the old principle of conservation of energy with his now-famous equation, $E = mc^2$, where E stands for energy and m for mass, and c is a constant. The new paradigm became "You can change matter into energy or energy into matter, but the total amount of matter and energy remains the same." Since matter changes to energy only under very unusual conditions, it didn't make much difference that the paradigm that guided chemists for a century was not "true." In fact, research chemists still assume that, except at very high temperatures, matter changes only in form and not in amount.

The principle of conservation applies in many sciences. The biologist assumes that energy absorbed from sunlight must be lost in some other form or stored in the chemical bonds of newly synthesized molecules. We measure the amount of energy a person uses when at rest (basal metabolic rate) not by measuring how much food is consumed but by measuring how much oxygen is taken in and how much carbon dioxide is breathed out. We assume that a certain amount of food had to be oxidized in order to produce the carbon dioxide released. In an ecosystem, we assume that the energy needed to sustain a hawk or coyote must come from small animals, and that these animals in turn get energy from plants.

Matter and energy are not the only things to which the conservation principle applies. If we apply a force to an object, we can increase the velocity of that object, and, as football players know only too well, a body moving at high speed hits with more force than one moving more slowly. The principle of conservation applies also to the field of economics, where, it has been argued, there is no such thing as a free lunch. Costs associated with production of goods or services must be paid by someone in some way. This principle will be applied in Chapter 6 as we examine alternatives in school instruction. Although total expenditure for education can increase, money allocated for staff salaries and physical plant is not available for instructional materials. Assuming a fairly constant supply of dollars for support of education, we must examine alternative ways to deploy these funds, for schools cannot spend the same dollar twice.[2]

We should also recognize that the principle of conservation does not apply to some significant areas of education. An instructional regime that increases one student's learning does not thereby subtract from the achievement of other students. Although alternative instructional approaches may differentially benefit students, it is in principle possible to find new approaches that enhance the learning of *all* students, and which also cost no more than less effective approaches.

Another important area in which the conservation principle is not applicable is the human relationship known as love. Children sometimes believe that love is a conservable commodity: parents who have several children must have less love to give each one than parents who have only one child, and a new baby will take love away from the older child. Mother's energy and time are conservable, and so a new baby may indeed capture more of her attention, but her love for her older children can increase. As Erich Fromm (1956) and others have shown, the more we love, the more we can increase our love for each person. Similarly, the capacity for learning is nonconservable. Proficiency in mathematics does not detract from proficiency in English or physics. In fact, the reverse is often true. Just as learning to love one person makes it easier to love others, most new learning will facilitate other learning, unless false propositions or poor strategies are acquired. The person who asserts that "someone must always fail" speaks as though there were just so much learning to go around and some students will get none. Of course, some students will always learn less or more slowly than others, and we need to seek alternative explanations for this problem.

---

[2] In New York State, some educational programs can be funded through a Board of Cooperative Educational Services (BOCES), and 80 percent of the dollars spent by a school district in BOCES-sponsored programs are returned to the school district. This system seems to deny the conservation principle, since schools can theoretically spend $100 five times. BOCES funds, however, are supplied by the state of New York—one reason, perhaps, that New York per-pupil instructional costs are the highest in the United States.

The Principle of Ecological Niche

The third scientific principle of value in education, the principle of ecological niche, has been described briefly in relation to Toulmin's views. In *Death at an Early Age* (1967), Kozol described what happened to poor children in Boston public schools. Although the children did not literally die, their educational aspirations were destroyed; these students were in the wrong niche for educational survival. Kozol's work, Nell Keddie's *Myth of Cultural Deprivation* (1973), and numerous other writings have made many educators keenly aware that educational failure is rarely the result of "bad seed" or poor inheritance. It is the result of forcing children into an educational niche for which their early training has not prepared them, and in which home and social pressures do not allow them to survive successfully. Head Start and other programs are attempts to force-feed disadvantaged youngsters so that they can meet the constraints of the public school niche. It has been argued that the niche represented by schools is the kind of environment that prepares students to live in contemporary societal niches. If we examine this argument carefully, we can observe that school is immensely more uniform, selective, and noxious to many people than is society at large. The niches available to individuals in society allow for a far wider array of behavioral patterns than does the school niche. Illich's (1970) recommendation to "deschool" society is at once impracticable and unnecessary. We do, however, need to increase enormously the variety of educational niches offered to children, and to profess avidly that educational and social survival is possible with a much broader spectrum of behaviors than the WASP ideal of American society would suggest. Some specific recommendations for educational changes are presented in Chapter 7.

Cognitive Learning

The philosophical issues examined up to this point could have implications for any discipline, not just for education. I should like to close this chapter with a brief synopsis of several philosophical issues that bear most directly on school learning.

Obviously, affective experience occurs in schools, and therefore affective learning occurs there. Much of this learning, however, is incidental to the business of schooling; whether good, bad, or indifferent, most affective learning in schools is not part of the curriculum. I agree with those humanistic educators who argue that the quality of affective experience in schools badly needs improvement; my quarrel with them is that they have little evidence to support the value of some of the activities about which they are so enthusiastic. They tend to diminish or ignore the useful things we can do to improve affective learning through cognitive learning. It is my contention that we should concentrate our efforts on improving at least those aspects of cognitive learning for which we have reasonable assurance of positive results; surely positive affective experiences will accompany our efforts. Successful cognitive learning produces positive affective response.

Central to Toulmin's view of human understanding is the evolutionary development of concepts. And although concepts change in time, and may vary from culture to culture, a person's grasp of a field's concepts is the basis for understanding in that field. There are no grand mental strategies by which a person can become omniscient. To understand all fields of human endeavor, a person must come to know the concepts in these fields, and acquire a correlated knowledge of the methods by which these concepts evolved. This view is at once optimistic and pessimistic. It is optimistic in that education to enhance human understanding can be a focused, deliberate effort to enhance the number and quality of concepts people have; it is pessimistic in that there is no single mental strategy that can be applied wholesale to all new learning tasks.

The only approximation of a grand mental strategy to augment new learning is a firm grasp of the broadest, most generally relevant concepts in our cultural heritage. This consideration is by no means trivial, for, as I have tried to show, some concepts—evolution and conservation, for example—are useful in the pursuit of understanding in widely divergent fields.

If the central element in human understanding is the individual's conceptual framework, we need to examine the knowledge claims of various groups of psychologists to see which group speaks most directly to the process of concept learning. We need, for the sake of parsimony, to see which psychological conceptions explain data from studies of learning and at the same time suggest optimal educational alternatives, including practicable alternatives for schools as they exist. This is why I believe Ausubel's theory of cognitive learning should be understood by all educational researchers and practitioners. His focus is on acquisition of concepts and on their hierarchical (qualitative) ordering in cognitive structure. I shall discuss this issue more fully in the following chapters, but first must, on philosophical grounds, deal with B. F. Skinner, for it is his type of thinking that has dominated educational psychology in this century.

In the next chapter I shall sketch the history of associationist psychology, including Skinner's operant conditioning. The central philosophical tenet of associationism is that we must not look within the organism for explanations of behavior. As Skinner (1938) put it, "Behavior is what an organism is *doing*— or more accurately what it is observed by another organism to be doing" (p. 6). And farther on he states: "We need to establish laws by which we may predict [external] behavior, and we may do this only by finding variables of which behavior is a function" (p. 8). Skinner goes on to describe some of the "laws" developed by associationists up to the time of his writing—for example, the Law of the Magnitude of the Response: "The magnitude of the response is a function of the intensity of the stimulus" (p. 13). Most so-called laws of behaviorists have been demonstrated to hold only under special circumstances and essentially to have explanatory value only in the experimental frameworks of the psychologists, certainly not in the classroom. As every schoolteacher knows, the ringing of the bell at the end of the school day brings an impressively different response from students than the ringing of the same bell at the start of school. The difference is in the internalized meaning that the ringing bell has for students, a meaning we cannot understand if we observe only their external behavior.

The insistence on restricting observation to external behavior is a psychological variation of the old philosophical doctrine of *peripheralism,* which emphasizes external sensorimotor processes rather than internal cognitive processes as determinants of behavior. This doctrine arose in part from psychologists' disenchantment with introspection, since one person's introspections too often do not agree with another's. Peripheralism was also fostered by the empiricists' view that only things publicly visible can count as observations. Given the theological and mystical origins of much dogma regarding human behavior, it is understandable that peripheralism flourished in intellectual circles, and indeed it served some useful purpose in advancing human understanding at one time. The problem is that cultures change, conceptions change, and peripheralism is an anachronism today. Unhappily, behaviorist doctrines continue to flourish in education, largely without awareness of their inherent peripheralist philosophy, and thus they crowd educational niches that might be utilized more fruitfully by other concepts. Kenneth Strike (1974) has examined this problem, and has criticized the farfetched extension of peripheralism into social planning in Skinner's *Beyond Freedom and Dignity* (1971).

Some people appear to be unalterably attached to a search for absolutes. They don't want good or better answers, they want the *right* answers. People in search of absolutes frequently feel frustrated by human recalcitrance. When such people work their way into high political offices, they can cause enormous damage, for their certainty of their goals leads them to believe that the ends justify any means they may use to reach those goals. But society is not formed of absolute truths, and those who think they have found some eventually come into conflict with the rest of humanity, a conflict they have always lost. The question is whether we can risk this type of entrepreneurship while stockpiles of nuclear weapons proliferate and the peoples of the world grow increasingly interdependent. Toulmin's evolutionary view of human understanding may help to expose the absolutists who would subject others to tyranny.

CHAPTER 3

The Central Role of Learning
Theory in a Theory of Education

A Search for Relevant Learning Theory

We have evidence indicating that all animals learn; the behavior of even protozoans appears to be modified by past experience. While there are many definitions of learning, all include the idea that learning is a change in the behavior of an organism resulting from previous experience. The study of learning, therefore, crosses many disciplinary boundaries including biology, psychology, sociology, anthropology, linguistics, education, and cybernetics (if we accept machines in the class of "organisms" capable of modifying behavior on the basis of earlier interactions). The focus of this book is on education of humans in institutions we call schools; however, it will profit any serious student of education to examine what we know about learning in a much broader context. Some misconceptions regarding learning in schools derive from a narrow focus of attention. As a result, curriculum organization, evaluation practices, administrative structures, and roles of teachers and students are viewed as the only relevant parameters affecting learning; one very important factor—the nature of the learning process per se—is ignored. Our best hope for the improvement of education derives from careful study of the learning process and from consequent implications for other factors associated with school learning.

The biological basis for all learning is some form of chemical or structural change in living cells. We do not know at this time whether signals accepted by an organism (be it a planarian or a human being) are coded and stored as special, complex molecules or whether changes occur in cell membranes and other cell structures, thus encoding the signals. The biological mechanisms involved in reception of sensory signals, coding and/or information reduction at the site of the receptor (be it the retina or a muscle proprioceptor), and storage of coded information in neural structures are today a subject of intense research. At some time in the future, research in neurobiology will undoubtedly answer many questions we now have on the biological (cellular) mechanisms involved in learning, but schooling goes on now, and we must move forward as best we can without these answers. We do not see this task as futile, for plant breeders produced hybrid corn, wheat, and other grains long before they knew the mechanisms by which deoxyribonucleic acid (DNA) codes hereditary information and regulates synthesis in plant cells. In fact, the elucidation of the role of DNA in plant heredity has made very little difference in the work of plant breeders.

We can and must move forward in our search for better human learning environments even though we do not understand what are the specific biological mechanisms in human learning. But we cannot proceed in a conceptual vacuum. Plant breeders knew that some kind of "genes" were transmitted from parents to offspring, and after Mendel's work of 1859 was rediscovered in 1900, they understood that there were regularities in the transmission of genes and in the expression of genetic constitution in the attributes of the plant. Things we now know about human learning should be a part of a rational approach to education. A partial list of concepts or principles that can be accepted as "basic truths" at this time follows:

1. One third of brain mass is present at birth and little significant increase in brain mass occurs after age seven.

2. The *biological* mechanisms involved in receiving and coding information are the same for all humans (and probably for all vertebrates).

3. Different regions of the brain perform special functions, but all regions appear to interact in learning.

4. The normal human brain contains more than one hundred billion neurons and appears to have a potential for storage of almost unlimited information.

5. The environment influences the development of learning capability, especially environmental conditions existing from ages zero to five years.

6. Except for severe cases of organic brain damage or malfunction (brain tumors or hereditary diseases such as phenylketonuria), the human brain has an enormous capacity for learning throughout most of an individual's lifespan.

A review of the research in biology that supports these assertions is beyond the scope of this book. Contemporary books in neurobiology and physiological psychology would be very difficult reading for most educators; a realistic and authoritative alternative is to be found in some semipopular articles from *Scientific American* collected in *Psychobiology: The Biological Basis of Behavior* (1967). We recommend this or similar books to any educator seriously interested in the process of learning. My conclusion is that heredity is not more important than environment (or vice versa) for learning but that a complex interplay occurs between genetic expression and environmental conditions, an interplay that changes over the lifespan of an individual. The arguments in the field of education, about the meaning or importance of I.Q. for example, take on differing degrees of plausibility when viewed in the context of the biological mechanisms involved in learning.

Focusing more closely on human learning, we must search for a theory or paradigm that is consistent with what we now know about neurobiology and that will guide our inquiries into phenomena associated with school learning. The general attributes this theory should possess were outlined in the previous chapter. An obvious first step is to examine existing theories of learning and to assess their potential as a paradigm for education. The classic book in this field is Ernest R. Hilgard's *Theories of Learning* (1948, 1956, 1966, 1975).

In the fourth edition of *Theories of Learning* (1975), Hilgard and Gordon H. Bower identify six "typical problems" confronting learning theories. Their list (pp. 22–23) is useful to consider:

1. What are the limits of learning? Here is raised the question of the capacity to learn, of individual differences among learners of the same species and of unlike species. There are questions not only of persistent differences in capacity, but of change in capacity with age. Who can learn what? Are the limits set at birth? Do people get more or less alike with practice? These are the sorts of questions it is natural to raise.

2. *What is the role of practice in learning?* The old adage that practice makes perfect has considerable historical wisdom behind it. Surely one learns to roller skate or to play the piano only by engaging in the activity. But what do we know about practice in detail? Does improvement depend directly on the amount of repetition? If not, what are its conditions? What are the most favorable circumstances of practice? Can repetitive drill be harmful as well as helpful to the learner?

3. *How important are drives and incentives, rewards and punishments?* Everybody knows in a general way that learning can be controlled by rewards and punishments, and that it is easier to learn something which is interesting than something which is dull. But are the consequences of rewards and punishments equal and opposite? Is there a difference between intrinsic and extrinsic motives in their effect upon learning? How do goals and purposes affect the process?

4. *What is the place of understanding and insight?* Some things are learned more readily if we know what we are about. We are better off as travelers if we can understand a timetable or a road map. We are helpless with differential equations unless we understand the symbols and the rules for their manipulation. But we can form vowels satisfactorily without knowing how we place our tongues, and we can read without being aware of our eye movements. Some things we appear to acquire blindly and automatically; some things we struggle hard to understand and can finally master only as we understand them. Is learning in one case different from what it is in the other?

5. *Does learning one thing help you learn something else?* This is the problem of formal discipline, as it used to be called, or of transfer of training, to use a more familiar contemporary designation. Some transfer of training must occur or there would be no use in developing a foundation for later learning. Nobody denies that it is easier to build a vocabulary in a language after you have a start in it, or that higher mathematics profits from mastery of basic concepts. The question is really one of how much transfer takes place, under what conditions, and what its nature is.

6. *What happens when we remember and when we forget?* The ordinary facts of memory are mysterious enough, but in addition to familiar remembering and forgetting, our memories may play peculiar tricks on us. Some things we wish to remember are forgotten; some things we

would be willing to forget continue to plague us. In cases of amnesia there are often gaps in memory, with earlier and later events remembered. Then there are distortions of memory, in which we remember what did not happen, as is so strikingly demonstrated in testimony experiments. What is taking place? What control have we over processes involved? *

My study focuses on school learning; hence, for my purposes, I must add four more problems:

7. *What parameters of learning are most important in designing a school curriculum?* Schools cannot include more than a sample of the knowledge contained in our culture. How do we select from this pool of knowledge what is worth studying most and how do we order the sequence of subjects to achieve the maximal learning?

8. *How do different instructional practices influence learning and under what conditions?* Do we "individualize" instruction using technology, concentrate on better training of teachers, write better books and study guides—do we do all of these things, and in what form?

9. *How does school organization influence learning?* Should we have "open" schools, paraprofessional and student tutors, twelve-month or nine-month programs, highly prescribed curricula, or student-selected studies? Or no schools at all?

10. *Is all subject matter learned in the same way, or do learning mechanisms differ significantly in science, literature, mathematics, history?* This issue is important, and frequently ignored, since experimentation in school learning is almost always in areas of specific subject matter. How much we can generalize from principles supported by research in mathematics education, for instance, to apply them in history or music education is of fundamental importance in school learning.

Hilgard and Bower describe a dozen different learning theories. Several are based essentially on some association between a *stimulus* acting on an organism and the consequent *response* of the organism. These S-R or "connectionist" theories were among the earliest formulated (and they continue, with some modification, to be supported) and were based on research with rats, cats, or other small animals used in laboratories. Empirical verification of S-R theories derives from data showing

---

* Ernest R. Hilgard and Gordon H. Bower, *Theories of Learning*, 4th ed., © 1975. Reprinted by permission of Prentice-Hall, Inc., Englewood Cliffs, New Jersey.

that a given set of conditions (stimulus) operating on an animal will, in time, produce a predictable response. For example, a cat placed in a "puzzle box" will randomly move about, but will gradually learn to manipulate a latch or lever to free itself. Skinner (1938) argued that the specific stimuli which function in such experiments are not easily described, and it is more useful to focus attention on the operations the animal performs to receive his reward (escape, a pellet of food, or some other gratification). In time, the animal learns to associate a specific act or operation with the reward, so Skinner's theory becomes an O-R theory or, as he calls it, a theory of operant conditioning. The experimental setup for operant conditioning studies requires some kind of bar, disk, lever, or other gadget, which an animal operates. Data show that animals can be trained to exhibit a variety of operant behaviors in time sequences that are highly predictable.

The puzzle boxes used by Edward Thorndike in the 1890's and the "Skinner boxes" used by Skinner continue to be useful research tools in psychology. Thousands of experiments have shown that a wide variety of animals learn S-R or O-R behaviors in similar fashions, and that forgetting (or extinction, as it is called) of learned responses also occurs in predictable ways. These theories are consistent as models for learning with what we would expect in terms of the minimum *biological* assumptions we have stated earlier. The value of S-R or O-R theories for human learning, however, has not been demonstrated except in the simplest kinds of exercises. Much empirical data from classroom learning does not support S-R or O-R theories, nor in fact have any substantial efforts been made to link S-R theories with the learning theory issues (numbers 7 through 9 in the list) given earlier.

Skinner (1968) has argued for programmed instruction and the use of technology in teaching based on what he claims to be control of "operant conditions." The connection between his theory and recommended practices, however, is no more profound than the statement that students will tend to do what we require them to do. None of the so-called laws of operant conditioning have been shown empirically to work in schools. A colossal inferential leap is made in the suggestion that if pigeons can be trained to operate (peck) on specific sequences of colored disks in a Skinner box to obtain a food pellet, humans can be conditioned to exhibit desired behaviors by properly designed contingencies through which they will be rewarded. It is a neat intellectual "sleight of hand," but where are the data to support this contention? Since Skinner's theory says little more than that human behavior can be predictable, we cannot refute the theory. Furthermore, it is almost useless as a source of guidance in designing and planning curricula, instruction, and research in schools.

One important contribution to education, however, has been made by the behaviorist's emphasis on observable behavior: considerable literature has appeared emphasizing that we must observe what students can do after learning and that we must specify as clearly as possible what the learning tasks are. I shall return to these considerations later.

Two other "theories of learning" have been described since the earlier edition of Hilgard's book (1966): Gagné's *Conditions of Learning* was published in 1965 and Ausubel's *Educational Psychology* in 1968. Gagné has been widely read, and his views have found their way into many introductory psychology and educational psychology courses. Hilgard and Bower (1975) discuss Gagné's work, and a brief discussion of it is included later in this chapter. Hilgard and Bower, however, do not mention Ausubel's theory, and his work, as noted earlier, is either ignored or frequently misinterpreted in elementary texts. A dozen or so research workers in psychology and educational psychology have written papers dealing theoretically with one or more issues cited by Hilgard, but none has presented a comprehensive theory of learning. The work of Jean Piaget[1] in Geneva continues to influence thinking with regard to learning in children, but as extensive as his writing has been, Piaget has not constructed a general theory of learning, applicable at all age levels

---

[1] The work of Piaget has been described in many books and monographs by him and his coworkers (especially Barbel Inhelder). His ideas are woven together in these books, and general statements regarding his views of cognitive growth cannot be attributed to a single reference; in these cases, none is given.

and addressing all the issues cited by Hilgard. In this chapter I shall describe the major elements of Ausubel's theory of cognitive learning and subsequently show the relationship between Ausubel's theory and all ten learning issues presented earlier. Some of the learning issues cited (especially numbers 7–10) are closely related to problems of curriculum design and instructional methods; they will be discussed at greater length in Chapters 5 and 6.

My study of learning theories as a graduate student was a frustrating experience. There are subtle differences in the ways different behavioral psychologists define terms and laws of learning, and the many clever experiments that have been devised to prove certain laws are a challenge to the memory. Most frustrating of all, however, was that virtually none of this information appeared to have any relevance to school learning, which was my principal concern. Cybernetic models for learning appeared after Wiener's book (1948) laid the foundation for this development. The emphasis on information processing in cybernetic theory appealed to me, for problem solving is a major characteristic of human behavior and cybernetic theory focused on this issue. My early research studies (1955 to 1963) were based on various forms of cybernetic learning models.

An Interpretation of the Assimilation Learning Theory of David Ausubel[2]

When Ausubel's work came to my attention in the early 1960s, the emphasis on the role of concepts in meaningful learning appealed to me; but it took more than three years and six seminars in which Ausubel's work was emphasized before I began to feel comfortable interpreting his theory to others. His work began to make real sense after a five-day conference[3] on concept learning in 1965 at which I had the opportunity to talk

[2] Some of the ideas expressed in this chapter represent my views on Ausubel's theory. The description in this and subsequent chapters more closely follows that in a forthcoming description of Ausubel's assimilation theory of cognitive learning to be found in the second edition of his *Educational Psychology*.

[3] A report of this conference was published in Herbert J. Klausmeier and Chester W. Harris, *Analysis of Concept Learning* (New York: Academic Press, 1966).

privately with him. A sabbatical leave during 1965–1966 at Harvard University offered opportunities to study and analyze the work of Jerome Bruner and others. These experiences and particularly the new interpretations that my students and I were seeing in our research data led to a growing conviction that Ausubel's learning theory, especially as presented in his 1968 book, was a powerful model of learning to guide education.

One strength of Ausubel's theory is that it allows integration of many observations on learning into a single, coherent system. This coherence is a prime source of difficulty in grasping his theory—each part makes most sense when associations with other parts are understood. But how can one initially grasp the meaning of these associations? It is partly because of this difficulty that we have found schemas and diagrams to be valuable. A paragraph from Ausubel's book (1968) illustrates the problem:

The tremendous efficiency of meaningful learning as an information-processing and -storing mechanism can be largely attributed to its two distinctive characteristics—the nonarbitrariness and the substantiveness of the learning task's relatability to cognitive structure. First, by *nonarbitrarily* relating potentially meaningful material to relevant established ideas in his cognitive structure, the learner is able effectively to exploit his existing knowledge as an ideational and organizational matrix for the incorporation, understanding, and fixation of large bodies of new ideas. It is the very nonarbitrariness of this process that enables him to see his previously acquired knowledge as a veritable touchstone, for internalizing and making understandable vast quantities of new word meanings, concepts, and propositions with relatively little effort and few repetitions. Because of this factor of nonarbitrariness, the potential meaning of new ideas *as wholes* can be related to established meanings (concepts, facts, and principles) *as wholes to yield new meanings. In other words, the only way it is possible to make use of previously learned ideas in the processing (internalization) of new ideas is to relate the latter nonarbitrarily* to the former. The new ideas, which become meaningful, in turn, also expand the base of the learning matrix. [p. 58; Ausubel's italics]

Probably most words in this paragraph are familiar to any college sophomore; but what does the paragraph say? One must go back and explain how Ausubel uses the terms efficiency, meaningful learning, nonarbitrariness, substantiveness, cognitive structure, ideational matix, incorporation, fixation, established meanings, and learning matrix. Cognitive structure develops from nonarbitrary incorporation of meaningful learning material, but meaningful learning material is that which potentially can be incorporated nonarbitrarily into cognitive structure. Where do we break the cycle? Is it any wonder that recent textbooks of educational psychology make *no* mention of Ausubel? Too many educational psychologists have not taken the trouble to understand his theory. A rather monotonous public speaking style has not helped to arouse popular enthusiasm for Ausubel's arguments. One can only speculate on the position his theory would occupy in education if he had the stage charm, humor, and forensic skills of Jerome Bruner or B. F. Skinner.

Viewed in a broader context, we recognize that humans receive information through a variety of sense organs. Rarely do individuals receive input of only one type. When we eat, we not only taste our food, we also smell it and feel it in our mouths. We also experience some internally derived signals. The pleasure we experience in eating popcorn, for example, may be more from the odor and crunch than from the taste of the popcorn. Eating is not usually considered a cognitive learning experience, but it most surely would be that if we were judges of a popcorn-tasting contest or food specialists analyzing alternative products or methods of preparation. In skill learning, such as roller skating or ice skating, information from our proprioceptors is highly important, but we also engage other sensory mechanisms. Most cognitive learning, however, results from visual or auditory input. All forms of external sensory input are accompanied by some internal input which is recorded in the brain as pleasure or pain.

Deaf and blind individuals, of course, must rely on other sources of information for cognitive learning, and many talented people have surmounted this limitation admirably. In any case, signals impinging on our sensory mechanisms are not all "internalized"; we see, hear, feel, smell, and taste only some of these stimuli, partly because of the physical limitations of our organs (humans do not hear sounds with frequencies over 17,000 hertz nor do they see X-rays and infrared light). Other limitations are our focus of attention and past experiences with similar stimuli. For healthy persons, by far the most important determinant of what is seen or heard is the individual's experience history. What an adult senses from a book or at the theater is physically the same as what a two-year-old child senses, but what the adult internalizes into the brain is profoundly different. It may also be profoundly different from what is internalized by one's peers. The information that passes through our perceptual barriers is selected both by physical limitations of our perceptual systems and by the kind and quality of our past experiences (Powers, 1973).

In the model of learning used in this book affective learning is restricted to the storage of information from internal signals. This very narrow definition of affective learning will show functional value as my discussions proceed.

Meaningful Learning

The central idea in Ausubel's theory is what he describes as *meaningful learning*. To Ausubel, meaningful learning is a process in which new information is related to an existing relevant aspect of an individual's knowledge structure. Although we do not know the biological mechanisms of memory (or the storage of knowledge), we do know that information is stored in localized regions of the brain and that many brain cells are involved in the storage of knowledge units. New learning results in further changes in brain cells, but some cells affected during meaningful learning are the same cells that already store information similar to the new information being acquired. In other words, the neural cells or cell assemblies active in storage during meaningful learning are undergoing further modifications and are probably forming synapses or some functional association with new neurons. With continued learning of new information relevant to information already stored, the nature and extent of neural associations also increase.

Figure 3.1 shows a schema illustrating a cell assembly to

which new information is being added. The *biological* basis of meaningful learning involves changes in the number or character of neurons participating, or in the cell assembly involved; the *psychological* phenomenon involves the assimilation of new information within a specific existing knowledge structure in the individual's cognitive structure. Ausubel defines these psy-

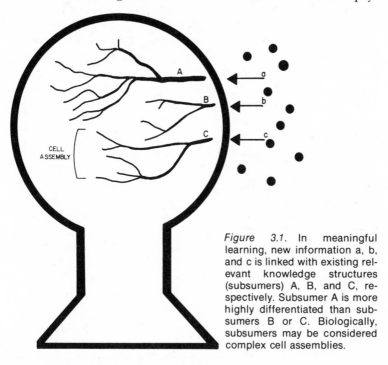

Figure 3.1. In meaningful learning, new information a, b, and c is linked with existing relevant knowledge structures (subsumers) A, B, and C, respectively. Subsumer A is more highly differentiated than subsumers B or C. Biologically, subsumers may be considered complex cell assemblies.

chological entities as *subsuming concepts* in cognitive structure, or more simply *subsumers*. During meaningful learning, then, new information is assimilated into existing relevant subsumers in cognitive structure. New meaningful learning results in further growth and modification of an existing subsumer. Depending on the experience history of the individual, subsumers can be comparatively large and well developed, or they may be limited in the amount and variety of elements (cell assemblies) they contain. In Figure 3.1, subsumer A shows the greatest differentiation and subsumer B the least complexity.

Ausubel makes no attempt to relate elements of his theory to neurobiology; in fact, he rejects such associations as speculative and misleading. In my experience many students want to know what possible relationships may exist between psychologically described learning phenomena and their neurobiological basis. Donald Hebb (1949) and Jacques Barbizet (1970) among others attempt to show how psychological behavior may be related to brain functioning. There is now substantive knowledge on the biology of brain mechanisms and we should examine some plausible relationships between psychological phenomena and brain mechanisms. I shall also discuss how "meaningful learning" is related to Piaget's ideas of assimilation and accommodation and to Gagné's work on conceptual hierarchies.

Ausubel has not been the first to recognize the importance of meaning as a factor in learning. D. O. Lyon (1914), M. G. Jones, and H. B. English (1926), and others are cited by Ausubel as early research workers who demonstrated that meaningful learning does not proceed in the same way as rote learning. Peripheralist philosophy, however, has been the dominant psychological dogma during the twentieth century. In an address to the Psychological Division of the American Association for the Advancement of Science, H. B. Reed (1938) argued that more attention should be paid to meaning as a factor in learning. He acknowledged that there was much "mystery" in such terms as insight and understanding, but pleaded for more psychological research on learning of meaningful material. History has shown that Reed's solicitation went largely unheeded, for most research continued to be of S-R and associationist nature, and Skinner's peripheralist philosophy, expounded in his *Conditions of Learning* (1938), has dominated the field of psychology in North America.[4]

[4] Ausubel received the E. L. Thorndike Award from the American Psychological Association in 1976 for "outstanding contribution to educational psychology." This followed a period when most of his research papers and books were rejected by editorial boards with prominent APA members.

Rote Learning

When relevant concepts do not exist in the cognitive structure of an individual, new information must be learned by rote. That is, each knowledge bit or unit must be arbitrarily stored in the cognitive structure. In rote learning, new information is not associated with existing concepts in cognitive structure, and therefore little or no interaction occurs between newly acquired information and information already stored.

Rote learning is always necessary when an individual acquires new information in a knowledge area completely unrelated to what he already knows. Also, some types of information are inherently meaningless; telephone numbers, nonsense syllables, and other information cannot be linked in substantive ways to existing cognitive structure elements and hence must be arbitrarily stored in cognitive structure. Knowledge elements learned by rote are arbitrarily distributed in cognitive structure; they are not linked to specifically relevant concepts in cognitive structure.

Where Do Subsumers Come From: Concept Formation

This question is frequently asked whenever I attempt to describe Ausubel's theory briefly. If meaningful learning is desirable and if it requires relevant concepts (subsumers) in cognitive structure, how does the process start? The answer is that, in young children, *concept formation* is the principal process by which concepts are acquired. This is a type of discovery learning involving hypothesis generation and testing as well as generalization from specific instances. For example, through repeated encounters with dogs, or chairs, or hot objects, so labeled by older children and adults, the young child gradually discovers the criterial attributes that characterize these concepts, and their language labels. After a child has acquired one or two thousand concepts (usually recognized as the child's functional vocabulary) through concept formation, additional differentiation of these concepts and development of new concepts proceeds principally through concept assimilation. Those who have been around two-year-old children know how repetitious their questions can be as they try to sharpen their understanding of simple concepts and the appropriate language labels. By school age, most children have an adequate framework of concepts to allow meaningful reception learning to proceed and although concept formation may occasionally occur, most new concepts are acquired through concept assimilation, progressive differentiation, and integrative reconciliation.

Cognitive Bridging: Advance Organizers

When Ausubel published his first paper (1960) recommending the use of advance organizers, he described these as "more general, more abstract, and more inclusive" than the learning material that was to follow. Advance organizers should serve to provide anchorage in cognitive structure for new knowledge. If relevant concepts were not available, the advance organizer would serve to anchor new learning and lead to development of a subsuming concept which can function to facilitate subsequent relevant learning. If appropriate concepts were already available in cognitive structure, advance organizers could serve to link new learning with specific, relevant subsumers. In the latter instance, advance organizers would serve as a cognitive bridge, which would allow ready linkage between existing relevant subsumers and new material to be learned. This is shown in Figure 3.2.

Much research in education has been based on the early twentieth-century model of agricultural research where yields of crop plots were compared with or without substance X. An obvious research question then is how effective is learning with or without advance organizers? This has been the most researched question associated with Ausubel's theory; the research produced a confusing mass of information, because many important variables were overlooked or went uncontrolled. First of all, Ausubel never claimed advance organizers would facilitate learning of "meaningless" information, but rather that subsequent information must be "potentially meaningful" and that the learners must have a meaningful learning set. Second, as

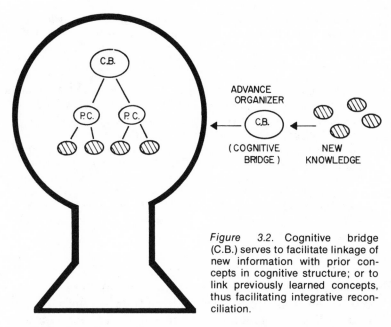

Figure 3.2. Cognitive bridge (C.B.) serves to facilitate linkage of new information with prior concepts in cognitive structure; or to link previously learned concepts, thus facilitating integrative reconciliation.

evidence has accumulated on the value of advance organizers, it has become increasingly clear that facilitation of new learning is very much a function of the adequacy of existing concepts in cognitive structure. Advance organizers probably function only to the extent that some relevant subsumers exist, and association between existing subsumers and new information is perceived by the learner (which requires a little more than just a meaningful learning set). When researchers ask for my opinion of the advance organizers they have prepared, I explain that their question cannot be answered without knowledge of the type and extent of relevant subsumers in their target population, and without sufficient information about the learning materials to be presented. Our research group has come to view advance organizers as functional only to the extent that they facilitate explicit cognitive bridging. This view is supported by other studies, which will be cited in Chapter 8 and by more recent writings of Ausubel (1968), including the following:

As pointed out earlier, the rationale for using organizers is based primarily on: (a) the importance of having relevant and otherwise appropriate established ideas "already" available in cognitive structure to make logically meaningful new ideas potentially meaningful and to give them stable anchorage; (b) the advantages of using the more general and inclusive ideas of a discipline as the anchoring ideas or subsumers (namely, the aptness and specificity of their relevance, their greater inherent stability, their greater explanatory power, and their integrative capacity); and (c) the fact that they themselves attempt both to identify already existing relevant content in cognitive structure (and to be explicitly related to it) and to indicate explicitly both the relevance of the latter content and their own relevance for the new learning material. In short, *the principal function of the organizer is to bridge the gap between what the learner already knows and what he needs to know before he can successfully learn the task at hand.* [p. 148; Ausubel's italics]

The Rote/Meaningful Learning Continuum

Except perhaps in a newborn infant, absolute rote learning probably never occurs. Even telephone numbers are linked to the knowledge structure that specifies that all phone numbers in the United States and Canada now have a three digit area code and a seven digit local number. We might memorize by rote that *karandash* is the Russian word for pencil, but "pencil" is something we know as a writing instrument that comes in a variety of colors, with soft or hard leads, usually with an eraser. We have developed a concept "pencil," and the word *karandash* links with this concept in a nonarbitrary, substantive fashion. It is very important to recognize that rote → meaningful is a continuum and not a dichotomy. This is a fundamental idea, since we doubt if any school learning occurs in an absolutely rote fashion. The real issue in school learning is not whether new information will be learned meaningfully or by absolute rote; the problem centers on the extent of meaningfulness in new learning. In our view, the idea of rote learning should be retained but applied only to those learnings where acquisition of new information takes place by linking to comparatively small elements in the existing cognitive structure. In some cases, whether some new information is learned by rote or meaningfully may be primarily a function of the individual's learning set, rather than a function of the learning material. (See also Figure 4.1, p. 101.)

Learning Set

The extent to which new information can be associated with elements in existing cognitive structure is at least partly under the control of those who learn. In the city of Ithaca, New York, for example, the first three digits of phone numbers are 256, 257, 272, 273, 274, or 277. This means all phone numbers now begin with one of these six series, plus four more digits, and not with one of the 994 other possibilities that exist for the first three digits. If people are disposed toward trying to learn new information as meaningfully as possible, they will search for ways to form associations of the type suggested here. Furthermore, all 256 numbers are Cornell University numbers, and other groups tend to be located in specific geographic areas. Knowing this, learners can reduce the rote memory load by narrowing the possibilities for the first three digits of a phone number and then learning by rote only the last four. We would say they have a meaningful learning set, even though some of the information must be stored by rote (arbitrarily) in cognitive structure. Alternately, people can learn definitions of new terms, descriptions of phenomena, or plots of stories by rote without attempting to discern how each new knowledge element is related to existing knowledge in their cognitive structures.

In my view, *rote* learning occurs when no conscious effort is made to associate new knowledge with a framework of concepts or knowledge elements already in the cognitive structure. Thus, the extent to which learning is rote or meaningful is partly a function of the learner's predisposition toward the learning task or what psychologists have called learning set; it is also a function of the degree to which relevant concepts in cognitive structure have been developed, as indicated earlier, and the potential range of linkages between new information elements and existing cognitive structure. (Phone numbers, for example, have little potential for meaningful learning.) Increasing the potential for meaningful learning should be a primary consideration in the design of curriculum and instruction, which will be discussed in Chapter 5.

Our learning set can also influence what we perceive in a given experience. A classic example is the "reversible goblet," which may be seen as a goblet or as two opposing faces, depending on our momentary cognitive set. Advance organizers can serve in part to focus the learner's attention on elements or attributes of study materials that might go entirely unnoticed without the set induction that can be offered. In a broader context, guiding students to establish a meaningful learning set can significantly influence the way in which information is internalized in cognitive structure. This guidance should be one of the most important roles of the teacher and should be emphasized in teacher education.

Subsumption and Obliterative Subsumption

In the course of meaningful learning, new information is linked with concepts in cognitive structure. In order to place emphasis on this linking phenomenon, Ausubel has introduced the terms subsuming concept or subsumer into the literature. The justification for adding these terms lies in the primary role that subsumers play in the acquisition of new information. A subsuming concept is not a kind of mental fly paper to which information is stuck; the role of a subsuming concept in meaningful learning is an interactive one, facilitating movement of relevant information through the perceptual barriers and providing a linkage between newly perceived information and previously acquired knowledge. Furthermore, in the course of this linkage, the subsuming concept becomes slightly modified, and the stored information is also altered somewhat. It is this interactive process between newly learned material and existing concepts (subsumers) which is at the core of Ausubel's assimilation theory of learning. Ausubel describes the subsumption process symbolically thus:

New information a	$\rightarrow$	Related to and assimilated by	$\rightarrow$	Established Concept A in cognitive structure	$\rightarrow$	Interaction product $A'\,a'$ (modified subsumer)

Over a sequence of time when several new knowledge elements are subsumed, substantial alteration of the original subsumer can occur as symbolized in this expression:

$$A + a_1 \rightarrow A'a'_1 + a_2 \rightarrow A''a'_1a'_2 + a_3 \rightarrow A'''a'_1a'_2a'_3 + a_4 = A''''a'_1a'_2a'_3a'_4$$
$$\text{time} = 0 \quad \text{time} = 1 \quad \text{time} = 2 \quad\quad \text{time} = 3 \quad\quad \text{time} = 4$$

In the course of meaningful learning a subsumer becomes modified and differentiated further. Differentiation of subsumers results from assimilation of new knowledge in the course of meaningful learning. Concept differentiation also occurs as new linkages are formed between concepts. This process is discussed in the next section.

Meaningfully learned information is usually retained longer than information learned by rote (information not associated with a subsumer), but in time, conscious retrieval of associated elements is not possible. When subsumed elements can no longer be retrieved from memory, Ausubel says, obliterative subsumption has occurred. This does not mean that the residual subsumer has returned to the condition it had prior to the subsumption process. Thus, although there is an apparent loss of a subordinate element, the subsumer has been modified by the prior meaningful learning experience. To continue our symbolic representation, obliterative subsumption can be shown thus:

$$A''''a'_1a'_2a'_3a'_4 \rightarrow A''''a'_2a'_3a'_4 \rightarrow A''''a'_3a'_4 \rightarrow A''''a'_4 \rightarrow A''''$$
$$\text{time} = 4 \quad\quad \text{time} = 5 \quad\quad \text{time} = 6 \quad\quad \text{time} = 7 \quad \text{time} = 8$$

An interesting research question would be to study whether the subsumer at $t = 4$ can facilitate learning of a new relevant element (a_5) better than can the subsumer at $t = 8$. There would be some difficult methodological problems to overcome, such as eliminating or minimizing any significant learning related to this subsumer between $t = 4$ and $t = 8$, but this kind of study is possible in principle. Based on some of our research findings and the work of others, we could expect that new meaningful learning relevant to subsumer A would occur most rapidly at $t = 4$, but more rapidly at $t = 8$ than at $t = 0$.

Forgetting

Most information we learn cannot be recalled at some time in the future. Although the debate continues as to whether the biological mechanisms accounting for forgetting result in physical destruction of stored memory traces or whether forgetting is purely a psychological phenomenon, for purposes of education the fact that information becomes irretrievable some time after learning is of primary concern. Most careful research on retention has been done in laboratories where subjects are given nonsense syllables or word pairs to memorize and are then tested for later rote recall of information. Some studies have used poetry, story passages, and ordinary school materials for analysis of retention. These studies show that substantial forgetting occurs in a matter of hours for nonsense syllables; for poetry and story passages, much is lost in a matter of days; and for science, history, or other classroom information, retention drops to a fraction of original learning in a matter of weeks. Some information, however, is retained for months or years.

In Ausubel's theory variation in rates of forgetting depends primarily on the degree of meaningfulness associated with the learning process. Information learned by rote (nonsense syllables and meaningless word pairs) cannot be anchored to major elements in cognitive structure and hence form a minimum linkage with it. Unless materials learned by rote are restudied repeatedly to achieve overlearning (continued study after error-free recall has been achieved), they cannot be recalled several hours or several days after learning. Information that is learned meaningfully (associated with subsumers in cognitive structure) can usually be recalled for weeks or months after acquisition. The process of subsumption results in some modification of the stored information, however. As a result recalled information may appear in a form slightly different from that originally learned. In time, recalled information may take on more general attributes of the subsuming concept(s) into which it was assimilated, and after obliterative subsumption has occurred, the specific messages learned are no longer retrievable.

Rote learning has one important advantage over meaningful

learning; we have already noted that sometimes it is useful to recall knowledge learned in precisely the same form as the original message. This process is all too frequently required in school testing.[5] Meaningful learning has three important advantages over rote learning. First, knowledge acquired meaningfully is retained longer—much, much longer in many instances. Second, subsumed information results in increased differentiation of subsumers, thus adding to the capacity for easier subsequent learning of related materials. Third, information that is forgotten after obliterative subsumption has occurred has left a residual effect on the subsuming concept, thus facilitating new related learning even after forgetting has occurred.

The last point in favor of meaningful forgetting is very important. Laboratory studies have shown that information learned by rote inhibits subsequent learning of additional similar information. Moreover, even information learned by rote that is forgotten inhibits learning of similar new information. The reverse effect operates with meaningful forgetting. While it is true that restudy or relearning of the same information is facilitated by prior retention in both rote and meaningful learning, the "savings" (as psychologists refer to this facilitation) in rote learning is only for relearning of precisely the same material, whereas meaningful learning will result in savings for relearning and facilitation (rather than inhibition) of learning new, similar (relevant to the same subsumer[s]) information.

Many students experience the feeling of being snowed under. Usually this feeling becomes most intense six to eight weeks into a course. Some studies (see Howard Hagerman, 1966) indicate that most information learned by rote in schools is lost within six to eight weeks. As a result students recognize that they have forgotten much of the information presented earlier *and* that their earlier but now lost learning is interfering with new learning. They must force themselves into review and meaningful restudy of earlier materials, cram for hours to overlearn earlier material, or give up hopes of passing the course.

[5] Banesh Hoffman has written an interesting critique of this issue in *The Tyranny of Testing* (1962).

The same phenomenon may occur at the beginning of a course when it is highly related to similar previous courses, and prior learning was rote in character.

Progressive Differentiation and Conceptual Hierarchies

As meaningful learning proceeds, development and elaboration of subsuming concepts necessarily occurs. In Ausubel's view, concept development proceeds best when the most general, most inclusive elements of a concept are introduced first and then the concept is progressively differentiated in terms of detail and specificity. For example, to introduce the concept of culture, we might begin by explaining that all the knowledge, skills, and habits passed on from parents to children constitute the culture of the human race. We could subsequently discuss Samoans or American Indians or urban American cultures, describing the methods and agencies by which the general cultural elements are transmitted.

Determination of what in a body of knowledge are the most general, most inclusive concepts and what are subordinate concepts is not easy. In Chapter 5, I shall argue that good curriculum design requires an analysis first of the concepts in a field of knowledge and second consideration of some relationships between these concepts that can serve to illustrate which concepts are most general and superordinate and which are more specific and subordinate. One reason school instruction has been so ineffective is that curriculum planners rarely sort out the concepts they hope to teach and even more rarely do they try to search for possible hierarchical relationships among these concepts. As stated before, my premise is that concepts are primarily what we think with, that concept learning is the principal function of schooling. Therefore, we must sort out from the mass of knowledge those major and subordinate concepts we wish to teach. Attitudes and skills are necessary and supportive elements for concept learning, but for most education, these are associated or concomitant learnings and do not constitute the primary structure of school curriculum. Even in trade schools, in the study of auto mechanics, for example, learning concepts in the field is at least as important as learning skills, such as acquiring competence to use a torque wrench or to remove a brake shoe.

To illustrate the idea of progressive differentiation, the concepts associated with school learning are shown in hierarchical arrangement in Figure 3.3. The concepts shown are related to a larger conceptual matrix in which school learning is seen as part of more general human culture, these relationships are not sufficiently clear to us to allow satisfactory specification in a hierarchy. The concepts at the lowest level of the hierarchy in Figure 3.3 are not unitary concepts but clusters of concepts that achieve specificity at the level of instructional practice. Thus, learning to appreciate color values in the art studio would be one form of direct experience involving one form of elemental concept learning.

The form of a conceptual hierarchy derived will be partly a function of the purpose for which it has been developed. In later sections on curriculum planning I shall show that what concept

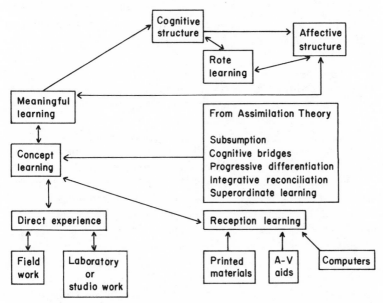

Figure 3.3. Conceptual hierarchy for learning used in this book.

we place at the top of our conceptual hierarchy and what concept is at lower levels is somewhat arbitrary. This choice does not mean that the idea of progressive differentiation has no value; the sequence of examples, the kind of examples or exercises chosen, and relative emphasis given to specific topics or concepts may be substantially different if instruction is based on one conceptual hierarchy rather than another. The central point is that efficient learning of concepts requires explication of relationships between concepts and progressively greater development of the most salient concepts. The specific sequence of experiences provided to achieve concept differentiation is only one of an almost infinite variety of learning sequences. This process is well illustrated by children as they acquire concepts. For example, young children may call everything with four legs and a tail a doggie when they are two, but soon they learn to differentiate among dogs, kittens, cows, horses, and so on. Young children nicely illustrate how progressive differentiation of concepts occurs spontaneously where the environment provides the necessary learning experience. I shall return to questions of concept differentiation and conceptual hierarchies in the section on integrative reconciliation.

Superordinate Learning

As new information is received and associated with a concept in cognitive structure (subsumption) the concept grows or differentiates. This subsumption process may continue until the concept is differentiated to the point that, to refer back to the example above, not all dogs look the same and new concept labels are applied to subordinate elements, kittens, cows, horses, for example. At some point in learning, the child may recognize or be guided to see that all these animal groups he can now distinguish are hairy and belong to a group called mammals. The concept mammal can now develop in a superordinate relationship to the concept of dogs, cats, and so forth. Superordinate learning occurs when previously learned concepts are recognized as elements of a larger, more inclusive concept. Similarly, children may learn that beets, carrots, beans, and tomatoes are all vegetables, and as biology students later in life, when the concepts of root and fruit have been articulated, they may learn that carrots and beets are both types of plant *roots* whereas beans and tomatoes (as well as pumpkins and oranges) are plant *fruits*. Superordinate learning is not common in school learning simply because most teachers and textbooks start with more general, more inclusive concepts; however, they often fail to show explicit relationships to these inclusive concepts when subordinate, specific concepts are presented later.

Integrative Reconciliation and Cognitive Dissonance

During concept differentiation, new meanings will be acquired for one or several concepts. By new meaning I mean that information that previously would not have been recognized as relevant to a given concept now is perceived as relevant and subsumable under this concept. In the example of plant fruits noted above, beans must be recognized as a kind of plant fruit as well as a vegetable. Bean pods, as other fruits, develop from the mature ovary of a flower. A student of botany must reconcile two meanings associated with bean pods.

At first a student of botany is faced with *cognitive dissonance;* how can beans be both a fruit and a vegetable? How can a corn kernel be a fruit when it looks like a seed? Whenever two concept meanings appear to be in contradiction or in some way antithetical, a learner experiences a negative emotional response or dissonance resulting from what appears to be conflicting meanings. This dissonance can be resolved when relationships between subordinate and superordinate concepts are clarified. In our example, a student can be shown that a dietary or nutritional classification scheme places beans in the category (concept) of vegetables, whereas botanical classification places beans in the category (concept) of plant fruit. We see how concept hierarchies can vary, but clear delineation of relationships in these hierarchies is important as progressive differentiation of concepts proceeds. The nature of cognitive dissonance and problems associated with reducing dissonance have been described by Leon Festinger (1957).

To avoid or minimize cognitive dissonance, instruction must be sequenced to provide not only for progressive differentiation of concepts but also to show how new concept meanings are related to alternative superordinate concepts. We must explicitly illustrate how new meanings compare and contrast with more restricted earlier meanings, and how higher order concepts now take on new meaning. Cognitive dissonance occurs when two or more concept labels are used to express the same concept, or when the same label is applied to more than one concept. For example, fruit is a concept label for a nutritional concept and also for a botanical one. In this book, subsumer, anchoring concept, subsuming concept, and concept all refer to the same thing—an organized element in cognitive structure to which new relevant information can be incorporated. I have tried to achieve integrative reconciliation by repeatedly expressing this synonymy and by stressing that the term concept is not restricted to narrow psychological meaning such as redness or triangular. Ausubel has a useful statement that may elucidate what I have said regarding integrative reconciliation (1968, p. 155):

The principle of integrative reconciliation in programming instructional material can be best described as antithetical in spirit and approach to the ubiquitous practice among textbook writers of compartmentalizing and segregating particular ideas or topics within their respective chapters or subchapters. . . . Hence, little serious effort is made *explicitly* to explore relationships between these ideas, to point out significant similarities and differences, and to reconcile real or apparent inconsistencies. Some of the undesirable consequences of this approach are that multiple terms are used to represent concepts that are intrinsically equivalent except for contextual reference, thereby generating incalculable cognitive strain and confusion, as well as encouraging rote learning; that artificial barriers are erected between related topics, obscuring important common features, and thus rendering impossible the acquisition of insights dependent upon recognition of these commonalities; that adequate use is not made of relevant, previously learned ideas as a basis for subsuming and incorporating related new information; and that since significant differences between apparently similar concepts are not made clear and explicit, these concepts are often perceived and retained as identical.

To achieve integrative reconciliation more surely, we must organize instruction so that we move "up and down" the conceptual hierarchies as new information is presented. We might do well to start with the most general concepts, but we need to illustrate early how subordinate concepts are related, and then move back through examples to new meanings for higher order concepts. This cycling up and down the conceptual ladder is schematized in Figure 3.4, which shows only one reasonable sequence and only a portion of what would occur in a semester course or in a given textbook. Planning instruction to optimize

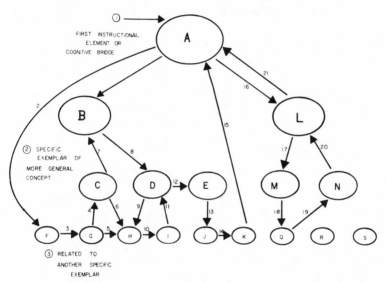

Figure 3.4. Schema of a conceptual hierarchy (letters) showing instructional sequences (numbers) for the achievement of progressive differentiation of higher order concepts and integrative reconciliation of concepts.

integrative reconciliation is discussed at some length in Chapter 5. I shall show later that careful development of instructional objectives and explicit presentation of these objectives to students is necessary for them to achieve integrative reconciliation. The use of appropriate cognitive bridges as we move from one concept to another is essential. Learning objectives, in the form in which they are now presented to students, rarely make explicit association between subordinate and superordinate con-

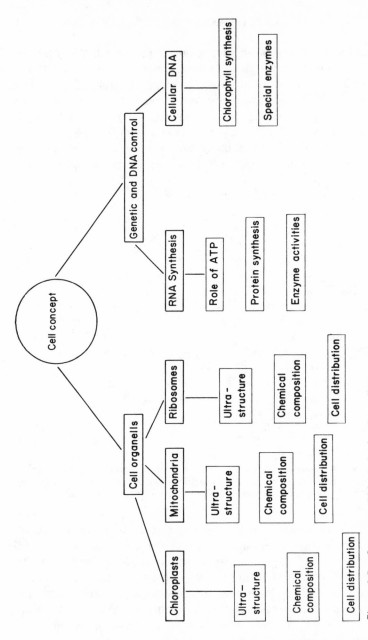

Figure 3.5. Conceptual hierarchy for the cell concept.

cepts.[6] The student is left eventually to discern relationships between concepts; the most able succeed, but others are forced into rote learning patterns or into acquiring each concept as a relatively independent entity, which thus severely restricts subsequent transfer of learning.

In the schema shown, students should learn that concepts G and H are both special aspects of concept C, and similarly, that concepts I and H are special aspects of D. They should also learn that concepts G and I are related not directly but rather through concepts C and D, which are more general concepts but also are special aspects of concept B. Conceptual hierarchies are extremely difficult to establish, even in the sciences where associations between concepts may be more evident than in history or English. Figure 3.5 shows an example of a conceptual hierarchy for the cell concept. Readers with training in biology will see how the relationships noted above hold in this scheme. The scheme is incomplete, however, for I have not mentioned some cell parts and some metabolic activities, not to mention cell differentiation into tissues. This concept hierarchy is only part of a larger conceptual hierarchy dealing with organisms, which would be part of a grand hierarchy dealing with the organization of all forms of matter in the universe. It could be argued that *all* knowledge is related and that the conceptual framework of the sciences is only a small part of the intellectual fabric of man's culture. If we proceed with this "unity" of knowledge as a premise, consider the enormity of the task of designing instructional sequences to guide students to see such relationships.

The idea of integrative reconciliation, together with the idea of progressive differentiation of concepts, has important implications for all ten questions (raised earlier in the chapter) which I believe a sound theory of learning should address.

---

[6] The writings of Robert Mager (1962) and others who have stressed behavioral objectives in education are rooted in S-R or associationist psychology, and this "peripheralist" orientation precludes concern for hierarchical organization of concepts in cognitive structure and the necessity for progressive differentiation and integrative reconciliation of concepts.

CHAPTER 4

Crucial Psychological Issues for a Theory of Education

Some of the requirements for a sound learning theory applicable to education can be found in Ausubel's assimilation learning theory for two reasons: (1) epistemologically, concepts seem to be the most important component of cultural exchange and Ausubel's theory is specifically addressed to concept learning, and (2) many educational issues can be resolved into factors that deal primarily with the quality and extent of progressive differentiation and integrative reconciliation of concepts. These key ideas, together with the basic concept of meaningful learning, can be used to see many educational issues in a new framework.

An Extension of Ausubel's Assimilation Theory
Logical vs. Psychological Organization

Although some teachers and textbooks move from general to more specific concepts, the procedure used is seldom optimal for progressive differentiation of concepts or for enhancement of integrative reconciliation. Most teachers and textbooks proceed in a *logical* order rather than in a *psychological* order. A good logical organization might place all information relevant to a concept in a single location, and all information relevant to subordinate elements in that same location. Thus, an American history book may discuss "colonial America" in a single section; the needs of people and the social institutions developed to meet those needs have changed over the past three hundred years, however, and the events during colonial times could well serve to show the evolution of social institutions. Chronological organization may help students to remember the dates when events occurred in history, and this does have some logic, but sequencing instruction progressively to develop concepts of economic systems, transporatation, and political organizations might help students much more to learn important social-historical concepts. Similarly, a biology course that describes group after group of plants from bacteria to trees and animals from amoeba to man may be logically organized, but the important concepts of ecology, genetics, evolution, metabolism, and behavior may be completely buried.

In the previous chapter it was indicated that integrative reconcilation is best achieved when instruction deals with concepts at all levels of the conceptual hierarchy in a cyclic fashion. Logical presentations present information instead in a serial order. In the cell biology example, a logical presentation sequence would look like this:
1. Cell-defined
  2. Cell Organelles
    3. Chloroplasts
      4. ultrastructure
      5. chemical composition
      6. cellular distribution
    7. Mitochondria
      8. ultrastructure
      9. cellular distribution
   10. Ribosomes
     11. ultrastructure
     12. chemical composition
     13. cellular distribution
 14. Genetic Control—DNA
   15. RNA Synthesis
     16. Role of ATP
   17. Protein synthesis
   18. Enzyme activation
 19. Cellular DNA
   20. Chlorophyll synthesis
   21. Special Enzymes

Although logical organization is better than no organization at all, most integrative reconciliation of concepts is left to the learner. One reason successful students continue to be successful is that they have somehow mastered the art of transforming logically presented information into a psychological organization. This ability, of course, is to be valued, but how do we deliberately teach to achieve it? One claim for the value of inquiry or discovery learning is that students learn how to learn. Some students do. If we understood more clearly the processes involved in progressive differentiation of concepts and their integrative reconciliation, we probably could design very good programs to teach inquiry skills, but these programs would be very different from what critical thinking, inquiry learning, discovery learning, and process education enthusiasts have been concocting. Chapters 5 and 6 will describe strategies for better psychological organization of instructional programs.

Readiness

One popular research question in education has been: When are children ready to learn a particular subject matter, such as reading, addition or multiplication, ancient history, English literature, or calculus? Despite hundreds of studies on this issue the answers are at best equivocal. The confusion arises from the question; it arises from a lack of learning theory relevant to classroom subjects, which in turn leads to formulation of the wrong questions. Ausubel's theory of learning suggests a promising reformulation of questions of readiness.

Rote learning of most subject matter can occur at almost any age. Radio quiz shows in the past popularized "wizard" children who could recite historical facts or do specific mathematical computations. As it turned out, most of the quiz shows were rigged, with children responding to "impromptu" questions on the air—after they had been carefully coached on answers prior to air time. In narrow subject matter areas, it is true, young children can demonstrate surprising knowledge; some children know the batting averages and playing positions, for example, for dozens of baseball players. But this is essentially rote learning and is limited by all the constraints described in the section on forgetting. It is a meaningless question to ask when a child is ready to learn by rote a given subject matter.

Ausubel's theory centers on the process of meaningful learning. When he recommends that we "ascertain what the learner already knows" and "teach him accordingly," he is speaking to the issue of the child's *readiness* for meaningful learning. According to this theory, a child is ready for meaningful learning in any subject area for which he has some specific, relevant subsuming concepts. The issue is related to age only because older children tend to have more and better developed concepts than younger children. This view is not peculiar to Ausubel. A group of scholars interested in education met in Woods Hole in 1959 and the report of this conference, prepared by Bruner (1960), has been widely circulated. The opening paragraph of the chapter "Readiness for Learning" reads: "We begin with the hypothesis that any subject can be taught effectively in some intellectually honest form to any child at any stages of development. It is a bold hypothesis and an essential one in thinking about the nature of a curriculum. No evidence exists to contradict it; considerable evidence is being amassed that supports it" (p. 33).

The key phrase here is "some intellectually honest form"; what does it mean to teach *any* subject this way? Bruner suggests that we must teach "basic concepts" and not "recipes":

What is most important for teaching basic concepts is that the child be helped to pass progressively from concrete thinking to the utilization of more conceptually adequate modes of thought. But it is futile to attempt this by presenting formal explanations based on a logic that is distant from the child's manner of thinking and sterile in its implications for him. Much teaching in mathematics is of this sort. The child learns not to understand mathematical order but rather to apply certain devices or recipes without understanding their significance and connectedness. They are not translated into his way of thinking. Given this inappropriate start, he is easily led to believe that the important thing is for him to be "accurate"—though accuracy has less to do with mathematics than with computation. [pp. 38–39]

We can see that what Bruner is describing sounds very much like an advocation that instruction be directed toward *meaningful* learning and not at *rote* learning. How this instruction is to be achieved, however, is never explained in his book, for Bruner flounders on the rocks of Piaget's stages of children's cognitive growth, which focuses more on the age of children than on the adequacy of specific subject matter concepts. I shall return to this issue in a later section on Piaget's work, and also in the chapter on empirical studies.

Motivation

Readiness to learn does not imply that learning will necessarily occur; an individual must also be motivated to learn. Although authors differ in the ways motivation is described, we see three principal types of motivation operating in schools: ego enhancement, aversive, and cognitive drive. *Ego enhancement* motivation occurs when learners recognize that they are in some way demonstrating competence or achieving success.[1] It is probably the most important form of motivation in learning or for achieving success in adult life. It is the way individuals enhance their images of "I'm OK," to borrow a phrase from Thomas A. Harris' popular book, *I'm OK—You're OK* (1967). *Aversive motivation* derives from an individual's desire to avoid unpleasant consequences, be it an ego-degrading experience or some form of punishment (penalties, low grades, and so forth). *Cognitive drive* motivation derives from the recognition of success in learning.

The three forms of motivation are not mutually exclusive. For example, successful mastery of a unit of instruction may result in cognitive drive motivation to study further, but if the individual is the first in the class to complete the unit, ego enhancement motivation may also be obtained. Conversely, the necessity to pass a subject to graduate or advance in some form, or to avoid failure, may also lead to success in learning and consequent cognitive drive motivation. Some forms of ego enhancement motivation require that others be denied this kind of motivation. Conventional grading procedures on a curve may be ego enhancing to the top students in the grade distribution, but they are ego destructive to the students at the bottom. For the

---

[1] Some authors, including Ausubel, also identify *affiliative drive* as an important form of motivation based on an individual's desire to perform to receive recognition by teammates, parents, teachers, or others with whom there is group identification. We see this, however, as essentially another form of ego enhancement motivation involving the individual simultaneously with some group image.

latter students, there may be some aversive motivation to work harder before the next exam, but what if they continue to be at the bottom of the curve?

Mastery learning programs, where students have variable amounts of time to achieve success in learning a body of subject matter, can provide cognitive drive motivation to all students. There will still be some ego enhancement and aversive motivation operating for the quick or slow learners, but the primary motivation in this mode of instruction is shifted to where it most properly belongs—in the satisfaction that comes with the realization of success in learning.

Another advantage of cognitive drive motivation is that it is *intrinsic* to the very process of learning. It does not require that a teacher administer or deny rewards, and it can continue to motivate learning in formal school settings or in independent study. Successful learning is in itself rewarding.

Too many school practices in the past have used aversive motivation (dunce caps have given way to tracking schemes and posting of grade point averages) or ego enhancement motivation (dean's list, honors sections) as primary means of motivation rather than directing efforts to achieve nondiscriminative ego enhancement or cognitive drive motivation. The latter derive from careful diagnosis of growth in competence against some fixed criterion, and not with reference to other students. We have justified aversive and selective ego enhancement motivation on the premise that this is a "dog-eat-dog" world and children must learn to live in it. The question remains if motivation for school learning should condition students for a competitive kind of societal existence for ten, twelve, or sixteen years. It might be appropriate to ask if competitive practices are inherent in man's existence or if they derive from human value structures engendered by years of schooling. As peoples of the world recognize increasingly that natural resources are finite and diminishing in supply, we may witness more aggressive competition, perhaps with ultimate nuclear holocaust—or we may see societies moving toward realistic standards of satisfying life styles. To what extent changing the emphasis in school motivation to cognitive drive motivation for learning would influence positively the value structure of future generations is an interesting conjecture.

Reception Learning and Discovery Learning

You, as a reader of this book, are engaged in *reception* learning; you are receiving information assembled by me in a form in which you can admit this information into your cognitive structure. Ausubel places heavy stress on the role of reception learning in all education, but especially in school learning. This is not to deny the value of *discovery* learning, where the content to be learned (internalized) is selected and acquired by the learner. Ausubel's emphasis on reception learning is pragmatic; he contends that most of school learning is reception learning and, therefore, that we need to analyze this type of learning with the goal of improving reception teaching and reception learning. This idea is central to the thesis of this book, although the value of discovery learning especially for purposes of affective development will also be stressed.

One of Ausubel's important contributions is his careful distinction between *rote* reception learning and *meaningful* reception learning. He is at least as unhappy with the common practice of rote reception learning as most proponents of discovery learning. However, rather than clarifying methods by which reception teaching and, hence, reception learning could be improved, enthusiasts of discovery learning have thrown the baby out with the bath water; they would prefer that students be given a minimum of guidance in directing their learning efforts, although few today would go so far as to make no effort to guide students in the selection of study material.

Figure 4.1 illustrates that rote learning and meaningful learning represent a different continuum from reception learning and discovery learning. The failure to recognize that the former represents the form in which information is acquired in cognitive structure, whereas the latter represents the instructional approach employed has resulted in much confusion in education. Examples of activities which vary in degree of meaningfulness and/or discovery are shown in Figure 4.1.

Discovery learning can also be rote learning; we can discover

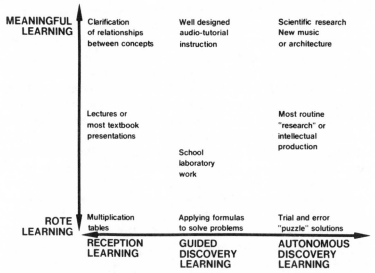

MEANINGFUL LEARNING	Clarification of relationships between concepts	Well designed audio-tutorial instruction	Scientific research New music or architecture
	Lectures or most textbook presentations	School laboratory work	Most routine "research" or intellectual production
ROTE LEARNING	Multiplication tables	Applying formulas to solve problems	Trial and error "puzzle" solutions
	RECEPTION LEARNING	**GUIDED DISCOVERY LEARNING**	**AUTONOMOUS DISCOVERY LEARNING**

Figure 4.1. Reception and discovery learning are on a continuum distinct from rote learning and meaningful learning. Typical forms of learning are shown to illustrate representative different "positions" in the matrix.

a solution to a puzzle or algebra problem by trial and error and not associate this "discovery" with existing knowledge in cognitive structure. A "discovery" made by a scientist is not a discovery until the new information can be related to concepts already familiar to scientists or to a new concept that encompasses or supercedes earlier concepts. Rote discovery learning may be involved in games with desirable social or affective learning outcomes, but it cannot be justified as an important mode for cognitive learning. Meaningful discovery learning, as when an individual sees, on his own, how attributes or functions of some instrument or object relate to concepts in his cognitive structure, can not only lead to cognitive growth (concept development and/or elaboration) but also provide the individual with a strong positive affective experience that can motivate further study and contribute to his self-image of adequacy.

During the 1960s we observed in education a conspicuous rush to inquiry or discovery methods. Lee Shulman and Evan

Keislar (1966) edited a conference report, *Learning by Discovery: A Critical Appraisal,* in which varied viewpoints were expressed about the nature of discovery learning and the methods to encourage it through instruction. In our view, discussions on alternatives for fostering discovery learning get mired down as a result of poor definition of what should be the primary goal of discovery learning—the development of the individual's conceptual framework through meaningful learning. The determination of how much guidance is permissible before learning ceases to be discovery learning is thus translated into a concern for efficient programs, to assimilate new information into existing or developing concepts in students' cognitive structures. The concern for transfer of learning from one set of tasks to new problems becomes principally a curriculum issue of determining which concepts, once developed, will have maximum relevance for the widest array of subsequent concept learnings or problems. Thus, we have seen in the almost perennial arguments on discovery learning[2] a focus on instructional elements rather than on cognitive learning elements, with the result that empirical studies fail to support many alternatives tested and we remain confused about how best to promote discovery learning. Here is a classic example of the chaos that can occur in education when we lack a paradigm for the study of learning and consequently raise the wrong questions in our research.

Learning Style

Given the same new information to learn, one individual may form few or no linkages with concepts he already has (that is, learn by rote), and another individual may consciously relate the new information with one or more elements of his conceptual framework that seem relevant (that is, learn meaningfully). We could say that the first person has a rote learning style whereas the second has a meaningful learning style. Of course, any individual can vacillate from rote to meaningful styles from time to

---

[2] Over the years the essential features of discovery learning have been debated and advocated under the labels of critical thinking, problem solving strategies, inquiry learning, divergent thinking strategies, and, most recently, process education.

time depending on his learning set, so the learning style of an individual is more appropriately characterized by his modal behavior and not by performance on a single learning task. In the previous section we distinguished between rote reception learning and meaningful reception learning. Undoubtedly, each of us has on some occasion received information that we learned essentially by rote rather than meaningfully. A common problem today is to convert temperature from centigrade to Fahrenheit. We can learn by rote that $F° = 9/5C° + 32$, but we may forget if the value is 5/9 or 9/5, or if we add or subtract 32°. When one can recall that $0°C. = 32°F.$ (freezing point of water) and that $100°C. = 212°F.$ (boiling point of water), then the conversion factor for centigrade to Fahrenheit or vice versa has more meaning and can be remembered better. Certainly all of us can think of instances in which we once learned something by rote and later possessed the conceptual structure to acquire this same knowledge meaningfully. Although concepts are retained much longer than facts learned by rote, we do forget concepts in time and occasionally we must resort to rote learning things we once learned meaningfully. Our style of learning has reverted from meaningful reception learning to rote reception learning, and the associated affective response is usually negative. Not uncommonly we observe that we once understood why some fact was true or why some formula was written in a specific form, but that later we forget the explanatory concept(s).

As with reception learning, every reader has probably engaged in some rote discovery learning as well as in some meaningful discovery learning. In assembling a puzzle, for example, a person usually constructs the border first, since the straight edges of these pieces reduce the need for random search and trial-and-error fitting of pieces. If it is a picture puzzle and the picture is kept in view, a kind of guided discovery proceeds since the colors or design will reduce the possible alternative locations for any given piece. If the puzzle has no picture or design, or if work is proceeding on a large area of blue sky, almost random trial of pieces may occur, although the stamp pattern does provide a limited conceptual framework to guide assembly. The positive emotional response that comes from completing a puzzle varies with individuals and with the difficulty of the puzzle. Some individuals want essentially no guidance with puzzles or games whereas others seek assistance to the point that the task becomes one of reception learning. The discovery strategies involved in puzzle solving or other recreations are usually pursued for the affective dividend an individual receives and only secondarily for cognitive growth, whereas discovery learning in school might be pursued primarily for concept learning. Some people who enjoy difficult puzzles or games are repelled by tasks of discovery learning in subject matter fields which others enjoy. We see, then, that discovery learning as a style of learning may be selected by an individual depending on the extent to which affective rewards are perceived to compensate for the inefficiency of this method of learning as opposed to reception learning, if a choice of either method is available.

In the literature on learning styles, reference to *convergent* versus *divergent* thinking is common. Convergent thinking is characterized as that which leads to stereotyped responses or interpretations, whereas divergent thinking is associated with novel or creative associations. For example, to say bricks can be used to make a building is to give a convergent response, whereas to suggest that a brick can be used as a measuring rod would be considered a divergent response. The literature on convergent-divergent thinking is an intellectual morass, for it lacks precise association between the uses of these terms and specific learning performances. If the terms are worth salvaging, convergent thinking could be described as learning that tends to be rote in character, and hence, responses appear to be standardized or stereotyped. In divergent thinking learning is meaningful in character, and hence, responses are drawn from a much broader cognitive network or framework of concepts.

Problem Solving

Problem solving takes many forms. Motor skills may be required, as in the case of artistic representation of "solutions" or in tracing maze patterns. Most commonly, however, problem solving involves reorganization of stored information in cognitive structure to reach some specified goal. Where new information is required for a solution, problem solving may include search procedures such as hypothesizing or experimentation. Stress on the latter procedures characterizes the writing of Karl Pearson (1900) and John Dewey (1910), and continues in contemporary thinking as embodied in the American Association for the Advancement of Science elementary school curriculum, *Science: A Process Approach* (1968). While it would be foolish to ignore the role of motor skills or procedures used in experimentation, especially in some forms of problem solving, the most salient issue, in my view, is to explore how hierarchically arranged cognitive structures (conceptual structures) function in the process of problem solving.

My early views of problem solving, based on a general cybernetic view of learning, placed stress on two separate components of cognitive functioning: information storage and information processing. As I viewed the process then, improvement in the ability to solve problems could occur by either acquisition of new knowledge or by improvement in information processing skill. The latter skill I thought might be improved by appropriate school instruction in which students were frequently presented with problems and guided in their solution. My thesis research (1957) was based on an experimental project centered method of teaching college botany, wherein progressively more open-ended laboratory exercises were given followed by a six-week period for a major botanical project with only individual tutoring taking place. To measure problem solving ability in a manner consistent with cybernetic theory, a problem solving test was designed that required students to select the most probably correct alternative in the successive and related choices. The test consisted of six problems, each presenting a problem statement and then successive pairs of answer statements. A student was to read the problem, choose the most plausible alternative answer for Part I, move to Part II answers based on the previous choice and choose another alternative, and then select a final choice at Part III. Each answer statement contained some new information, so in accordance with cybernetic theory, correct problem solving required successive information processing, storage, and retrieval. Evidence for reliability and validity was obtained (Novak, 1961), and data on error patterns were analyzed. The theory was that good information processing ability was much more important than the amount of information an individual had stored in cognitive structure. Therefore, good problem solvers (that is, those who get correct answers on most of the problems) would be more successful in making successive correct choices and using information gained from Parts I and II in the problems; the result should be that most of the errors would be in the final choice. On the other hand, we theorized that poor problem solvers would not process new information obtained in Part I adequately and make their first error in Part I of the problems. The answers were scored so that a problem was marked wrong if all three selections were not correct. Figure 4.2 shows the results obtained. One can see that

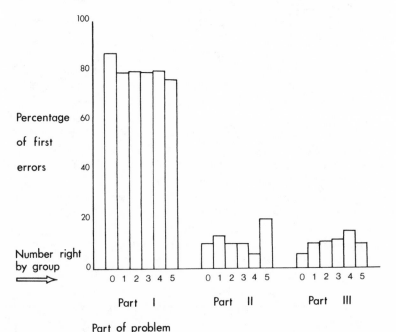

Figure 4.2. Percentage of "first" errors made on each of the three parts of a problem for each of the score groups.

both good and poor problem solvers made their errors in the same place on problems that were missed—students missing the most problems (score group 0) and students missing the least problems (score group 5) made about 80 percent of the errors in Part I. In 1961 I wrote:

It should be pointed out that the failure of the error patterns to correspond to that expected under the theory given earlier may be due to the structure of the test problems. As they are presented, the successive choices may be relatively obvious if the subject selects the "correct" alternative at the first part of the problem. If this were true, we would expect most of the errors would occur at the first step of the problem. In checking through the comments of the validation group, it was found that several of the scientists felt that the alternatives at each step were very "close" and that frequently a final decision on the answer for the first part of a problem could not be determined with a satisfactory degree of certainty until all three parts were studied and the selections made. No member of the validation group commented that the answers to the second and third parts of the problems were obvious once the first selection was made.

With the above considerations, it remains possible that the good problem solver differs from the poor in that he more successfully considers the information of preceding behaviors (choices to parts one and two of the problem) in determining what is most likely the "correct" answer to the problem. The data available in this study do not show whether or not the good problem solver actually explores more possible "solutions" than the poor problem solver. It is possible that the individual with problem solving skill actually explores more possible answers, mentally or through overt behavior, and/or derives more information from each answer (behavior) he attempts. [p. 129]

Now that we are using Ausubel's theory as a basis for our research, we see my earlier results in a new light.

If the degree of cognitive differentiation (that is, the number and extent of differentiation of hierarchically ordered concepts) is the primary determinant for meaningful learning and if this cognitive differentiation proceeds gradually as a person matures, it stands to reason that the comparatively small amount of new information presented in the test problems would have little or no bearing on the relative adequacy of an individual's total cognitive structure. Hence, all individuals would tend to exhibit a kind of all-or-none performance, either answering the problem correctly or failing at Part I. Ausubel's ideas seemed to explain the data I obtained on problem solving. Further analysis of empirical studies that support Ausubel's theory will be given in Chapter 8.

I had learned that it is probably incorrect to isolate information storage and information processing activities into two separate characteristics of cognitive functioning as was suggested by cybernetic theory. I now see them as essentially two elements of the same functional cognitive framework. Meaningful information acquisition is dependent on availability of relevant subsuming concepts in cognitive structure and, as was stressed in Chapter 2, concepts are what we think with in solving problems. Good problem solving ability, therefore, requires well-differentiated relevant concepts, concepts relevant to the problems we wish to solve. What characterizes the person who is good at solving new problems is probably the tendency to develop higher order concepts, which through their greater generality and inclusiveness necessarily become relevant to a wider array of problems; also important is the adequacy of relevant prior learning, either meaningful reception learning or discovery learning. Because problem solving often requires incorporation of new information into cognitive structure, I see problem solving as essentially a special case of meaningful learning.

There is, then, no simple magic formula for training students to become good problem solvers, but the search for some special method goes on. We need instead to focus on improving the process of meaningful learning and developing evaluation programs that reward successful problem solvers more than rote memorizers.

Creativity

The number of meanings for the term "creativity" is almost as large as the number of people describing this trait. However, all writers hold in common that creative behavior results in some kind of interpretation (in words or products) that is novel; it is in a form not commonly expressed or evident to all. Creative behavior would also be evidenced as "divergent thinking." There have been many attempts to characterize creative individuals; E. Paul Torrance (1962) has reviewed some of this literature and compiled a composite list of eighty-four characteristics of creative individuals.

Ausubel (1968) takes the position that "although creativity undoubtedly varies along a continuum, only the rare individual who makes a singularly original and significant contribution to art, science, literature, philosophy, government, and so forth, can be called a creative person. The creative person is, by definition, a much rarer individual than the intelligent person" (p. 552). Thus, Ausubel has a very restrictive definition of the creative person. I agree with Ausubel that "creativity undoubtedly varies along a continuum," but I see no reason to restrict description of the creative individual only to those who are singularly outstanding. It may be easy to recognize the extremely creative person, but how does this kind of person function mentally to achieve results? Ausubel asserts that creativity is primarily an inherited ability:

This is not to deny the important role of environment in the development of creativity; many potential Mozarts, for example, have spent their lives as peasants or cobblers. But even assuming an optimal environment, creative individuals would still be extremely rare. The principle [sic] determinant of creative persons, in other words, is genetic within a specified range of environmental influences. These latter influences function more as limiting rather than as directive factors. [pp. 552–553]

A truly creative individual is rare not primarily because he lacks appropriate experience to develop his creative potentialities, but because he is, by definition, at such an extreme point in the distribution of creative potentialities that he is *qualitatively discontinuous* from persons exhibiting lesser degrees of creativity. [p. 552; italics mine]

The history of sciences and the humanities shows the dependence of eminently successful thinkers on the work of the contemporaries or predecessors who were less exceptional. James Watson in *The Double Helix* (1968), when describing the creative work leading to elucidation of the molecular structure of DNA, nicely documents an intellectual race where, in effect, he and Francis Crick were the lucky winners, and not singularly creative. Rarely is such candor shown by creative persons in describing their work, and even though a few critics may be correct in challenging some of Watson's perceptions, we owe him thanks for an illuminating description.

My primary reason for disagreement with Ausubel's emphasis on accounting for creativity primarily in terms of genetic factors is that no explanation of mental functions is achieved by divorcing creative behavior from other cognitive or affective processes; genes must act in some explainable manner to produce creativity. My view of creative behavior is that this behavior occurs when an individual makes unique associations across concepts at higher levels in a conceptual hierarchy. Creative behavior is to us a form of superordinate learning which allows perception of new relationships between subordinate concepts. The superordinate learning occurring in creative production is necessarily discovery learning and not reception learning. However, we may fail to recognize much creative work that is not original, for we may often assume that the student acquired superordinate concepts through good teaching (or writing), when in fact the latter may have failed to teach. Conversely, we sometimes think we have a creative insight only to learn later that we probably received (by reception learning) the conceptual relationship from some teacher or writer we failed to recall. Extraordinary creativity occurs when very broad concepts at high levels in two or more conceptual hierarchies are related to each other through some still higher level of generalization. For example, Einstein's recognition that mass and energy are conserved but that a new relationship is possible wherein mass can be converted into energy ($E = mc^2$) drew on concepts familiar to all physicists but also allowed new associations to be formed in a manner not recognized until Einstein described the fundamental relationship.

In short, we see creative behavior as a tendency to build hierarchical conceptual structures and to seek relationships between higher order concepts (to achieve superordinate learning). What may be inherited are a facility to structure knowledge in hierarchical fashion, an emotional predisposition toward hierarchical structuring of knowledge in cognitive structure, or both. The highly creative person seeks to find relationships between knowledge elements or low-level concepts and to form high-level superordinate concepts. Emotionally, the creative person is disposed to persist in this meaningful learning activity even when, for example, rote learning would have good payoff in an instructional setting. We see in the descriptions of creative behavior by Jacob Getzels and Philip Jackson (1962), Torrance (1962), and others the characterization of a person who persists in meaningful rather than rote learning, sometimes to the consternation of his teachers, who want verbatim answers. The creative person achieves overall success in school not by playing the game the way the teachers and most students would expect, but by using the long-term power of meaningful learning to achieve ultimate success. Figure 4.3 illus-

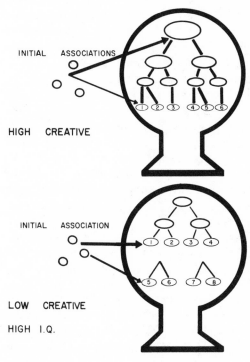

INITIAL ASSOCIATIONS

HIGH CREATIVE

INITIAL ASSOCIATION

LOW CREATIVE

HIGH I.Q.

Figure 4.3. Schema showing differences between highly creative individuals and low creative individuals. High creatives tend to form initial linkages with "high order" concepts, and to build complex hierarchical structures. Low creatives tend to internalize information by linkage to specific, low-order concepts or by rote learning. High creative students tend to form strong hierarchical linkages (heavy lines) in concepts, whereas high I.Q. subjects tend to form numerous specific, low-order concepts with weak linkages to other concepts. A student may be high (or low) in one or both of these aspects.

trates schematically the high creative and low creative learner. There is parsimony in the view that creativity and creative behavior can now be described in terms of rote versus meaningful learning behavior. School environments that favor rote learning or that place little reward in hierarchical ordering of knowledge not only restrict creative expression by students (whatever their genic potentials may be), but tend to be more positive emotionally for the least creative and more negative emotionally for the most creative students. Is it any wonder that such critics as Illich (1970) call for "deschooling society"? I shall reconsider the relationships among intelligence, creativity, and school achievement in later chapters.

Intelligence

The number of definitions of creativity is easily exceeded by that for intelligence. Moreover, efforts at measurement of intelligence have a history of seven decades, to say nothing of the thousands of studies that correlated measures of intelligence with measures of school achievement, personality traits, creativity, and personal adjustment. Sometimes intelligence is described simply as what intelligence tests measure but there are a variety of intelligence tests. Early intelligence tests developed by Binet and Simon were designed to select French children who could profit from schooling, and most subsequent intelligence tests have been validated largely by their power to predict school achievement. But what mental faculties are required for school achievement? The elementary school at the turn of the century was primarily an experience in rote learning, wherein the master dictated lessons to children (textbooks were scarce) and children memorized by rote information to recite when called upon. Unfortunately, even with our enormously greater potential resources for learning, much of school learning continues to be listen (or read)—memorize—recite—forget.

In our discussion of the continuum between rote learning and highly meaningful learning, we stressed that the latter was dependent upon the availability of relevant, hierarchically arranged conceptual structures. Rote learning, or essentially rote learning, occurs when new information is arbitrarily stored in a cognitive structure or is associated with weakly differentiated concepts at low levels of abstractness and inclusiveness. An individual can have a good facility for rote learning as a product of inheritance, but little facility for forming high order conceptual relationships or for effecting superordinate learning and integrative reconciliation. A person can be highly intelligent (that is, facile in acquiring information by rote or at low levels of conceptual abstractness) and yet have very little creative ability as we have described it. On the other hand, well-differentiated subordinate concepts can substantially enhance meaningfulness resulting from superordinate learning at higher conceptual levels; however, I agree with Ausubel that the highly intelligent person may not be creative.

We can represent differences between the high I.Q. individual and the highly creative individual as shown in Figure 4.3. If testing monitors only or primarily information stored at the lowest conceptual levels, the high I.Q. individual will perform well, whereas if testing involves problem solving necessitating use of higher order concepts, the highly creative individual will be favored. Most I.Q. tests and most tests of school achievement (including Scholastic Achievement Tests and Graduate Record Examinations) tend to require information from only the lowest levels of conceptual abstraction. Partly for this reason, the dean of the Graduate School at Cornell has found a zero correlation between Graduate Record Examination scores and professors' ratings of doctoral students' achievement.

There has been continuing controversy on the nature and meaning of I.Q. test scores. Intelligence test scores are scaled so that the average score obtained divided by the average age of the subject will equal 1.00 for a normal population. Multiplying by 100 we obtain an average I.Q. of 100, with about two thirds of our group falling in the range of 84 to 116 on the I.Q. scale. Consider what this means in terms of Ausubel's model of cognitive learning. It means that the person of average intelligence will possess in cognitive structure twice as many dissociable knowledge bits at age fourteen as at age seven. Of course, administrative and scaling problems are associated with using the same test across widely differing age levels, so some test-item juggling is necessary. What the I.Q. test does not tell us is the specific conceptual hierarchies an individual possesses, the extent of differentiation of concepts in these hierarchies, and the individual's proclivity to learn meaningfully rather than by rote. The inevitable result is that correlations between I.Q. scores and school achievement tend to be around $r = 0.5$ (and hence $r^2 = 0.25$, which means at best that 25 percent of the variance in school achievement is accounted for by the I.Q. factor and 75 percent by something else) and correlations between I.Q. and adult performance drop to near zero.

We are not saying that I.Q. tests have no validity or that it is useless to consider the meaning of various I.Q. test results. We do feel that measurement of I.Q., including most of the more recent work in psychometric measures, suffers seriously from lack of foundation on mechanisms of learning and of a theoretical learning framework. In later discussions on research it will be recommended that all testing programs, including intelligence testing, need to be re-examined with respect to the extent to which they utilize specific conceptual structures and the levels of conceptual hierarchies at which items are targeted.

Value Learning

During the 1950s and early 1960s, schools in the United States became preoccupied with the knowledge explosion and the need to teach more contemporary knowledge to students. The 1970s have been a time of reassessment, and we expect that the 1980s could very well become a decade in which value education is a major preoccupation. In my view, these changes in educational fads derive in part from the muddy view most educators have about both cognitive and affective learning. I see values held by a person as a composite of his cognitive, psychomotor, and affective learning experiences.

We can easily illustrate how one learns to value golf, as skill and knowledge of the game are acquired and positive emotional experiences ensue. The same could be said about values regarding chess or music or literary criticism. In other instances, the interplay of knowledge, skills, and affective experience may be more subtle as, for example, in valuing truth or environmental quality.

Societal values evolve as the concepts held by the society evolve. This could be illustrated by the growing world-wide interest in birth control and related values associated with women's liberation and population control. The alleged preoccupation of Western culture with material values is, in part, a product of conceptual evolution in the sciences and the subsequent development of technology. It is easy to see how societal values have changed over centuries as new knowledge came into being. It is often more difficult to recognize how an individual's values change as he or she acquires new knowledge. Moreover, the experience in which an individual acquires new knowledge may bring about either strong positive or negative emotional experience, with the result that one person places high value on a particular area of knowledge (mathematics or literature, for example), while another does not.

Educational programs cannot be neutral. Whenever we succeed in teaching new knowledge, we necessarily influence students' values. The challenge faced by educators is to give attention to the effect of new knowledge and the emotional context of the learning upon students' values. To ignore these issues is to go forward blindly, influencing values frequently in socially undesirable ways, which may contribute to delinquency, crime, or personal inadequacies that will be costly to both the victimized individuals and the society as a whole.

Piaget's Developmental Psychology: Value and Limitations

Although Piaget began writing on children's learning more than a half century ago, interest in his work has exploded on the American scene largely in the 1960s. The delay in American awareness of his work can be in part attributed to the fact that much of his early writing was in French. Piaget's *Language and Thought of the Child,* however, was published in English in 1926, and other important works appeared in English in the following five years. But Piaget's writing is not easy to read, as he mixes theory, observation, and logical descriptions. Why, then, the burgeoning interest in Piaget during the 1960s?

In my view, American educators were widely promulgating discovery or inquiry teaching and, in the absence of data to support this method of instruction, they were seeking some authority figure to justify what might be referred to as the cult of discovery learning. Piaget's studies have been based on careful observation of children doing things and on careful questioning of children as they manipulated objects. Since discovery teaching emphasizes free exploration of study materials by children, advocates of discovery learning seized upon Piaget's theory to justify their position. We doubt if many such enthusiasts read one book or paper by Piaget, but they learned to invoke his name to buttress their claims for the power and validity of discovery teaching.

This "marriage of convenience" of discovery learning and Piaget, unwarranted as it has been, is not without its redeeming value; it has served to draw attention to the important work of Piaget and also to the value of clinical investigation, in contrast to the widely popular multivariate educational experimentation of the 1950s and early 1960s. The latter type of research, prodded to a frenzied pace by large financial grants from the U.S. Office of Education and aided by new, high-speed computers, allowed certain educational research workers to display statistical sophistication that obscured the conceptual emptiness of their research questions. The rising popularity of Piaget's simple clinical methods was to many educators a blessed relief from the psychometric and statistical barrage symbolized in the leadership of the American Educational Research Association. If Piaget had anonymously submitted a proposal for funding of one of his studies to the U.S. Office of Education in 1955 or 1960, the review panels would probably have regarded it as some kind of practical joke. How absurd. It would have contained no data on sample size or randomization, no indication of the reliability of the "assessment protocol," and no information on the type of experimental design or statistical tests to be employed.

Piaget's Clinical Interview

Piaget's autobiography (1952) describes his childhood interests in plants and animals and relates his careful studies of mollusks, including his doctoral degree studies between 1915 and 1918. Whether from heredity or through experience in natural history, Piaget showed great capacity for careful observation and description of organisms. When employed in 1920 to help standardize intelligence tests in France, he was intrigued not by the psychometric problems involved in item selection and normalization procedures but by the individual responses of students and especially by the wrong answers they would give. This experience led Piaget to study carefully and systematically the types of responses children gave to questions, with much of his work involving manipulative materials. He found not only that older children answered more questions correctly but also that their answers were qualitatively different from those of younger children. Our research group has adapted Piaget's clinical interview method in some studies, and Figure 4.4 shows one colleague administering a Piagetian interview using materials related to our audio-tutorial elementary science program discussed in Part II. In a clinical interview, children are asked to explain what is occurring in a situation, or what they would expect to happen if the situation were manipulated in some way. Interviews are usually tape-recorded for later analysis.

The following description illustrates the kinds of things Piaget learned: very young children shown a ball of clay rolled into a sausage shape will frequently say that the "sausage" has more clay—because it is longer; or that the ball has more clay—because it is thicker. In short, the children do not conserve substance and do not see that changing the form of the clay does not change the amount. By age six or seven, however, most children will recognize that no clay has been lost in a transformation and that the ball and sausage forms are the same substance, and by age ten they will know that the various forms of clay will have the same weight.

Studies using the clinical interview, as well as naturalistic studies during which Piaget and his coworkers simply observed

Figure 4.4. Piagetian interview with materials related to our audio-tutorial elementary science program.

carefully and recorded the spontaneous behavior of children in an environment containing materials with which to interact, have led Piaget to describe developmental stages of children. Although transition from earlier to later periods is gradual and sometimes vacillating, four general periods in the development of children's cognitive structure have been described by Piaget and his coworkers.

Piaget's Developmental Stages

1. Sensory-Motor Period (birth to two years). During this period, a child progresses from inherited behaviors, characterized by sucking, prehension, and crying, to more specific motor patterns controlled deliberately by the child. By the end of this period, the child can manipulate physical objects in the environment to satisfy hunger or curiosity and can imitate various adult behaviors. The child can respond to things not in direct view, and hence, physical objects have taken on a cognitive as well as a physical reality.

2. Preoperational Period (two to seven years). Children develop their ability to form mental symbols which stand for or represent things or events, even in the absence of the latter. Playing house and other symbolic play characterize this stage. Language development progresses and is actively used in symbolic play. Children continue to be egocentric in perspective, seeing reality largely as it affects them; consequently, explanations may be in terms that are consistent with the children's experiences—the tall toy house has more blocks than the flat building because the toy house is bigger (taller)—and may or may not be consistent with reality.

3. Concrete Operational Period (seven to eleven years). During this period the child gains precision in comparing and contrasting objects of concrete reality and can come to predict correctly which stick in a series is longest or which jar holds the most water. However, explanation and prediction, while no longer based on children's egocentric view or the mood of the moment, still require comparison and contrast with real things; they cannot handle such symbolic contrasts as if all A's are bigger than C's and C's are bigger than B's, all A's are bigger than B's. In other words, children have cognitive representations of reality, but they can manipulate relations between these reality objects only when the objects are present.

4. Formal Operations Period (eleven plus years). In this period the child can compare and contrast among alternatives that may exist only in the mind. Increased language development also makes possible better interpretations. Piaget stresses that the important characteristic of this final period (that continues through adulthood) is the ability to manipulate mental constructs and to recognize relations between these constructs. To understand that a car traveling fifteen miles on one gallon of gasoline could travel one hundred fifty miles on ten gallons of gasoline requires formal operations.

Piaget and Ausubel

Piaget emphasizes that children do not abruptly move from one period to another. On the contrary, they may as teenagers or adults exhibit all four types of behavior on occasion, although their predominant mental activity will be formal operations. Children may occasionally behave in ways characteristic of earlier periods, but their modal behavior will be in a pattern characteristic of their age group. I.Q. or other ability indicators and differences in cultural settings can show small variations in the *age* at which a child reaches each period, but the *order* of the periods will be invariant for all children. Moreover, one should rarely expect that a child in one period will exhibit behavior characteristic of two periods later; in other words, individuals can always exhibit behavior at lower levels but not at substantially higher levels of cognitive functioning.

My Ausubelian-based views[3] on cognitive development place more stress on language development. In this respect, Ausubel and I are closer to the thinking of Lev Vygotsky (1962) and Benjamin Lee Whorf (1956), who place stress on the role of language in mediating higher levels of cognitive functioning. Both Piaget and Vygotsky were born in 1896 and Whorf in 1897; however, Vygotsky died in 1934, and Whorf in 1941. Undoubtedly, their work would have had much wider influence on cognitive psychology had they continued their brief but productive careers. Vygotsky and Whorf saw language development as the primary vehicle for higher order cognitive functioning whereas Piaget minimizes the role of language and, instead, places focus on physical maturation (age related) and experience. It is unfortunate that so many Piaget enthusiasts are unfamiliar with the works of Vygotsky and Whorf, to say nothing of the recent work of Chomsky (1972) and other contemporary linguistic scholars.

Experience with concrete objects is to us an important requisite for cognitive growth. Ausubel stresses the need for "concrete empirical" props in the process of forming *primary abstractions*. A child's concept of dog, for example, derives from direct experience with specific dogs and only later does the generic concept of dog emerge. Similarly, the primary abstraction "triangle" takes on initial meaning from specific experience

---

[3] I see some minor differences between my views regarding Piaget and those of Ausubel in that I place somewhat more stress on the fundamental importance on the degree of differentiation of specifically relevant concepts in cognitive structure in the facilitation of learning or problem solving.

with "triangles." The development of primary abstractions includes, in Ausubel's view, acquisition of verbal labels, and once these are sufficiently stable and differentiated, children can use the concept label by itself in their thinking, without reference to specific "concrete props."

Young children (ages up to four) are limited to use of primary abstractions in Ausubel's view and hence, they are "preoperational" in that their thinking is tied to concrete empirical props directly or to concept labels whose meanings are tied to recent experience with concrete props. Although Piaget and his co-workers tend to continue emphasis on the role of concrete props in new learning of preoperational children, my view allows for meaningful verbal learning whenever new learning can be related to existing primary abstractions that are adequately differentiated. Thus, meaningful reception learning of abstract concepts is possible with preschool youngsters but only in specific concept areas and not generally across all subject matters.

By the age of six or seven, Ausubel holds that children can easily form secondary abstractions; they can form concepts whose meaning does not derive from specific concrete empirical props. For example, we could define mammals as animals with fur and mammary glands for nursing offspring, and the child would be able to discriminate between examples of mammals and nonmammals when presented with choices. The child is in effect *applying* the concept to exemplars rather than using exemplars to *acquire* the concept. Of course, secondary abstractions require that specific primary abstractions already exist at adequate degrees of differentiation. The concept of mammal would have no meaning if a child had not acquired primary concepts of dogs, cats, insects, worms, and so forth. Again, I see the development of secondary abstractions as highly specific in content and dependent on prior development of specific primary abstractions, whereas Piaget and coworkers see the development of "concrete operations" as more age-related maturation than specific cognitive differentiation.

As children acquire more and better differentiated secondary abstractions, they can begin to form associations between these concepts without reference to concrete props. At this stage—the

abstract logical stage in Ausubel's terms and the formal operations period in Piaget's terms (about age eleven on)—the child
can deal "internally" with ideas about ideas. An example would
be a child who could see that one car traveling twice as fast as
another would reach the same destination in half the time, or
any similar relationship.

In our view, a six- or eight-year-old child could conceivably
demonstrate abstract logical thinking provided that the secondary concepts needed had been acquired adequately. Since
overall learning depends at least somewhat on time, most children cannot engage in broadly ranging abstract logical thinking
much before the age of eleven or twelve and, indeed, adults
cannot perform in this way in subject matter areas where they
lack adequate secondary concepts. I shall show in Chapter 8
that confusing data on "nonconservation" by adults does not
present a dilemma in developmental psychology so long as we
use our Ausubelian spectacles—we simply observe instances
where learners lack the specific relevant cognitive structure to
acquire new knowledge meaningfully or to solve problems that
require well-developed secondary concepts.

In our view, no operational conflict exists between the ideas
of Piaget and Ausubel. What Piaget and his coworkers have described in a half century of careful observation are numerous instances in which specific primary and/or secondary abstractions
were not developed in the subjects observed, and hence their
cognitive functioning was characteristic of preoperational or
concrete operational thinking. Since the general experience
background of most children in Western society is comparable,
necessary varieties of primary and secondary abstractions are
acquired by normal youngsters at approximately the same ages,
and hence Piaget's developmental periods have a descriptive validity, even though they may not be the most useful functional
characterization of cognitive learning processes.

I shall not invoke the additional constructs of preoperational,
concrete operational, and formal operational thought since all of
these periods can more parsimoniously be explained in terms of
development of specific cognitive conceptual hierarchies with
progressively greater degrees of inclusiveness and differentia-

tion. This interpretation thereby subsumes apparently qualitatively different forms of cognitive functioning under the general framework of progressive cognitive differentiation. Because of the enormous growth in specifically differentiated cognitive structures from ages two to fourteen, quantitative differences in cognitive differentiation appear to have qualitatively differing functional capacity. In an analogous way, the modern digital computer is only a glorified adding machine, but the enormous quantitative difference in storage capacity and processing imbue the computer with manifestly unique capabilities. Piaget's developmental periods have descriptive value to characterize modal states of the degree of cognitive differentiation, but it is misleading and nonparsimonious to view these periods as unique episodes in the ontogeny of brain development. With our current knowledge of the biology of brain functions, we find it unlikely that any new neural mechanisms could be introduced in the maturing child. The biological mechanisms for information coding, storage, and processing are in all probability the same from birth to senescence or death. What does change is the number and relations between functional neurons, and this is quantitative development over time, not qualitative change. The parsimonious view—that apparent new cognitive capacities become manifest as the result of quantitative growth in cognitive structure as children mature—is consistent with our knowledge of biological brain mechanisms. I shall show in Chapter 8 that this view is also consistent with data from studies on school learning.

Piaget's work has stressed that children's cognitive growth proceeds through *assimilation* and *accommodation*. New experiences, when they are perceived by the child, lead him to accommodate the experience into his existing cognitive structures. Piaget views the development of the child's cognitive structures as invariant in sequence, from sensory-motor to formal operations stages although differences in individuals of the same age and some differences between cultures may be found. Assimilation occurs when experiences have led to modification of cognitive structure and hence early accommodated experiences later become an integral and functional part of developing cognitive structures. Experiences of the kind that some months or years earlier might have been accommodated are later assimilated into the child's cognitive framework and a new stage of equilibrium is achieved. However, new experiences will lead to new accommodations, later assimilation, and a new state of cognitive equilibrium. This equilibration goes on until formal operations are achieved and continues in some areas of experience into adulthood.

We see in Piaget's views a kind of psychological preformationism, not as absolute as the ancient concept that the homunculus of the sperm cell contained the miniaturized human which grew and unfolded into a human in time, but philosophically rooted in a kind of a priorism. As Toulmin (1972) points out, "for both Piaget and Kant, therefore, the final 'necessary' forms and operations map the bounds of any thought which can claim to be fully 'rational'. The two men differ only in this: that, after 150 years of historical and psychological inquiry, Piaget prefers to speak of these bounds as defining, not the inescapable structure of any properly 'rational' thought, but rather the common destination of rational development in human individuals and communities alike" (p. 425).

In contrast, Ausubel's meaningful learning (assimilation of new experience with existing relevant concepts in cognitive structure) is *idiosyncratic,* and the development of cognitive structures that will allow new experience to be incorporated meaningfully into an individual's structure will be dependent upon the past sequences of his experiences and on the kind of cultural heritage in which he is embedded. Conceptual ontogeny of the individual proceeds not in a definitive pathway, but rather in a pattern determined by experience, dependent on the transect of specific experience the individual has had in encounters with evolving cultural heritages. Thus, on the basis of both empirical studies and on philosophical grounds, I shall argue that Ausubel's views should supplant Piagetian interpretations of cognitive differentiation.

The Psychology of Robert Gagné

In 1965, Robert Gagné published his first book, *The Conditions of Learning*, which was responsible in part for his quick rise to national prominence in educational psychology. In this book Gagné described eight types of learning and conditions that are necessary for learning. Moving from a description of *signal* learning (type 1) where a child may learn, for example, that a bell at the end of a class period is a signal for dismissal to *problem solving* behavior (type 8), Gagné's argument has a character of authoritativeness by virtue of melding early views on animal S-R learning with contemporary issues in school learning.

The plausibility of Gagné's descriptions of signal learning, stimulus-response learning, chaining, verbal association, and discrimination learning—all based on S-R theory—obscure an intellectual sleight of hand as he moves to descriptions of rule learning (involving combinations of concepts) and problem solving. In the latter two types of learning, S-R explanations are essentially dropped; rule learning is described as an *"inferred capability* that enables the individual to respond to a *class* of stimulus situations with a *class* of performances" (p. 191; emphasis mine); and problem solving is "not simply a matter of application of previously learned rules" but also a "process that yields new learning" (p. 214). We shall see that the "inferred capability" of rule learning looks very much like Ausubel's subsumption and that new learning in problem solving resembles Ausubel's superordinate learning and integrative reconciliation.

Gagné's theory, based on progressively larger units of S-R connections, leads him to postulate that learning is best when we move from mastery of the smallest conceptual units *to* the more general and more inclusive, whereas Ausubel recommends that we proceed *from* the more general, more inclusive to specific subordinate concepts in the process of progressive differentiation of cognitive structure. This contrast between Ausubel's and Gagné's views is schematized in Figure 4.5.

As a consequence of Gagné's emphasis on moving from "lower level" rules to "higher level" rules, one must construct

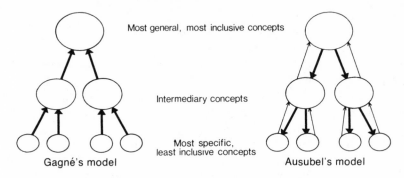

Most general, most inclusive concepts

Intermediary concepts

Most specific,
least inclusive concepts

Gagné's model

Ausubel's model

Figure 4.5. Comparison of Gagné's and Ausubel's models of progressive concept development.

"learning hierarchies." Figure 4.6 shows a hierarchy for basic reading (p. 271). Notice that all arrows in this hierarchy point upward, indicating the sequence in which learning must proceed. However, a learning sequence evidently could be designed for young children which would proceed from the top of this hierarchy downward, if we were carefully to select words that have been an important part of the child's experience and then move to unfamiliar words or letters. Such a learning sequence could be meaningful in Ausubel's terms and result in efficient learning. The crucial factor is that, in whatever direction we proceed in teaching some knowledge hierarchy, our instruction must be planned so that relevant subsuming concepts exist or are developed, and integrative reconciliation occurs. This problem becomes one of careful planning of instructional materials for whatever sequence we choose to follow.

Gagné contends that the design of instruction should be such that we proceed from S-R connections to chains, to concepts, to rules, to problem solving. The very foundation of all learning in his model is an S-R association basic to all other learning. Gagné recognizes "there can be little doubt that Watson's ideas that most forms of human learning could be accounted for as chains of conditioned responses is *wildly incorrect*" (p. 13; emphasis mine). Nevertheless, the S-R theory that underlies Gagné's views is not fundamentally different from Watson's

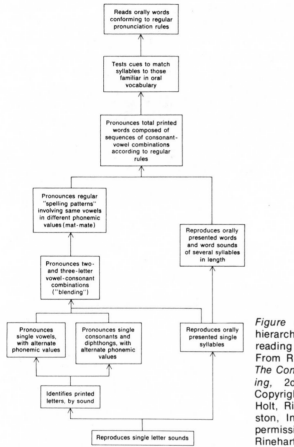

Figure 4.6. A learning hierarchy for a basic reading skill (decoding). From Robert M. Gagné, *The Conditions of Learning*, 2d ed., p. 270. Copyright © 1965, 1970 by Holt, Rinehart and Winston, Inc. Reprinted by permission of Holt, Rinehart and Winston.

views on the establishment of neural associations between stimuli and responses, and it is on this S-R base that Gagné constructs his model of school learning.[4]

In my view educational psychology would be miles ahead of where we are today if Skinner's operant conditioning and various S-R based learning theories were laid to rest and more

---

[4] Gagné's new book (1977) uses a cybernetic model of learning and hence, in my view, represents some advance in his thinking.

of our energies were directed toward elucidating cognitive processes that cannot be reduced to series of S-R chains. In Chapter 2, I indicated that the S-R and operant conditioning models of learning derive from a peripheralist philosophy. To start with behavioral absolutes—stimulus S produces response R—and to chain successively more complex processes into logical sequences reduce the effort to a priorism. When we find that initial stimulus S does not necessarily lead to response R, the whole chain of reasoning collapses. Instead, I believe it would be better to use a relational interpretation of learning which rests on evolving cognitive structures and societal conceptualizations.

CHAPTER 5

The Design of Curriculum and Instruction

A Need for Theory

We cannot transmit all our cultural heritage to all students; therefore, curriculum planners must consider what knowledge is of most worth for most students, what instructional methods may be employed most effectively to transmit this knowledge, and finally, what kind of school should our society have, if any. Specific discussion of this third issue will be postponed until Chapter 7. Here the focus will be on methods by which we can make rational decisions on *what* to teach and *how* to teach it.

Rational decisions in selecting content and instructional methods require that we employ methods whereby the recommendations arrived at by one individual (or group) are not based solely on private information available only to that person (or group) but show a logical correspondence between assumptions and recommendations that can be recognized by another individual (or group). We seek a process whereby some concensus can be reached about valid and relevant evidence or assumptions in the selection of what is to be taught and in the method of teaching this selected subject matter. In this chapter, I shall present concepts that can be useful in selecting knowledge and methodologies from disciplines and in designing instruction. It is an effort to present theories of curriculum and of instruction that draw on concepts applicable to educational planning and consistent with the concepts of learning presented earlier.

Education groups often refer to "curriculum and instruction" simultaneously, as though they represented a single entity. Johnson (1967) and others have emphasized that we have been careless and have not delineated those educational issues that are principally curriculum (that is, content) issues from those that are principally instructional (that is, teaching approach) issues. My experiences in the design of curriculum and in instructional planning strongly support the kind of distinctions Johnson has recommended. I have found it valuable to identify carefully the ideas or concepts that are to be taught and the possible hierarchical relationships between these concepts and to keep them *distinct* from the examples chosen to illustrate a given concept or idea. The choice of exemplars is largely a problem of effective instructional design, whereas the selection and hierarchical ordering of concepts is a matter of curriculum design. For example, my colleagues and I have chosen to teach primary school children the concept of the particulate nature of matter; the instructional approach we have used has been audio-taped guided lessons, selecting the materials and appropriate language for the lessons on the basis of observation and empirical tests. The decision to teach the concept of the particulate nature of matter was a curriculum decision and the decision to use audio-guided lessons with various specific activities was an instructional one. We could have chosen other teaching approaches and from an almost infinite variety of alternative activities to teach the concept; moreover, one can make curriculum decisions independent of methods of instruction and without specifying the activities in which learners will be involved.

Curriculum theory building is a relatively recent phenomenon. Although occasional reference to curriculum theory can be found in the literature of the early 1900s, the first organized effort to clarify it came in 1947 and appeared as a published monograph in 1950 (Virgil Herrick and Ralph Tyler). George Beauchamp published a book on curriculum theory in 1961; other books proposing models for curriculum building were published by Tyler in 1949 and Hilda Taba in 1962. None of them emphasizes a close relationship between learning theory and curriculum or instruction—a dominant emphasis in this chapter. Unlike Johnson's work, the theory books mentioned do not clearly distinguish curriculum and instruction, and therefore I shall draw on Johnson's writing (1967) as a primary source for some ideas presented in this chapter.

Johnson's Model for Curriculum and Instruction

Figure 5.1 shows a simplified version of Johnson's model. We see that the curriculum (a structured series of intended learning outcomes) is a product of a curriculum development system in which criteria of selection and ordering are used to choose knowledge from the available culture and to organize this knowledge into a curriculum. The product of the curriculum development system is used in turn for instructional design. Drawing specific activities and examples from the available culture, an instructional program is developed. As students are involved in the instructional program, learning hopefully occurs and actual learning outcomes (ALO's) can be evaluated. The information obtained from evaluation can in turn be used to redesign the curriculum and/or instructional components.

When Johnson's model first came to my attention in 1967, several aspects were attractive to me. Already mentioned was my experience that curriculum decisions can, to some extent, be considered separately from instructional decisions. Also, Johnson's stress on selecting knowledge from the total available culture and on ordering this knowledge was consistent with my experiences in designing elementary, secondary, and college science programs. The explosive growth of new knowledge in the sciences over the past thirty years has necessitated careful analysis of what knowledge may be of most worth and what relationships may exist between disciplines and subdisciplines. For several years I had attempted to construct conceptual hierarchies or frameworks that could guide science curriculum planning, and I saw this work as directly relevant to Johnson's curriculum processes of selection and structuring of knowledge. In my view the identification of frameworks of concepts was fundamental and must precede curriculum planning in science. This emphasis on concepts derived partly from views on the nature of science presented in Chapter 2 and partly from empirical studies that have led me to see Ausubel's learning theory as a valuable explanatory model for concept learning.

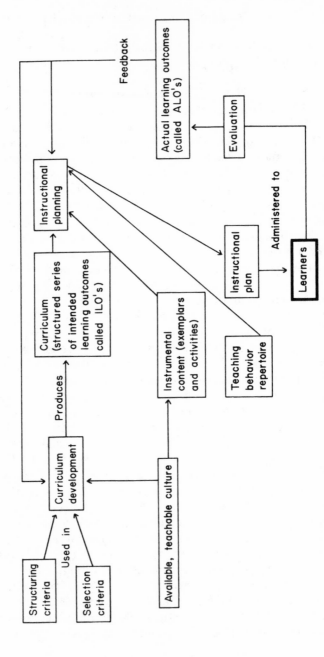

Figure 5.1. A simplified version of Johnson's (1967) model for curriculum and instruction.

Another aspect of Johnson's model consistent with my experience was the instructional program's essential neutrality with respect to the concepts to be taught in that a wide array of exemplars, student activities, teaching strategies, and technological support could be used to teach any specified concept. Some of these ideas were included in a paper (Novak, 1966) in which I proposed that effective science instruction was, in essence, dependent upon the extent to which the concepts (or paradigms, to use Kuhn's term) developed by scientists become the superordinate concepts of students' cognitive structures. Three figures were used to schematize the educational process and are included here in somewhat modified form. Figure 5.2 shows the general process of science education where I create a kind of

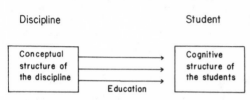

Discipline

Student

Conceptual structure of the discipline

Education

Cognitive structure of the students

Figure 5.2. A representation of the process of education when viewed as the transfer of conceptual structure as it exists in the discipline to the student's cognitive structure.

knowledge isomorphy between the conceptual structure of the sciences and the cognitive structure of the student. Here I suggest that education is a process by which the knowledge generated by man over centuries can be transmitted to youth. Figure 5.3 schematizes the traditional science education pro-

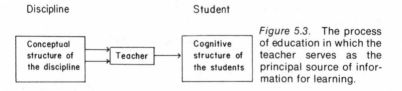

Discipline

Student

Conceptual structure of the discipline

Teacher

Cognitive structure of the students

Figure 5.3. The process of education in which the teacher serves as the principal source of information for learning.

gram, which is largely dominated by the teacher who selects what will be learned by the student, conferring many of the teacher's cognitive limitations in a kind of filtering that takes place in the process. Figure 5.4 schematizes the emerging pattern of teaching that attempts to make use of a wide array of learning resources to individualize instruction. In this scheme the teacher is a learning counselor—guiding, advising, tutoring, and providing emotional support. Students' cognitive growth should be enhanced over the traditional scheme partly as a function of the quality of available learning materials and the teacher's skill in obtaining appropriate materials and guiding students in their use, and partly as a function of the students' prior relevant experiences.

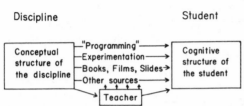

Figure 5.4. A representation of the process of education in which the teacher plays a mediating role, assisting students to select and use learning resources and providing human interaction.

Figure 5.4 can be redrawn to illustrate correspondence between this scheme for science teaching and Johnson's model. Figure 5.5 shows that we draw from the disciplines of science to form our curriculum and to select specific instructional activities. We also plan instruction from the discipline of education and hope that our instructional program will result in positive growth in the cognitive structure (conceptual structure) of our students and in positive affective responses toward science.

The Role of Learning Theory in Curriculum and Instruction

No curriculum theorist in the past has shown the relevance of learning theory in the design of curriculum. Although Taba (1962) devotes considerable space to the discussion of learning theories, subsequent application of learning theories to curriculum design is ambiguous at best. Our explanation is pragmatic: the learning theories that preceded Ausubel's were not particularly relevant to curriculum and, therefore, were not a substantive part of curriculum planning. With respect to instructional theory, the situation has been only slightly better, with most of

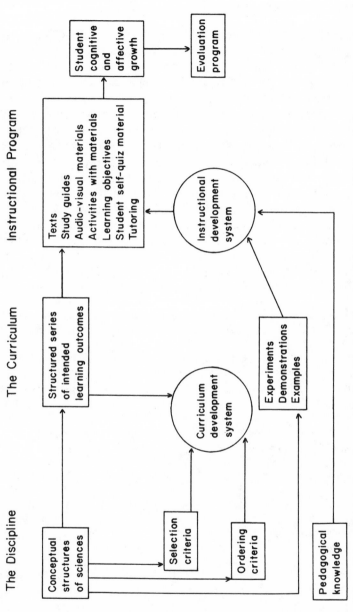

The Discipline   The Curriculum   Instructional Program

Conceptual structures of sciences

Selection criteria

Ordering criteria

Curriculum development system

Structured series of intended learning outcomes

Experiments
Demonstrations
Examples

Pedagogical knowledge

Instructional development system

Texts
Study guides
Audio-visual materials
Activities with materials
Learning objectives
Student self-quiz material
Tutoring

Student cognitive and affective growth

Evaluation program

Figure 5.5. A schema for science education showing elements of Johnson's model for curriculum and instruction.

the literature giving hardly more than passing acknowledgment to any connection between learning theory and the theory of instruction. Bruner in *Toward a Theory of Instruction* (1966) actually puts the cart before the horse and says that "a theory of instruction, which must be at the heart of educational psychology, is principally concerned with how to arrange environments to optimize learning according to various criteria—to optimize transfer or retrievability of information, for example" (pp. 37–38). But it is specifically to the issue of "how to arrange environments to optimize learning" that useful educational psychological theory (and not instructional theory) should apply. Educational psychology should be at the heart of instructional theory, and not vice versa. Before we can design a learning environment to optimize learning of some specific element of knowledge, we must know how students learn in general.

After reviewing briefly some more common learning theories, Taba (1962) makes the following observation:

As was pointed out earlier, these theories suggest diverse ideas about learning but have not yet produced a science of learning—a coherent set of explanations, laws, and principles to guide education. The more "scientific" behavioristic observations in experimentally confined situations cannot be used to understand or to guide learning of a more complex nature, such as the development of cognitive processes or the formation of attitudes. On the other hand, field theories of learning present too great a complexity of variable factors, with the result that it is difficult to examine adequately their regularities to translate them into appropriate principles and laws. If the possibility of drawing educational applications were limited only to what the experimental psychologists consider precise laws and explanations, one would have to conclude that there can be little correspondence between the studies of learning and the practice of education. One reason for this is the fact that although there are wide varieties of learning, experimental psychology, which is primarily concerned with developing a theory of learning, deals with only a limited range. [p. 85]

I concur with her statement as it describes the situation in 1962. However, I contend that Ausubel's theory of human learning has heuristic value not only for further research in learning mechanisms as they operate in the classroom but also for guiding school curriculum development, instructional design, and evaluation practices. His theoretical work in educational psychology published since 1962 stands as a largely unrecognized but thoroughly adequate foundation for curriculum and instructional planning based on learning theory. Ausubel's learning theory focuses on the role of concepts (subsumers) for effecting meaningful learning. His additional stress on progressive differentiation of concepts, superordinate learning, and integrative reconciliation further lends relevance to curriculum planning and instructional planning. If learning is to be meaningful, then new knowledge to be learned must have relevant anchoring concepts available in the learner's cognitive structure. Since an enormous array of information is to be learned in any discipline, only the most general, most inclusive concepts are likely to provide anchorage in a wide variety of learning situations. Johnson's stress on selection criteria for curriculum planning can be related to Ausubel's stress on subsumption, starting with the most general, most inclusive concepts. And Johnson's equal emphasis on ordering criteria can be linked to Ausubel's description of progressive differentiation of concepts in cognitive structure. The correspondence between Johnson's model and Ausubel's theory is shown in Chart 5.1.

Chart 5.1. Corresponding elements in Johnson's model and Ausubel's theory of learning.

Johnson's Model Component	*Ausubel's Learning Theory*
Selection criteria for knowledge in our culture	Stress on concepts implies need to identify major and minor concepts in a field of study
Ordering criteria for knowledge selected	Meaningful learning and progressive differentiation require the most general, most inclusive concepts be presented early and subsequent information be provided to clarify meaning and show connections to subordinate concepts. (Recall distinction between logical and psychological order in Chapter 4.)
	Superordinate learning and integrative reconciliation require that subordinate concepts be presented in a manner that allows association with more inclusive concepts (superordinate concepts), and meanings of apparently dis-

Chart 5.1. Corresponding elements in Johnson's model and Ausubel's theory of learning. *(Continued)*

Johnson's Model
Component

Ausubel's Learning Theory

parate concepts will be clarified to show distinctions and relationships between subordinate concepts (integrative reconciliation).

For young learners, care must be taken to assure that primary abstractions are available in the learners' cognitive structures prior to instruction in concepts requiring secondary abstractions.

Curriculum
Intended learning outcomes (ILO's)

Although Johnson does not specify the form of ILO's, Ausubel's theory would indicate that these should be concepts to be learned, for with them we effect meaningful learning. In other words, Johnson's "curriculum matrix" produced by the curriculum development system should be a matrix of concepts. To the extent possible, this matrix should suggest hierarchical and subordinate relationships between concepts, although this feature is in part confounded with the sequence in which concepts are taught and the specific exemplars used in instruction. Skills, attitudes, and values should be considered especially as they bear on learning of the concepts specified.

Instructional planning system
Selection of exemplars (instrumental content)

Ausubel's theory requires that examples used meet the following conditions: (1) necessary motor skills are available or practiced, (2) relevant primary abstractions are available or taught, (3) secondary abstractions presented do not ignore (1) and (2) above, and (4) explicit association between new learning and existing cognitive structure is provided (cognitive bridging).

Selection of teaching approaches

Concrete props, when needed, require teaching approaches that introduce these props in proper order.

Development of primary and secondary abstractions will be somewhat idiosyncratic, hence teaching approach must allow for varying rates of learning, for alternative exemplars, variation in exposure to concrete props, and adjustment to motivation patterns of students.

Johnson's Model Component	*Ausubel's Learning Theory*
Actual learning outcomes	Achievement will be a function of the general cognitive maturation (degree of overall cognitive structure differentiation) but primarily dependent on initial or developed relevant subsumers in learner's cognitive structure. Presence of meaningful learning set will lead to growth in relevant subsumers, in contrast to rote learning, and should facilitate problem solving capabilities to the extent that progressive differentiation and integrative reconciliations of relevant concepts has occured.
Evaluation	Rate of new learning will depend on quality of existing or developed relevant subsumers, and motivation for learning. Transfer of learning to new problem solving situations will be a function of the degree of concept differentiation, superordinate subsumption, and integrative reconciliation achieved. Genic variation in learners will be confounded with achievement of the above.
Feedback to curriculum planning	Concepts selected may require (1) more general cognitive structure development than typically present in the learners, (2) alternative sequences of concept presentation, (3) better clarification of relationships between concepts in the matrix and/or better description of salient aspects of the concept(s).
Feedback to instruction	Failure to achieve concept mastery (as evidenced by lack of transfer to novel, relevant problems) may indicate a curriculum problem as above or (1) poor selection of exemplars (not easily or extensively linked to existing cognitive structure of learners), (2) inappropriate pacing leading to rote learning or failure to learn (too fast) or boredom and decline in motivation (too slow), (3) necessity for provision for more motor skill development, greater use of concrete props for primary concept development, more extensive development of secondary abstractions and/or relationships among the latter. (4) Selection of alternative instructional strategies to better achieve above items, for example, tutorial assistance where existing relevant cognitive development of learners is highly variable or unusually idiosyncratic.

We must structure our curriculum so that major concepts are introduced early and thus serve to facilitate meaningful learning of a wide array of information as well as learning of new subordinate concepts. Recall the contrast between Ausubel's theory and that of Gagné's presented earlier. Gagné's theory would lead to different ordering criteria, and the simplest, least inclusive concepts would be presented first. However, Gagné shares with Ausubel a stress on the importance of concepts in the curriculum plan, although he is less consistent and emphatic in his stress on concepts or, as he calls them generalizations.

We have already discussed the problem of readiness and the fact that early learning in any discipline must proceed from development of primary abstractions based on experience with concrete empirical props to instruction that leads to development of secondary abstractions. Moreover, Ausubel stresses that there is no age at which all learners can handle secondary abstractions in any subject matter area. Piaget's work is sometimes misinterpreted to suggest that once a person reaches the stage of formal operations (about age fourteen), concrete props are not necessary for new learning. Ausubel's stress that meaningful learning is specific in content means that curriculum planning cannot ignore either the learner's general level of cognitive development or his specific fund of primary and secondary abstractions in the discipline to be learned. Even adult learners need some experience with concrete-empirical props when they enter a new area of study.

Ausubel's theory gives more freedom and at the same time more constraints to the curriculum planner. In principle, any disciplinary subject matter can be learned meaningfully by any student. However—and this is a large qualifier—we must organize the curriculum to assure that all the necessary motor skills—and primary and secondary abstraction needed at any stage of the learning sequence—are available, and this can be prohibitively time consuming, costly, and/or inefficient. For example, I tried to design some audiotape guided lessons to teach elementary concepts of electrostatics to first-grade children. The children's motor proficiency was so poor that most could not get a good electrostatic charge on a plastic rod except with extended instruction (three or four twenty-minute lessons) which showed them how to charge the rod and hold it close to (but not touching) a pith ball. I could see that in time (perhaps about fifty twenty-minute lessons) I might have been successful in teaching some concepts of electrostatic charge, but my patience ran out. I decided to work with third-grade children instead. With their much better motor coordination, they could easily charge a glass or plastic rod, test its effect on a suspended pith ball, and follow other instructions on the audiotape. Here motor skills were at least as limiting as available cognitive structure for first-grade youngsters. Because it is well known that training in many simple motor skills is a waste of time (all children eventually learn to walk), I made a curriculum decision (that is, not to teach concepts of electrostatics to first graders) on the basis of my experience and not on a priori grounds. We see in this example an interplay between instructional and curriculum planning. Some concepts we may wish to teach to students are best placed later in a curriculum plan to avoid undue difficulties in executing instruction in these concepts. We must avoid, however, the common practice of making arbitrary decisions on the theoretical issues or without empirically tested instructional alternatives. When instruction in basic concepts that can effect meaningful learning of a wide array of knowledge is postponed unnecessarily, the common school practice of rote learning occurs when, on the contrary, meaningful learning could be achieved. The design of instruction to teach fundamental concepts in science, mathematics, social sciences, and other fields is no easy matter. At least two hundred hours of design (and testing) time were needed to develop each fifteen-minute lesson in our audio-tutorial elementary science program, discussed in the next chapter.

To plan curriculum and design instruction consistent with Ausubel's theory, as suggested in Chart 5.1 above, a primary and exceedingly difficult task is to identify concepts in any given discipline and to organize them into some hierarchical or relational scheme. This task requires the best available talent with respect to knowledge of the discipline and also skillful guidance by curriculum experts in the process of "unpacking" knowledge from a discipline.

If we cannot identify salient concepts in a field of study, distinguish among concepts, and isolate relatively trivial or subordinate concepts, curriculum planning is likely to proceed from a list of topics, such as one finds in the table of contents of most books. Sometimes topics are also concepts, for example, "Cells—Structure and Function" or "Mercantilism," but more often they represent a conglomeration of concepts, perhaps with some logical coherence but without psychological organization. In other words, in topically organized instruction we often cannot show how the learning sequence would facilitate hierarchical ordering of the concepts. Furthermore, seldom in topically organized instruction does integrative reconciliation occur, wherein apparently disparate meanings of a concept are recognized as aspects of the same concept, or as essentially different and thus integrated with another concept.

"Unpacking" Knowledge in a Discipline

A colleague at Cornell University has developed an approach to help students understand the problem of unpacking knowledge from a discipline. Whether in the form of books, papers, lectures, or discussions, knowledge is not easily extracted from a discipline and put into a form appropriate for instruction. Gowin (1970) has devised five questions useful in helping teachers to unpack knowledge:

1. What is (are) the *telling question(s)*?
2. What are the *key* concepts?
3. What *methods of inquiry* (procedural commitments) are used?
4. What are the major *knowledge claims*?
5. What are the *value claims*?

Gowin describes telling questions as those which identify the topic under study. Sometimes the telling question is explicitly stated, perhaps in the title of the book or article. Often it is not the question the author says he plans to consider, and is buried in the text.

From a psychological standpoint, telling questions represent superordinate concepts or propositions that will be explicated through presentation of new knowledge and/or subordinate concepts. Thus the telling questions should have some generic meaning to the learner and should be relatable to concepts already present in the cognitive structure of the learner. Other material in the book or report will serve primarily to differentiate further existing concepts or to facilitate new integrative reconciliation of existing concepts. For example, telling questions of this book would be "how do people learn?" and "how can cognitive learning theory guide curriculum and instruction development?"

Key concepts are not always explicitly stated or defined, and any book or report requires that some minimal set of concepts are already familiar to the learner. Other key concepts are stated or explicated in some way. For example, school, test, student, and knowledge are concepts used in this book which are already familiar, while meaningful learning, curriculum, and mastery learning are concepts I have defined. One of the difficulties the novice encounters in unpacking a book or report is that he lacks expertise or knowledge to recognize salient concepts, or to see the relevance of concepts that are not specified but are assumed.

Methods of inquiry are important to recognize, for they help to provide an understanding of the context in which events are observed and records of events are made. In education, for example, many experimental studies fail to describe carefully the sampling procedures used, the characteristics of measuring instruments (including reliability, validity, and score range over which discrimination between individuals can be obtained), and anecdotal comments on observations during the experiment. Since students cannot be locked into climate controlled chambers nor selected for homogeneity of genic background, the scientific research models are not easily applied to education. Most research reports in education fail to provide sufficient explanation of the methods of inquiry used either to permit precise replication (validation) of the study or to allow for drawing reasonable inferences. (See earlier discussion on advance organizers as an example.)

Knowledge claims are the result of the inquiry combined with the use of concepts (stated or covert) that lead the reporter to make assertions. For example, in Chapter 1, I showed data from a study (Ring, 1969) and asserted that prior knowledge of chemistry was a significant variable influencing success in elementary college chemistry. Chapter 8 will assert that individualized instructional methods can remediate initial deficiencies in knowledge of physics with the result that pre-instruction scores on a physics test show no correlation with achievment in the physics course. Obviously these apparently conflicting knowledge claims can be understood only when concepts of traditional instruction are recognized as different from concepts of criterion-referenced evaluation used in individualized instruction, which will be discussed in Chapters 6 and 8.

Value claims are a combination of knowledge claims and emotional (affective) interpretations. For example, I have made the value claim that future improvement of education is more likely if new educational alternatives and research are based on a coherent theory of education. While some empirical evidence for this claim is provided, a significant element is my own emotional predisposition to favor application of contemporary scientific models of research and application to the field of education. In Chapter 1, I noted that Roszak (1969, 1972) and others probably would not agree with this value claim.

Although in many respects Gowin's "five questions" may appear trivial and obvious, my experience in working with students and educators is that these questions are profound. Rarely do teachers at any educational level have a clear conception or the structure of knowledge of their field, and even more rarely have they made explicit attempts to help students understand the structure of knowledge in the discipline.

Developing a Curriculum Matrix: An Example from Science

During the late 1950s and early 1960s, there were intense efforts in the United States to improve science and mathematics programs, in part because of the successful orbiting of a satellite by the USSR in 1957, in part because of the wide disparity between what was known in science and mathematics as a result of the post–World War II "knowledge explosion" and what was being taught in schools. The National Science Foundation sponsored several science curriculum development projects, but in keeping with their strong bias for "inquiry" based programs, none of these developed a carefully articulated conceptual framework as a curriculum base (see Novak, 1969). Although the content of the NSF sponsored projects was much updated and laboratory work was improved, there was no emphasis or clear explication of science concepts nor any effort to articulate instructional programs to enhance progressive development of science concepts from kindergarten to grade twelve.

Many school districts adopted the "alphabet" programs, as they were called since the first letters of the science programs were used to identify them (BSCS, PSSC, CHEM, for example). It became increasingly evident that the difficult task of articulating science programs fell squarely into the lap of local school districts. Science teachers and science supervisors sought help from national programs, and it was natural that they should turn to the largest professional organization, the National Science Teachers Association, with some 25,000 members. NSTA established a Curriculum Committee to study the important problem of K–12 integration of science programs, as well as other issues.

The Curriculum Committee of NSTA attempted to obtain NSF funding to convene a conference of scientists to identify important major concepts that could serve as an organizational framework for K–12 curriculum planning. Committed to a philosophy of "inquiry" oriented curriculum, NSF personnel discouraged any proposals for support of such a conference. As a result, NSTA used its own limited resources to convene a conference of distinguished scientists and science educators to prepare and publish a document that could serve as a basis for K–12 curriculum planning. The conference results were published in an abbreviated form in the NSTA journal (Novak, 1964) and as a separate monograph (NSTA, 1964). The reaction to these documents was mixed; school science teachers and supervisors generally responded favorably, but persons in leadership roles in national curriculum projects were critical (see Bentley Glass, 1965). To be sure, this preliminary effort to identify a conceptual framework for science instruction program planning had its limitations. However, there continues to be much of value in the original "conceptual schemes for science" published in 1964. The seven "conceptual schemes" are:

1. All matter is composed of units called fundamental particles; under certain conditions these particles can be transformed into energy and vice versa.

2. Matter exists in the form of units which can be classified into hierarchies of organizational levels.

3. The behavior of matter in the universe can be described on a statistical basis.

4. Units of matter interact. The bases of all ordinary interactions are electromagnetic, gravitational, and nuclear forces.

5. All interacting units of matter tend toward equilibrium states in which the energy content (enthalpy) is a minimum and the energy distribution (entropy) is most random. In attaining equilibrium, energy transformation or matter transformation or matter-energy transformation occurs. Nevertheless, the sum of energy and matter in the universe remains constant.

6. One form of energy is the motion of units of matter. Such motion is responsible for heat and temperature and for the states of matter: solid, liquid, and gaseous.

7. All matter exists in time and space and, since interactions occur among its units, matter is subject in some degree to changes with time. Such changes may occur at varying rates.

One of the criticisms leveled at the NSTA conceptual schemes was that they were too broad and abstract (Ausubel, 1965) and hence could be of little value to the average science teacher, especially the elementary school teacher, whose background in science is usually weak. The NSTA conceptual schemes were never intended to guide day-to-day classroom instruction, but were intended to guide specialists in science curriculum planning. Their purpose was to serve as a framework for ordering and selecting intended learning outcomes, as Johnson's model was later to suggest. In our view, the schemes should continue to be useful in this respect, albeit some modifications and additions would undoubtedly be useful. Although some elementary science programs have been developed from a conceptual framework similar to that of the NSTA schemes (consult Paul Brandwein, 1962; Novak, 1966, 1972a), there remain today serious problems with the design of articulated science programs for grades K–12. No national instructional development projects for preparation of K–12 integrated science programs are currently underway. No private enterprise effort for a K–12 articulated science program is in production, so far as we know, and such an effort probably could not succeed in the face of heavily subsidized and reasonably popular NSF supported programs.

The Curriculum Planning of Senesh

One of the most able educators I have known is Lawrence Senesh. A trained economist, Senesh had turned his energy to education and, while teaching at Purdue University, he developed a concept-based program in economics for grades one through twelve. He believes that knowledge of economics is as important in our society as is knowledge of mathematics, literature, or any school subject presented more or less continuously throughout the grades. Yet, many important economic concepts—such as market, goods, services—either are not taught or are garbled into some folklore about Indian wampum and Uncle Sam's currency. To counter this, Senesh began writing a series of books which would encompass what he saw as fundamental ideas of economics. He wanted to produce an "organic curriculum" in which the relationships between economic principles would be explicit and the meaning of these principles would be indelibly planted in children's cognitive structures.

Figure 5.6 shows Senesh's scheme for relationships among fundamental ideas of economics. When this scheme was published, Senesh received much criticism from economists who complained that the scheme was incomplete, omitted important concepts, and could not possibly be taught to students below grade twelve. But Senesh proceeded to write his books,[1] and although this project is still in progress, children in grades one

---

[1] The books are published by Science Research Associates (SRA), Chicago.

through six are already learning the differences between producers and consumers, labor and capital, and private or public support of institutions and services. Economists can judge better the accuracy or adequacy of Senesh's scheme, but as a curriculum effort, his idea makes good sense. It is one of the few efforts in which curriculum planning began with a careful analysis of the important ideas in the field, and instruction was devised to present these ideas at progressively greater degrees of elaboration and sophistication. Although Senesh was not aware of Ausubel's work, he devised a creative program that was based on concepts, that systematically planned for progressive differentiation of concepts and enhancement of superordinate learning and that made deliberate efforts to achieve integrative reconciliation of concepts to facilitate meaningful learning of economics. His major obstacle has been tradition-bound school curricula that insist on Dick and Jane readers, repetitious arithmetic drill, and memorization of dates and names, with no time for economics.

Through the leadership offered by Senesh and with the organizational support of the Social Science Education Consortium (now located in Boulder, Colorado), fundamental idea relationship schema have been described for political science, sociology, anthropology, social psychology, and law and jurisprudence. Figure 5.6 is an example of the schema as they are presented in the SRA literature (1973). That scholars in these fields found it necessary to show only *relationships* among these fundamental ideas suggests that a strict hierarchical ordering of concepts does not always characterize the organization of knowledge in a discipline. Gagné's (1970) theory of learning postulates that a specific hierarchy of learning tasks is needed to design instruction. From the standpoint of Ausubelian learning theory, however, the nonhierarchical form of Senesh's relationships presents no difficulty since efforts to achieve progressive differentiation of major concepts and integrative reconciliation among concepts require explicit instruction on interrelationships among concepts, and not sequential presentation from most elementary to most inclusive concepts, as Gagné's theory indicates.

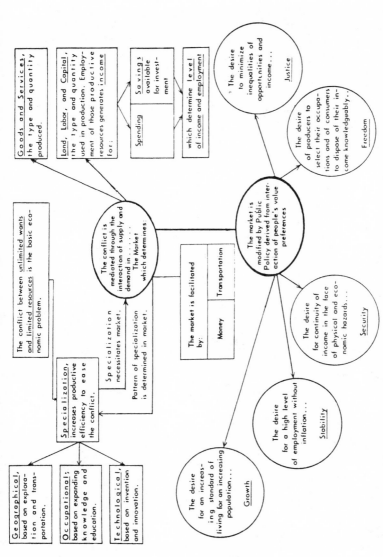

Figure 5.6 Fundamental ideas of economics. Reproduced with permission from Laurence Senesh.

I have suggested in this chapter that we can now proceed from theory to design of better instructional programs. It should be evident that an enormous task for redesign of school programs lies ahead of us if we are to effect the promise indicated by this theory in American schools.

CHAPTER 6

Planning for Instruction

Selecting Activities for Meaningful Learning

The interdependence of the elements shown in Johnson's model (Figure 5.1) becomes evident as soon as one plans a specific piece of instructional material. Not every possible contingency can be considered simultaneously, and hence the first question must be, where does instructional planning begin? Our experience has been that the best program begins with consideration of one or two major concepts to be illustrated. For example, we might decide to begin a science course with field study because the early fall is a pleasant time to have classes outdoors in most regions of the United States. If our student audience is sixth graders, we consider which of the five or six major concepts of science can be illustrated best through field work for students with the general maturation of sixth graders. We can see that at least initial choices of concepts to be taught (curriculum decisions) can be very much a function of what kind of instructional material may be most meaningful to a given group of students at a certain time of the year (instructional planning decisions). However, we cannot ignore that substantial development of one major concept (changes that occur in the structure of matter over time, for example) cannot be realized until some progress has been made in the development of other major concepts (the hierarchical organization of units of matter, for example). Any arbitrary curriculum planning decisions pertaining to the sequencing of concepts to be presented might result in undesirable or unmotivating instructional alternatives, and conversely, arbitrary decisions on topics or activities in instructional planning might obviate any chance for concept differentiation or integrative reconciliation. This starting dilemma in curriculum and instructional planning is schematized in Figure 6.1.

As shown earlier, one set of instructional exemplars may illustrate two or more concepts. In choosing activities or examples for instruction we should consider the extent to which maximum payoff can be achieved for the development of one or

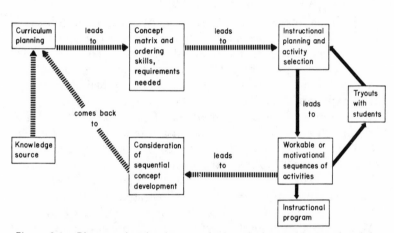

Figure 6.1. Diagram showing how curriculum design and instructional design decisions are interrelated and how successful planning requires "cycling" back and forth through the two design systems.

more significant concepts. Some exemplars are rejected even though they work well with a student group when other successful exemplars can be found from which a greater range of conceptual differentiation is possible. On the other hand, some exemplars may relate to a dozen or more concepts in our curriculum plan, but the learning experience with these may result in conceptual confusion. For example, one difficulty with educational games is the discrepancy that often exists between learning the strategies of the game and learning the concepts or relationships between concepts that are supposed to be illustrated by the game. Karen Busch (1973) found that students playing a game showed some gain in understanding sociology concepts, but the students who worked with her to design the games showed a better understanding of the concepts and relationships among the concepts. In most reports on the use of instructional games, however, no results are reported as to the extent of concept growth.

The Need for Concrete Props

We know from the work of Piaget and others that young children need experience with real objects (props) to understand phenomena affecting the objects. An elementary school child needs experience with clay to learn that the volume of clay does not change when a clay ball is flattened into a pancake. In Ausubel's terms, the child needs concrete experiences to establish meaning for verbal concept labels or to establish *primary abstractions*. Only later can the child use a concept label generically and without reference to concrete props that serve as individual exemplars of the concept. At this stage, *secondary abstractions* (concepts) are formed, and a child can recognize class membership of a new exemplar without comparing and contrasting with other exemplars. Finally, at about age twelve, most children can see relationships between secondary abstractions without reference to concrete props and are capable of abstract thinking or formal operations, to use Piaget's term. On the basis of research and interpretation of other studies, we see this reduction in dependence on concrete props as a function of the degree of relevant cognitive structure differentiation, related to age only because cognitive structure differentiation is to a considerable extent related to age. We find that young children (six years old) can manipulate secondary abstractions in narrow subject matter areas in which primary and secondary abstractions have been carefully developed. Conversely, a growing body of evidence suggests that college students and other adults cannot perform abstract thinking or formal operations in subject matter areas in which they have inadequately differentiated cognitive structure (Eugene Chiappetta, 1976).

The instructional implication of the above is that, except for the most homogeneous classes, instruction must provide vary-ing amounts of experience with concrete props at all age levels whenever topics are presented that include new concepts or concepts that cannot be associated easily with those existing in cognitive structure, that is, existing concepts of a more general, more inclusive nature. Too often our science and mathematics courses introduce concepts or relationships among concepts for which the student has neither the relevant subsumers nor the necessary concrete referents to establish the new concepts in cognitive structure. This practice occurs also in such subjects as history, when cultural attributes or governmental units are described and relationships between these are made with no ef-fort to relate the new concept labels to existing concepts in cog-nitive structure and to real life experiences of the students. As a result, learning must proceed in essentially a rote manner even though the students may possess the general mental maturation for meaningful learning and an inclination to learn in this way.

Another consideration in choosing and sequencing instruc-tional exemplars is the level of a conceptual hierarchy at which the exemplar is targeted. An exemplar that can be linked easily to a higher-order, more general concept is more likely to find a connection with the cognitive structures of the students than is an exemplar targeted at specific subordinate concepts. Although our learning is idiosyncratic, most of us have a similar general concept of "tree," for example, and an exemplar in biology targeted at this concept is more likely to find meaningful cogni-tive association than an exemplar targeted at the tracheid cell structure of gymnosperm xylem. Our instructional sequence might move from the cell types we find in the wood of trees (thick-wall, elongated, nonliving cells) to the tracheid cell struc-ture of gymnosperm woods (for example, the wood of pine trees). In general, initial instructional exemplars targeted at higher-order concepts are much more likely to result in mean-ingful learning than are exemplars which can be associated meaningfully only with highly specific subordinate concepts. We must plan instructional sequences to move from more gen-eral to more specific concepts, however, if we are to achieve pro-gressive differentiation and integrative reconciliation. It is a constant challenge—resolved only through a certain amount of trial and error—to select exemplars that are sufficiently general to be meaningful to a wide range of our learners and yet specific enough to effect some cognitive differentiation (and hence avoid boredom).

The Need for Skill Development

Cognitive growth in every field is dependent to some degree on skill development. The general skills of reading, writing, and listening are obviously important in learning, and they also involve a large cognitive learning component. Running, dancing, or basketball playing, on the other hand, require relatively low levels of cognitive involvement. In contrast to cognitive learning, skill development results in neurological changes in the lower portions of the brain (cerebellum, medulla) and in the spinal cord, as well as in areas of the cerebral cortex. Cognitive learning involves only neurological changes in the cortex (albeit, human behavior in many cases may be a complex of "gut" learning and cortical activity). From a functional standpoint, however, acquisition of some types of cognitive information is dependent on development of motor skills, be they simple control of eye movement needed for reading or the complex series of skills needed for electron microscopic study of structures.

Skill learning often involves the use of some materials on which the motor coordination components can be practiced. Mock-ups may be used, as in the case of computer-controlled flight simulators used to train pilots, but some experience with the real thing is usually necessary for development of functional skills. Moreover, tennis champions, golf pros, and dance instructors have recognized for generations that development of skill proceeds best when learning is carefully guided. No professional in any area of skilled performance recommends trial and error or discovery approaches as the best way to acquire proficiency in a skill or related set of skills. The centuries-old practice of apprenticeship has been a method by which the master carefully guides all elements of motor learning, as well as necessary cognitive learning, as the novice progresses. Our present-day aversion to guided instruction generally does not extend to development of skill. The penchant for discovery learning in school instruction derives from the recognized limitations of rote learning, but we have failed to distinguish this from the promise of meaningful reception learning through carefully planned instructional sequences.

An inevitable requirement for skill learning is practice. Only by accident can a beginner shoot an arrow into the bull's eye of the target.[1] Since the behaviors taught in skill learning and the subsequent performance of the learner is usually obviously manifest, guidance is easier than in most areas of cognitive learning; we can explain discrepancies between the learner's performance and the criteria for excellence, whereas in cognitive learning we cannot easily observe what the learner has acquired nor can we easily identify the discrepancies from our criteria for excellence. In fact, it is often a problem to characterize what output from a learner will indicate mastery of a concept, and it is an even more complex task to explain discrepancies between the observed and the desired cognitive functioning. We know from experience and research that proficiency in a skill comes with practice and that less practice is needed when the learner is carefully guided (see Fleishman, 1969). Variation in learning time for skill development has been generally recognized, but variation in time for cognitive learning tasks is still thought to be limited as evidenced by the fact that all students of a given age are in about the same school grade and study much the same material, although there may be low track and high track programs in secondary schools. We need to recognize that cognitive learning rates are at least as variable as motor or skill learning, and we need to account better for differential learning times in our instructional program.

Not all activity referred to as a skill involves substantial motor learning. Already noted have been reading and listening, which require primarily appropriate cognitive development. Sometimes we hear reference to the skillful card player or the skillful stock broker; in fact, these persons are either enjoying a run of good

[1] The combination of motor, cognitive, and affective learning required to become a "master" archer is well described in Eugen Herrigel's *Zen in the Art of Archery* (1973).

luck or they are employing cognitive processes that lead to correct (winning) decisions. In planning instruction, the extent and nature of the motor development involved must be distinguished from the cognitive processes involved. Unfortunately, much more research is needed in which motor proficiency is isolated from the cognitive adequacy for a variety of learning tasks. Some art students probably fail primarily because of their lack of skill in mixing paints, whereas others fail because of cognitive deficiencies.

Varying Learning Schedules

In Chapter 8, I shall show that some students gain much more knowledge in much less time than others, and they are at least two or three times more efficient in learning than some classmates. It inevitably follows that reasonable standards for achievement in any course must allow for varying rates of learning. In traditional instruction in which lectures, class drill, and discussion are the principal teaching strategies, study time varies either in out-of-class study or in attentiveness of students during instruction. Students who have cognitive structures relevant to the instructional material and/or skills needed to learn specific segments of the material may vary their study time by daydreaming, writing letters, or engaging in activities other than those necessary to learn what is being taught. Traditional instructional programs either require extensive out-of-class study for the majority of students or are often unchallenging or boring to the best-prepared learners.

It is commonly assumed that there are certain times of the day when students are most effective as learners. We are not aware of any reliable data to support this claim. At Purdue, where students were scheduled into laboratory or discussion sessions essentially at random, no significant differences in achievement between sections meeting at varying times throughout the day were observed in any consistent way. Some research results suggesting midmorning hours as best for learning are probably artifacts of related fatigue factors (students who began study at 8:30 A.M. may be fatigued by 11:30 A.M.) or of conditioned sleep cycles and the necessary time lag between awakening and full mental arousal. Since individual sleep habits vary considerably, real individual differences exist in learning efficiencies, and the best we can hope for to maximize learning is to allow some variation in the time of day a student chooses for study. Unfortunately, complete flexibility in learning time is seldom practicable, and most traditional instructional practices permit little accommodation for learner idiosyncrasies with respect to time of day when learning efficiency for a given subject may be at its peak. Even more impracticable in traditional teaching organization is to allow for study of a given subject at varying times during a week, semester, or school year. Just how important complete flexibility in learning schedules may be is primarily a matter for conjecture at this time. We know that one group of botany students learned at least as much botany in half as many class hours in individually scheduled audio-tutorial learning sessions as did another group in traditional lecture-discussion-laboratory format, but this difference may show only that students doze through half of their traditional classes or that the individualized program provided significantly better learning materials than the traditional program (Samuel Postlethwait et al., 1972).

Most students probably can learn efficiently at any time of the day or night, or on any day of the year, provided that their sleep cycles or personal agendas do not interfere. Living arrangements, recreation and work activities, and other factors limit individuals' schedules and hence their efficiency cycles. The best we can do is to plan an instructional program that maximizes flexibility in learning schedules without proliferating costly instructional resources.

Affective Development

Cognitive learning is accompanied by emotional experience; therefore affective development will be a necessary concomitant of cognitive learning. The emotional experience is most likely to be positive when instruction is planned to optimize cognitive learning, and hence positive affective development is greatest when conditions that favor cognitive growth are present. Other factors influence emotional response, and I shall examine these briefly.

1. Learning environment. Comfortable, attractive room decor with good acoustics and lighting is helpful. My study of secondary school science facilities (Novak, 1972c) found carpeted floors, study areas with upholstered furniture, and careful attention to room decor in the best schools visited. I do not know of any objective data which indicate that better learning occurs in better facilities, but students, staff, and administration were convinced that students were learning more in new, comfortable schools than in older, traditional settings. There would be so many uncontrollable variables in a study of the effect of alternative facilities on cognitive and affective growth in most schools that I question the value of such research at this time. The facilities study (Novak, 1972c) reported an evolving pattern toward more homelike learning environments and suggested that the collective experience of educators which has led to this type of facility, may reflect a composite of many individual observations favoring a "softer" environment with carpeting and comfortable furniture. Surprisingly, total costs (purchase plus maintenance and replacement) for comfortable learning environments are about the same as for traditional classrooms. The major obstacle to the improvement of facilities is the popular myth that learning must be unpleasant to be good and that facilities must be uncomfortable. In my view this myth contributes to the emotional difficulties suffered by many young people, and much more effort is needed in schools to enhance positive emotional experience.

2. Opportunities for human association. Although cognitive learning is necessarily an individual phenomenon, the richest sources of emotional experience are from human associations. These are the experiences that sustain us through our most difficult challenges. Positive associations fortify one's confidence and provide emotional support for other challenges.

We are witnessing a growing awareness of the importance of emotional development and the need for guiding affective growth in schools. Carl Rogers' *Freedom to Learn* (1969) is one of the good books on this subject. The writers of these books, together with a new type of school counselor, are beginning to convince school administrators and planners that we cannot ignore emotional needs of students and that schools can play an important role in fulfilling those needs.

I view positively the growing awareness for increased affective exchange in schools, although I see dangers in some of the sensitivity and T-group approaches—especially those that fall into the touching-feeling category—unless they have very competent leadership. Emotional exchange can occur through exchange of written material (up to and including love letters), verbal communication, eye contact and body expressions, various forms of touching, embracing, caressing (including sexual intercourse). The important element in all of these is that individuals must be deliberate in communicating their emotions to others. Much too little is done to stress this and to enhance opportunities for emotional expression in schools. While schools are not expected to include the last category in the near future, open college dormitories and coeducational physical education classes in secondary schools at least provide an opportunity for daily personal interaction beyond that available during athletic events and school dances.

In seminar sessions where we explored ways to enhance affective exchange, we did not agree on clear-cut approaches that can be used in schools. We did agree that our richest emotional experiences came from one-on-one association and not from group involvement. Where group experiences were strongly positive for a person, he or she could usually reduce them to one or a few positive individual associations, and to those experiences in one-on-one sessions.

The opportunity for nonsuperficial interaction between individuals is very much limited by the facilities available in most schools and colleges. Generally all students face the teacher, who is frequently shielded by a desk or lectern, and this arrangement minimizes the opportunities for affective exchange among students and between teacher and students.

In addition, instructional planning rarely includes deliberate efforts to enhance meaningful emotional exchange. One advantage in science laboratory sessions, physical education classes, and some classes in the humanities is that small groups of students often work together, sometimes in groups of two, thus providing the potential for significant one-on-one interaction which includes emotional exchange. Even in these classes one rarely finds deliberate instructional planning for positive emotional exchange. Only in a few instances have we seen study guide materials that asked students to express their feelings about some item of study or to observe how their classmates, teachers, or other individuals were reacting emotionally to their experience.

Affective development can be considered analogous to cognitive development in that growth and differentiation of an individual's affective structure proceeds over time, and this growth is more likely to be positive and extensive if we deliberately plan for it. A great deal is to be learned before we can design highly effective instruction to optimize positive affective growth as well as cognitive development. Nevertheless, to ignore this dimension from fear or ignorance is to blind ourselves to the inevitable emotional concomitant to cognitive learning and to the potential enhancement we might confer by applying at least our best intuitions in instructional planning. With minimum ingenuity we should be able to structure learner activities that are more direct and interactive than those commonly employed in school learning, while retaining reasonable order and decorum. Even in planning instruction for extension or home-study adult education programs, much more can be done to include human associations structured for potentially greater positive emotional interaction.

3. Evaluation of affective growth. Our evaluation practices are recognized by students as the real determinants of what counts in an instructional program. If all test items require only rote memorization, then developing concepts and relationships among concepts is not seen as valuable, except by creative students who have recognized that meaningful learning can be also more effective for acquisition of facts. Similarly, positive emotional involvement in learning will be retarded if evaluation techniques place no emphasis on this (or, indeed, discourage

such involvement by penalizing any form of cooperative student achievement).

We have no empirically tested guidelines for evaluating affective growth. The suggestions from writings in humanistic education include assessment of student commentaries on the quality of emotional expression experienced during a learning task or on the nature and extent of their personal emotional experience during learning. Another form of evaluation for emphasizing affective dimensions could be group reporting or panel discussions which include commentary on emotional experiences of the individuals during learning and preparation of the affective evaluation statement. So much remains to be learned in the evaluation of affective development that we can offer only the suggestion that this dimension be considered and that a variety of methods be tried out.

Value Orientation

To plan instruction that can influence students' value development requires consideration of both cognitive and emotional learning relevant to the phenomenon under study. A politically loaded issue among urban students may be legal penalties for drug pushing, or in farm districts, the use of price supports for farm commodities. Considerable relevant information is available for each, and each is likely to be associated with idiosyncratic emotional experiences. It is essential to isolate the cognitive elements from the emotional in planning instruction on value-loaded topics and to recognize that choice of information to be studied will influence student values.

In some value-laden areas, deliberate instruction can lead to unpleasant experiences with parents. Sex education, for example, which includes information on birth control methods— their reliability and use by various age and ethnic groups—almost inevitably leads to value conflicts. Some parents may view any information on birth control methods as an invitation to premarital sex, and their anxiety is likely to be even greater if data are presented on the frequency of sexual intercourse for various age and marital status categories. Even those parents who generally favor frank discussion of human sexuality may complain when statistics indicate the frequency of some behaviors. Some of our most pressing social problems require that future citizens meaningfully acquire information that necessarily has implications for value development in directions that conflict with contemporary family or community norms. Responsible educators cannot avoid all subjects that may lead to value conflicts, but good judgment must be shown in avoiding blatant confrontation of home or community values without adequate preparation.

Toffler in *Future Shock* (1970) describes the rapidly accelerating rate of change in society, a phenomenon that has important implications for education in the area of values. To illustrate this point, Toffler divides the 50,000-year history of modern man into eight hundred 62-year lifetimes and argues that more change has occurred in the most recent lifetime than in the preceding 799. In this eight-hundredth lifetime we have shifted from a predominantly agricultural population to a population of tradesmen and factory workers (blue collar) to the current population in which the majority of workers are in sales and service (white collar). With less than 6 percent of American workers engaged in agriculture, we have become an extremely mobile people, free to relocate, to find new work, and to make new friends. But this mobility and the continuing pressure of social change has reached a point where many people suffer a kind of psychosis of instability, a condition Toffler calls future shock, or what we might refer to as societal "change psychosis." The result is a desperate attempt to "stop the world," to hold steady some segment of society while other sectors inexorably go on changing. We cannot stop developed nations from using increasingly scarce natural resources, and hence many changes necessitated by energy and raw material shortages are thrust upon us. Some would try to maintain traditional political value structures (such as faith in the sanctity of the presidency) and school programs. Consequently, we are facing what may become an increasing public clamor to keep schools and curricula from changing, the response of people afflicted with change psychosis, who are attempting to hold one segment of society stable and to act in a manner consistent with their value structures.

This reaction is tragic because our best hopes to mitigate change psychosis are to help young people understand what is happening in society and to prepare them for rational decision making in the face of societal value shifts, rather than to pretend that somehow things will go back to normal. This problem is not unique to American schools; it is faced by all developed countries and increasingly thrust upon some poor countries, which have the fewest resources for dealing with it. Partly for this reason, the present population growth is most severe in countries least able to cope with the miseries associated with overpopulation. Schools in the developed countries should be providing guidance for schools in poorer nations to improve instruction in values and to help young people prepare for a lifetime of societal changes and accompanying value changes.

So far, we see little evidence that planned changes in instructional programs are toward more education in values. Probably the most important influence on a change in student values is the shift to coeducational dormitories and cohabitation, which is rapidly becoming the norm for colleges. When males and females live together in pairs or in groups, they may learn something about values that their parents were not likely to learn. This pattern, however, has been forced upon colleges by students and is not the product of educational leadership, nor is it part of the college curriculum. Some would argue that education in values is the job of the home and church or synagogue, and certainly values are learned there. Schools in free societies may never become the places where most of the values of students are acquired, but they should teach students to understand what values are, how they are acquired, and what some societal consequences of differing values may be. This will be a delicate task for the venturesome curriculum planners who pursue this work in public schools.

Instructional Objectives

One of the crusades in education in the 1960s called for specific statement of *instructional objectives*. This movement was powered to a considerable extent by Mager's *Preparing Objectives for Programmed Learning* (1962). The ideas in the book evolved from Mager's experience with vocational training programs and with programmed instruction which, together with educational television, were popular in the 1950s. Mager and his supporters believed that instruction was most likely to be effective if learning goals were carefully specified so that the student understood the criteria for successful achievement.

To facilitate clarity in instructional objectives, Mager recommended that they be stated in *behavioral* form—that is, the *activity* to be displayed by the learner should be manifest and comparable to a criterion behavior against which it is evaluated. Learning objectives so stated are characterized by action verbs, such as to identify, to diagram, to list. Objectives written with these kinds of action verbs are much less subject to ambiguous meanings than objectives written with phrases such as to fully understand or to show concern for. Mager's work does not call for stating objectives that aim at specific concept differentiation or at integrative reconciliation of concepts. Under Mager's guidelines, learning objectives become statements of the type illustrated below:

After the instruction the learner shall be able to:

1. *list* ten capital cities of the world
2. *construct* a bird house for wrens.
3. *differentiate* between angiosperm and gymnosperm
4. *identify* six attributes of Australian aborigines

Mager was correct, of course, in saying that this type of learning objective can be unambiguous to the learner and that evaluation based on these objectives is much less subject to varying interpretations. The primary difficulty, however, is that an entire instructional program can be planned using Mager-type objectives without giving any consideration to concepts to be learned or to hierarchical relationships between concepts. It is possible, in fact, to plan an instructional program of *rote* learning which will be most expedient for attainment of objectives, while meaningful learning will be discouraged and/or result in lower achievement. J. Myron Atkin (1968) and others have identified some problems associated with indiscriminate use of behavioral objectives. Mager's insistence on learning objectives that describe observable behaviors derives from the behaviorists' psychological orientation and hence a priori excludes concept learning as a major consideration (compare Strike, 1974)..

Looking at the problem in terms of Johnson's model, we see that use of behaviorally stated learning objectives can be useful in instructional planning and in evaluation. Most important is that we begin with a matrix of concepts (and/or skills) to be learned and then develop our behavioral objectives (Figure 6.2). Too many workshops for teachers have emphasized the action-verb form of behaviorally stated learning objectives and have ignored completely the problem of unpacking knowledge from a discipline and developing an appropriate curriculum matrix. In so doing, the emphasis has been on a pedagogical mechanics that ignore the central intellectual issues involved in instructional planning for meaningful learning.

In Chapter 2, I showed how a philosophical premise of peripheralism leads to S-R learning theory. Preoccupation with *behaviorally* stated learning objectives assumes the validity of peripheralism (usually without awareness on the part of the instructional planner) and ignores or denies the role of differentiated cognitive structure in mediating learning. Planning instructional objectives without consideration of the matrix of skills and concepts to be learned and the hierarchical relationships that exist in this matrix is to adhere unwittingly to a peripheralist psychology.

These reservations do not mean that Mager's work and behavioral objectives have no place in instructional planning. On the contrary, for all skill learning and most aspects of concept learning, behaviorally stated learning objectives are likely to be less ambiguous to the student; thus they facilitate meaningful learning and are more easily converted into an evaluation format that is objective and positively perceived by the student. A learning objective "to *compare* and *contrast* and *describe* the ac-

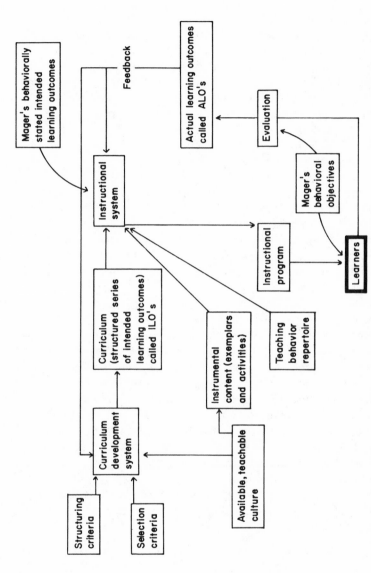

Figure 6.2. Johnson's (1967) model showing where consideration of Mager's (1962) behavioral objectives can be useful.

tion of osmosis, diffusion, turgor, and plasmolysis in plant cells" is immensely more helpful to the learner and evaluator than an objective "to *understand* osmosis, diffusion, turgor, and plasmolysis in plants." What I wish to emphasize, however, is that nothing in Mager's book (1962) or in most of the writings emphasizing use of behavioral objectives in education will help in *curriculum* planning. The selection, ordering, and emphasis for concepts to be learned is a task that must precede instructional planning and must be evaluated continually as instructional development and lesson tryout proceed.

I should also caution that one much too easily avoids confronting decisions on affective learning goals and value orientation of the learning material when undue attention is given to behaviorally stated instructional objectives. It is possible to write behavioral objectives for affective learning, but this is not easy. Mager (1962) offered no suggestions in this area, although other writers have published some useful material (see David Thatcher, 1973).

Instructional Strategies

Again we must emphasize the usefulness of separating instructional planning from curriculum planning, as indicated in Johnson's model. Once we have arrived at a curriculum including concepts and skills to be taught, we must find the most effective system to present this curriculum to students. Surveying the range of available instructional methods and resources, we need to decide about what combination of printed material, lecture, discussion, laboratory, studio or field work, and audiovisual support we wish to use. The role of computers in instructional planning has been negligible in the past, although new fourth-generation computers show high promise for the future; the Plato System developed in Illinois will be discussed later in this chapter.

Instructional Materials

1. Printed material. Except for children who do not read, printed materials have been and probably will continue to be the most important instructional tools. One advantage of printed

material is that students can skim over, read carefully and reread, spot check items that need review, and in many other ways adapt it to their individual learning styles. In a previous chapter I discussed the problem of logical organization and topical presentation in most printed materials, especially textbooks, but this problem is due to a limitation of custom, convention, and ignorance and not to the medium per se.

In recent years there has been a burgeoning interest in "instructional modules" or "learning activity packages" (LAPS) in secondary schools and colleges. The principal advantage to modular instructional material is that it is more flexible than textbooks or larger course study guides. Instructional modules will be discussed later in this chapter; the point of emphasis here is that a wide variety of printed material continues to be a primary instructional resource.

There has been increased use of overhead projectors, 35 mm slides, and 8 mm loop films as a result of federal money made available for this type of software and hardware. In preliminary versions of instructional material, audiovisual media may be convenient for the teachers and helpful to students. However, as lessons are refined, printed material can have the advantage of being available to students for continued study or review, in or out of the classroom. Moreover, illustrations can be placed into study guides at points where they are needed for immediate reference; students can mark or annotate illustrations; and since study guides are usually "consumed" by the student, new illustrations can be substituted without the expense of the investment associated with A-V materials. New, less expensive duplication technology has made possible convenient use of printed materials for many occasions in which audiovisual materials were needed in the past. The recent development of color xerography adds new potential for preparation of special printed materials.

2. Audiovisual (A-V) materials. The range of audiovisual materials available today is substantially greater than it was two decades ago. In general, A-V materials can be used for individual study or group instruction. However, much new A-V material is particularly adaptable for individual use, both in ease of opera-

tion and in terms of costs. Perhaps the best example is the small cassette tape recorder, which costs less than fifty dollars and uses cartridges that are priced at less than one dollar each. Cassette recordings are rapidly becoming the standard for tape recorders. In planning for and selecting A-V materials, we should consider whether group or individual use would be the best instructional mode. Accordingly, appropriate A-V materials would be developed and/or purchased. Also to be considered is whether a printed format would be less expensive and more useful in the operational/instructional program. The use of 35 mm slides, for example, gives the instructor flexibility in adding or dropping illustrations in early stages of instructional planning, but printed photos may be the best and most economical mode for wide student use.

Another important decision involves the value of motion in the instructional material. Most 16 mm films are a series of scenes that could be shown as well or better with slides or printed photos. Similarly, many 8 mm loop films contain little or no information that requires motion to be illustrated. My experience has been that information I initially thought would be best presented on movie film could be presented better on appropriate series of slides or printed figures. Cost is a factor usually operating against movie film, and maintenance of film and equipment can be an instructional nightmare. My colleagues and I have all but eliminated loop films in our instructional programs as a result of film and projector failures, and have had only marginally satisfactory results with cassette projectors. In spite of these limitations, movie film continues to be an important instructional aid, especially in early planning of new lessons.

3. Television. Television provides the same capability as movie film and has several important advantages. Video tape is usually less expensive than film since it can be erased and reused. No delays are encountered in processing, and hence a scene can be shot, reviewed, and retaped if necessary. The cost of video equipment, however, can be ten to one hundred times the cost of functional movie cameras and projectors, and even higher when color video equipment is used. The question is

often whether movie film can be cheaper and better in the long run, or whether printed illustrations are perhaps all that is needed. In visits to schools and colleges, we have seen video tape equipment relegated to closets. Instructors found that demonstrations formerly shown on video equipment could be photographed on 8 mm color film, edited, and used conveniently with much less chance of equipment failure. In many cases the video equipment is used only for a dry run attempt to devise instructional material and other A-V aids are employed for subsequent runs. On the group versus individual instruction issue, most TV equipment is not sufficiently reliable or is too expensive for individual use. Until more progress in design and lower cost makes cassette video tape practicable, video equipment is seldom worth the investment and may represent more of a showpiece for visitors than an instructional tool.

One value of television is as a substitute for or supplement to lectures. Especially in large classes (100 to 500 students or more) the use of television can circumvent the problem of physical distance between the student and the teacher. The teacher's manner and movements can indicate to students what the instructor regards as most important and as comparatively trivial. Also, the instructor's affective expressions during instruction can signal commitment and love of a discipline that might be contagious, if these expressions can be observed as in TV close shots. The use of television to bring students closer to a lecturer is probably one reason why some studies find that students prefer small-group viewing of televised lectures to large-group live lectures.

Numerous attempts have been made to use television for educational programs locally, regionally, and nationally. In general, these efforts seldom have shown substantial learning gains, and frequently other instructional formats would have been more effective as to cost. The Open University in England is finding that the contribution of TV to instruction does not appear to be worth the enormous costs (see Jeremy Tunstall, 1974). The problems associated with TV as an educational tool continue to be inherent in the medium. As a resource for substantial support of cognitive development, it has too many functional limitations. We must learn to use regional or national television for those aspects of education for which it is uniquely powerful, for example, when it provides timely examples and information and brings students close to inspiring personalities.

4. Computers. Computer technology probably has been the fastest moving area of technology. As a result educational applications that were not feasible with earlier computers have now become practicable, although relatively little use of computers is found in schools. In my study of 150 schools with exemplary facilities (Novak, 1972c), I found that less than half had any kind of computer facility and that most were using computers only in mathematics courses. In part this limited use of computers as a learning aid stems from unfavorable publicity associated with early efforts at computer assisted instruction (CAI); in part it reflects the general ignorance of educators regarding the cost and capabilities of new small computers and of time-shared terminals connected to fourth generation computers with almost unlimited data processing and storage capacity; in part we witness here the inflexibility of archaic school budgets that allocate 80 percent or more for salaries but only 3 or 4 percent for instructional equipment and materials.

Small, reliable computers can now be purchased for two thousand dollars or less, and while these are essentially electronic calculators, they have some programming capabilities. For less than fifteen thousand dollars computers can be obtained which have add-on data storage facilities and substantial potentials for enhancing instruction, especially as evaluation aids with which instructors can have test items generated in a wide variety for individualized testing, while simultaneously recording students' progress. Obsolescence has been a problem in the past, with new model computers rendering older models impracticable almost before teachers could learn how to use them. Although progress in computer technology will undoubtedly continue, present computer facilities are so versatile and reliable that they probably will have a useful life span of a decade or two rather than a year or two.

Teaching Approaches

Johnson (1967) points out that in developing an instructional program we select activities from the variety of examples available (instrumental content) and from the teaching behavior repertoire. For most college teachers, the teaching behavior repertoire is almost exclusively lecturing. Given four or more years of this kind of example, secondary school teachers imitate their professors, with the result that most teachers lecture most of the time (see Ned Flanders, 1960; Robert Travers, 1973). Our experience has been that secondary school intern teachers who may assist with laboratory work, discussion groups, and field trips do not believe they are teaching if they do not give lectures. To many students and teachers, teaching is synonymous with lecturing. From the standpoint of learning theory and instructional theory, however, lecturing is only one mode of teaching. Briefly, I shall review several teaching approaches and comment on their relationship to the theoretical structure of this book.

1. Lecturing. According to Ausubel's theory, lecturing may be effective in several ways. To the extent that learners have a framework of concepts relevant to the potentially meaningful lecture material, information can be learned meaningfully, provided that the lecture is suitably paced. Unfortunately, the adequacy of available subsuming concepts in a given subject matter area will vary considerably in any group of students, and hence the lecture will be too fast for some students to internalize the information meaningfully and too slow (hence boring or wasteful) for students with the best framework of relevant concepts. The result is a double penalty for the students with poor entry cognitive structure—they must take copious notes, thus draining their attention into writing rather than learning, and later accomplish in private study what they could not do in the group setting. This problem can be alleviated in several ways. If notes are duplicated and supplied to students in advance, they can come prepared to the lecture; they can study the notes beforehand to gain sufficient relevant cognitive structure to learn during the lecture, and they are spared the chore

of taking notes. Alternatively, or in addition, the teacher can provide a lecture syllabus in advance. This syllabus must, however, describe with sufficient clarity the concepts to be taught and provide pertinent references from which students can acquire the necessary subsumers. These subsumers can subsequently be differentiated further in the lecture. Moreover, some distinctions between subordinate concepts must be shown. Rarely are lecture guides more than a listing of topics to be presented, in serial order, with no attempt to describe rudimentary concepts and the hierarchical relationships between them. If textbooks were psychologically organized, they could serve as useful preparation for lectures planned to expand and integrate the concepts introduced in the textbook. Specially prepared prelecture study guides providing conceptual frameworks can do much to enhance the cognitive learning value of lectures. However, when relatively complete, conceptually focused study guides are prepared, lecture attendance tends to drop off (unless attendance is required), which illustrates in part the weakness and inefficiency of lectures for transmitting knowledge. The result can be not only a loss in useful elaboration of concepts but also a failure to transmit other desired learning outcomes.

In an earlier section we described the methods of work employed in disciplines. To the extent that the lecturer is a productive worker in his field or understands the methods of work in his field, he can, through description of examples of his work, characterize his approach to the identification of new facts, concepts, or skills associated with a subject of study. Personal insight into the methods of work in a discipline can be transmitted by lectures with great effectiveness—dramatically sometimes—especially when illustrations with slides, films, models, or demonstrations are used. Students who understand the methods by which new knowledge comes into being are more likely to learn meaningfully the concepts presented, partly because all learners must acquire primary abstractions with their verbal labels prior to meaningful learning of secondary abstractions in a subject of study. Illustrating the methods of work can serve to assist students in establishing primary abstractions and in associating concept labels to the phenomenon of interest. This process applies in music, history, and art, as well as in the sciences, where the association between methods of work and achievements may be more obvious. From the standpoint of instructional theory, lectures can be useful in presenting exemplars for concepts that are not easily presented in other ways. For example, should the morning news carry stories on peace negotiations, a lecturer can weave this news into a discussion of the role of the secretary of state in international affairs. The potential for identifying and selecting exemplars of immediate relevance to students is one of the important promises of the lecture. If appropriate lecture study guides were more commonly used, we might see more use of timely examples in illustrating lectures.

Finally, in the area of affective learning, lectures can be useful and effective. Except in very large classes (perhaps 500 to 1,000 students[2]) or in poor lecture rooms, a teacher can show his emotional disposition toward aspects of the discipline he teaches and toward students. His voice, intonations, smiles, sighs, and body movements can signal his emotional responses to the knowledge being presented and toward the students as recipients of this knowledge. In my view this personal projection in lecture settings is in itself of sufficient importance to justify the use of lectures at least four or five times a semester, but certainly not two or three times per week. The affective expression that can be transmitted in lectures needs to be studied more intensively, for this may eventually prove to be the most useful purpose of the lecture.

2. Discussion groups. Recognizing the idiosyncratic nature of every learner's cognitive and affective structures, good discussion group instruction can be immensely useful in education. On the cognitive side, we must recognize that the presence or

[2]The subject of optimal lecture attendance has been much researched, but criterion tests usually measure only cognitive learning. We are not aware of any studies that assess a student's ability to obtain "body language" cues in classrooms of various sizes. Within the limitations of the tests used, class size has seldom shown a significant influence on student achievement (see Travers, 1973).

adequacy of relevant subsumers in our students will vary, and hence the discussion group should provide help to students in identifying gaps or deficiencies in their conceptual frameworks and in understanding how new information relates to larger, more inclusive concepts. Before this can be accomplished successfully, the concepts to be learned and the possible hierarchical relationships between them must be identified clearly. In college teaching, discussion groups are usually led by graduate students, many of whom have not straightened out in their own minds what the significant concepts are in a given area of study, to say nothing about relationships among concepts. As a result, too many discussion sessions are either a rehash of lectures presented in a course, a kind of first aid for students who are conceptually lost in the discipline, or an ego display by the discussion leader of how simple a problem or technique may be. Wherever teams of teaching assistants or regular teachers are working together in multiple discussion sections, weekly staff planning sessions are needed to clarify concepts and skills to be learned, relationships among elements in the program, and important methods of work.

Discussion groups are sometimes small enough (about six to twelve students) that considerable one-on-one exchange may occur. We should consider the extent to which affective expression may be desirable and guide this expression to support the cognitive learning objectives of the course. Here again we see the importance of clarifying instructional objectives, both in the cognitive and affective domains. It may be very appropriate to have students describe their feelings about a given concept or set of concepts under study. In this case, it is useful to sort out those feelings that express concern or confidence with the individual's mastery of the concept from feelings toward the concept per se (the concept of apartheid is a good example here). The extension of the analysis might move to value issues and show how individual student value structures affect their perception of the subject.

When discussion groups are successful in clarifying concept meanings and relationships and in obtaining extensive individual expression of emotions and value orientations, they can serve as excellent vehicles for promoting closer human relationships between individuals. Milton Mayeroff (1971) stresses that to care for someone else requires that we get to know him: "To care for someone, I must know many things. I must know, for example, who the other is, what his powers and limitations are, what his needs are, and what is conducive to his growth; I must know how to respond to his needs and what my own powers and limitations are" (p. 13).

It should be evident that good discussion sessions can contribute substantially to the information a person needs to begin caring about some of his classmates. With the simple encouragement provided by distributing a class roster with names and phone numbers, a discussion class in one subject could lead to one or two valuable friendships for every member of the group. People need to learn to care more for people; we should capitalize on the potential in discussion groups to achieve this goal.

3. Laboratory or studio work. This instructional mode has potential for three important forms of learning. Laboratory work can provide direct experience with materials or props needed to develop primary abstractions. The concept terms such as color, hue, parenchyma cell, vascular system, pirouette, and plie take on substantially more meaning when observed in the laboratory or studio. Second, skills cannot be learned without practice of the motor performances required, and they are likely to be learned more quickly when example and correction are provided in close proximity. And finally, the laboratory or studio can illustrate the methods of work by which achievements are accomplished in a given discipline.

Although all three of the above learning functions can be achieved simultaneously, it is usually more profitable to focus on each separately and with clearly described instructional objectives. Too often laboratory sessions in science designed to clarify a concept require skills in the use of novel equipment, which results in neither acquisition of technical skill nor concept clarification. Laboratory work intended to illustrate the methods used by a scientist to obtain knowledge may not take into account that the scientist has a well-developed, relevant framework of concepts and a technical skill with the equipment, both of which may be deficient in the students, and hence the good intentions of the instructional planner go awry for he tries to do too much at once or fails to recognize the limitations inherent in his learners. The same problems exist in other laboratories and in studio work.

Laboratories and studios can be even more promising than discussion sessions for exchange of emotional expression and development of affective structure. Because life styles are moving toward more open relationships between people and because greater value is placed on developing relationships by young people, the laboratory or studio may hold an increasingly important role in education, even though their costs tend to be high.

4. Tutorial instruction. From the standpoint of assimilation theory, tutorial instruction could be the most effective method of teaching. In tutorial instruction with a single learner, new concepts or propositions can best be illustrated with examples that very obviously link to previous relevant concepts held by the learner, and the pace of presentation of new information will be most appropriate for the learner. In practice, however, teachers or graduate students seldom possess the broad fund of examples or the understanding of concepts necessary to present the most meaningful information for each tutee, at least not on the spur of the moment. Moreover, tutorial instruction, if used as the only method of teaching, costs more than society can afford, although it may be cost-effective under some circumstances (Ellson, 1976).

We have all experienced successful learning in groups or from reading, and hence tutorial instruction obviously is not necessary in spite of the idiosyncratic nature of learning. However, when judiciously employed as an adjunct to group instruction, especially when it is available immediately at critical moments, tutorial instruction can substantially enhance learning and may account for much of the positive experience with audio-tutorial strategies. Postlethwait (1972) and others have shown that audio-tutorial programs are also cost-effective.

5. Individualized instruction. Perhaps the most popular educational trend of the 1970s is individualized instruction. The

types of individualized instruction are almost as numerous as the books and articles on the subject; the generic meanings, however, all focus on one or more of the following aspects:

Students proceed at their own speed through segments of the program.

Students can select alternative lessons or activities to meet a given set of instructional objectives.

Students are instructed as individuals or in small groups for all or a major portion of class time.

Students can select when they wish to study a given subject and how long they want to spend in a given study session.

Students select or design their own learning activities.

An increased range of learning material is provided.

Technology is used to permit or increase individual study of materials.

Instructional materials are organized into distinct segments, blocks, or modules.

Didactic and direct experience activities are integrated into learning blocks or modules.

Instructional objectives and criteria for assessment or achievement are made clear to the students.

Student-student associations are encouraged.

Teacher's role primarily is to counsel and advise rather than to present information.

The methods of knowing in a discipline are at least as important as acquisition of knowledge.

Encouragement of individual creative expression is more common than in group instructional programs.

Some forms of individualized instruction have been labeled in ways that suggest their nature. "Learning activity packages" as used at Nova High School (Bethune, 1966), for example, consist of printed study guides and associated materials that allow for varying rates of student progress. (Some students complete a year's course in several weeks.) Optional study units provide variety in students' programs. The principal instructional tool is the printed study guide, but teachers are available for tutorial help, technicians provide laboratory packs, and a testing center staffed by clerical persons is used for evaluation.

A variation of learning packages has been developed for college courses under the label of Keller Plan instruction (Keller,

1968). With the Keller Plan, students are guided primarily by printed materials, although some programs also employ work with computers. The primary characteristics of these programs are that they usually permit students to move at their own speed through a course and they contain explicit guidance as to the objectives of study together with student evaluation checks to assess attainment of these objectives.

a. Modular courses. In recent years various forms of modular courses have appeared. A useful publication describing modules was prepared by the Commission on Undergraduate Instruction in the Biological Sciences (Joan Creager and Darrel Murray, 1971); much of this book would be helpful to teachers of any subject, at any grade level. It is suggested (p. 5) that a "module" consists of the following components:
1. Statement of Purpose
2. Desirable Prerequisite Skills
3. Instructional Objectives
4. Diagnostic Pre-Test
5. Implementers for the Modules (needed equipment, supplies, etc.)
6. The Modular Program (printed material, A-V material, etc.)
7. Related Experiences
8. Evaluative Post-Test
9. Assessment of the Module (by students and staff)

The centuries-old practice of dividing textbooks into chapters is an effort to make modular a course of instruction, but textbooks seldom contain all of the above elements. However, an easy way to conceive of modular courses would be to consider a textbook torn into separate chapters, with pages then added to provide all of the above elements. If the chapters were then rewritten carefully to elucidate each learning objective, with laboratory, studio, or field experience integrated and with appropriate evaluation material provided, we would have a good beginning for a modular individualized course.

b. Audio-tutorial instruction. One form of modular instruction worthy of special mention was developed by Postlethwait at Purdue University in 1961. He used a tape recorder to provide audio-guidance to students as they studied botanical materials. A description of his method was first published in 1962, and subsequently audio-tutorial instruction (or A-T, as it is known) has become probably the most widely used instructional innovation on college campuses since 16 mm educational films. One reason for the success of A-T instruction has been that it employs simple technology to augment individualization of instruction.

Postlethwait first began to use audio-tape for students who had missed lectures, or who could not grasp all of the material in the lecture at the rate it was presented. He recognized the value of providing charts and pictures along with the tape and the success of this supplementation soon led to arrangements for microscopes and microscope slides. When these supplements began to tax the facilities of the audio-visual center, Postlethwait decided to develop a learning center in the life sciences building, where the botany course was normally taught. As a result of the enthusiastic reception of audio-tape guided instruction by botany students, traditional lectures, laboratories, and discussion sessions, were abandoned, and A-T instruction was fully implemented. Instead of two lectures, one three-hour laboratory section and a one-hour discussion session, Postlethwait provided for most instruction to occur in a learning center where tutors were constantly on duty. Some lectures and discussion sessions were continued but these changed in form and purpose over the years. A description of the A-T program has been published (Postlethwait, et al., 1972). Figure 6.3 shows study materials used in addition to individual sets of materials provided in the carrels. Postlethwait's A-T approach provided for individualization of instruction through tutorial aid and through flexibility in study time. Each week a new study unit was available in the laboratory, and students could choose how long and how often they wished to work on the material during days and evenings of the week. More recently Postlethwait, together with Robert Hurst, has developed a biology program consisting of some eighty minicourses, which, together with a required "core," accommodates their varying interests or vocational objectives. Minicourses are essentially A-T units that contain all the components listed above for instructional modules. Minicourses for college biology have been developed by Postlethwait and associates with the aid of a National Science Foundation

Figure 6.3. Additional study materials used to supplement individual materials provided in the carrels.

grant, and have been published by William B. Saunders Company of New York (1976).

Chapter 8 includes a description of some of the research I conducted at Purdue, including studies done with students in Postlethwait's A-T botany course. My experience with A-T instruction as a research tool for the study of cognitive learning showed promise, although college students come to class with a very heterogeneous background in concept learning. They also have many interfering variables of motivation, love relationships, and competing class requirements. Young children who are just beginning to develop concepts relevant to natural phenomena are in many ways better subjects for study; here the difficulty is that most primary grade teachers know too little science to present appropriate instruction. One cannot study the process of concept learning if concept learning fails to occur. The A-T mode seems to hold promise as a research tool with six to ten year olds if successful programs could be developed.

Some of our research on audio-tutorial elementary school science is presented in Chapter 8.

c. Computer assisted instruction. Much of the excitement that existed in the late 1950s regarding the promise of computer assisted instruction (CAI) faded away as teachers and computer technicians became aware of the inadequacies of second-generation computers for instruction. These computers had more information storage capacity, faster response, and easier programming characteristics than early vacuum tube computers, but they were still too limited in information-handling capacity and reliability to function satisfactorily in teaching. Some improvement was achieved with third-generation printed circuit computers of the 1960s. More recently we are seeing fourth-generation computers employing new advances in solid state circuitry with capabilities that begin to match instructional needs. Since the 1950s, we have seen an enormous advance in computer technology. This rate of progress may continue; however, computers of the 1970s will probably continue to be used in schools partly because of their high reliability and partly because of their extraordinary data processing capability relative to present needs.

Today educators use small- or medium-size computers for calculating, controlling video displays, generating test questions and maintaining performance records for individual students, and directly instructing individual students. Computers in this size range can be used by individual departments or colleges for instruction and data processing. As staff members acquire more experience with computers in small- or medium-size range, and as more are purchased, we should expect to see an increasing percentage of courses using some CAI programs and also more instruction conducted in this mode.

The most spectacular CAI development is the work at the University of Illinois on the PLATO system (Programmed Logic for Automatic Teaching Operations). This program has been in development since the 1950s (see Alpert and Bitzer, 1970). The PLATO system has advanced as new computers and programming techniques have become available. The newest version, called PLATO IV, shows great promise for CAI instruction. It employs a special large computer developed by Control Data Corporation; up to 4,000 student terminals can be connected to it via telephone wires. The enormous capacity of the PLATO IV system for storage and data processing provides access not only to standard reference items, such as boiling points of materials, but to any or all portions of other courses already in storage. As a result, new course materials are comparatively easy to write. The immense capacity of the system means that when fully operational, CAI instruction can be available for about fifty cents per student hour. Considering the efficiency of learning that has been demonstrated with good CAI programs as compared to conventional teaching, the cost-effectiveness of the PLATO IV system is already attractive to schools. The state of Illinois is contributing to the development cost of this program and use of the PLATO IV system in all Illinois state colleges is planned.

6. Mastery learning. The practice of mastery learning (see Block, 1971) is a natural corollary to individualized instruction. A basic assumption in most individualized study programs is that a student will master the content of each block or module he attempts. Commonly, this means that the student must successfully complete 85 to 90 percent of the evaluation items for a given study unit. The student achieving this level has presumably mastered the content of the unit and can now proceed to other study units. If performance is less than the mastery level specified, the student restudies all or part of the unit and is then retested. The assumption is that most students can master any study unit or module, given adequate time. In practice, 60 to 75 percent of the students will show mastery on the evaluation schedule after one pass through a well-designed module. Most remaining students will succeed after restudy of all or selected parts of the module. A small percentage may find it necessary to bypass a given module—perhaps to return to it later—or to study an alternative lesson package that uses different examples or activities to achieve similar conceptual growth.

In mastery learning, achievement is based on successful completion of study units, not on comparative standing on a group test. Differences in student achievement exist, but these are differences in the number of study units mastered, and/or in the amount of time needed to complete the units successfully. Each student's evaluation is based on successful completion of evaluation items for each study unit rather than on group testing that ranks each student's class position. Students compete insofar as they strive to be the first to complete a set of units or to complete the most optional units. Realistic standards for passing a course, however, may permit the majority of students to receive A or B grades without extraordinary effort. This result in part comes from the fact that mastery of early units of instruction, although with more time needed for some students than for others, can lead to significant facilitation of learning in later units and to a minimization of initial student differences in background knowledge. In work with college physics students, I found that some students who required the most study time for early units in a related sequence were among those using the least study time to master later units in the sequence. Ausubel's principle of facilitation of learning through early development of relevant subsumers was evident. Further discussion of this work is included in Chapter 8.

Mastery learning practices employ *criterion-referenced* evaluation, whereas traditional instruction usually employs *norm-referenced* evaluation. In norm-referenced evaluation the student strives for a position on a curve, whereas in criterion-referenced evaluation the student is essentially in competition with himself. The important difference in evaluation is between the case in which the student knows explicitly what he is expected to master, and the other case in which he sees himself in an intellectual race with his peers. It is difficult to foster warm relationships among students when they view themselves in competition. It is also difficult for staff members to play the role of sympathetic facilitators of learning when they are identified with ranking students on tests that label one fourth or more as failures.

With the use of mastery learning strategies, course performance depends more on the quality of instructional materials and student's motivation to succeed than on individual differences in initial background knowledge. Grade distributions consequently can shift from the typical bell-shaped curve obtained in nonmastery instructional approaches with norm-referenced grading to highly skewed curves with the majority of students receiving A or B grades. In work with students in a college physics course we observed this change in grade distributions as shown in Figure 6.4. An obvious question is whether A students under criterion-referenced evaluation and mastery learning strategy actually know as much physics as A students under traditional approaches. We do not have a definitive answer, but we do know that the tests used under the mastery learning schedule were at least as difficult as those used in former norm-referenced evaluation; this information is based on item statistics comparisons and on the judgment of physics professors involved in both types of instruction.

On psychological grounds, mastery learning strategies make

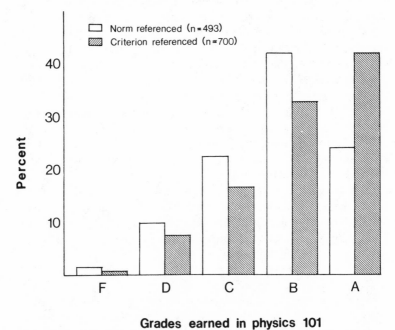

Grades earned in physics 101

Figure 6.4.   Norm-referenced achievement vs. criterion-referenced achievement.

very good sense. They tend to shift the primary motivation for learning away from *aversive* motivation associated with low grades (since now almost any student who tries hard can receive an A or a B) to *cognitive drive* motivation associated with explicitly recognized mastery of units of subject matter. *Ego enhancement* motivation may still operate for those who finish units quickly, but at least it is not at the expense of denying classmates the ego enhancement that derives from achieving an A grade, albeit with more time and effort.

Those who insist on classifying students into some ability rank system may ask how excellence can be judged if most students get A grades in a course. Clearly, criteria other than course grades are needed; we need to indicate the rate at which mastery (A grades) was achieved. The reader is reminded that meaningful learning is sometimes *slower* than rote learning because the individual is involved in reorganization of cognitive structures and differentiation of subordinate and superordinate concepts. A physics student who may be "slow" in introductory physics may later demonstrate the best capability for problem solving or new learning when physics concepts are required, long after information learned by rote is forgotten. Although genic differences is learning ability will determine rates of mastery of subject matter, evidence suggests that the relative adequacy of prerequisite concepts may be more important in achievement of any specific segment of instruction, as I shall show in Chapter 8.

Evaluation

In education, evaluation techniques often destroy what might have been a good instructional program. A curriculum that focuses on concepts of a field, with carefully chosen illustrative examples and activities, has the potential for meaningful learning of important concepts and of relationships between concepts. If, however, the only evaluation is the usual teacher-made test, which requires only rote recall of specific facts, students rapidly adjust their study patterns, and most fail to acquire the conceptual framework that has become buried in the program. The evaluation of an education program can be as crucial as the design of the program itself, although evaluation seldom receives such careful attention. Two kinds of evaluation are needed in education. The common and more obvious kind determines what knowledge and skills students have acquired from a given instructional program. Michael Scriven (1967) has called this *summative* evaluation to distinguish it from the second kind, *formative* evaluation. As an instructional program is developed, constant checking on strengths and weaknesses of the program is needed. Scriven, by stressing this need for continuous formative evaluation during development of the instructional program, has done a great service to education. Formative evaluation checks on how well the instructional program is fulfilling the purposes of the curriculum plan, whereas summative evaluation appraises the individual's success after completing the program or program segment.

The distinction between formative and summative evaluation can be seen clearly in the framework of Johnson's model (Figure 5.1). Formative evaluation determines to what extent the actual learning outcomes (ALO's) achieved by students match the intended learning outcomes (ILO's) of the curriculum plan. More specifically, we use formative evaluation to see if the examples chosen to illustrate skills, concepts, or relationships between concepts are functioning to achieve meaningful learning and for what fraction of the target population. If only 20 percent of the students acquire the skills or concepts we wish to teach, effective formative evaluation will suggest where the problem lies. If the problem is mostly with the examples chosen—which, as students suggested, were not meaningful to them—alternative examples could be tried. Or the examples may simply have been "uninteresting," so that more imaginative choices are needed. On the other hand, if the problem lies in the difficulty of the concept or skill we are trying to teach, some remedial preparation or an alternate sequence of presentation of topics may be required.

Summative evaluation primarily assesses the individual's success with the instructional program, usually for purposes of grading or ranking. Of course, properly designed summative tests can also provide formative evaluation in that they can point out which ILO's are not being achieved by a percentage of the students. In mastery learning programs, the desired level of achievement will not be reached by most students until the instructional program is adequately refined. This is one reason why we favor mastery-mode instructional programs, and why indolent teachers do not use such programs.

Educational evaluation currently does not use learning theory, curriculum theory, or instructional theory; in my view, it is in a shambles. The literature mentions very little learning theory and it usually has strong overtones of connectionist psychology, which has been discarded in earlier chapters. Educational evaluation needs a complete reassessment in terms of more acceptable cognitive psychologies. For example, if Ausubel's theory were employed as a basis for evaluation theory, emphasis would be placed on the extent to which test items measure concept differentiation and integrative reconciliation, rather than on the present narrow concerns with item difficulty and discrimination. Evaluation experts shy away from this emphasis because it obviously requires some understanding of concepts (and skills) in each specific field. More extensive discussion of better evaluation is beyond the scope of this book. I hope that some creative scholar interested in evaluation will examine how the theory of education presented here requires and might provide guidelines for a new educational evaluation discipline.

CHAPTER 7

The Future of Education

Evolving School Programs

The history of Western education shows that for at least two millennia great teachers have demonstrated concern for the student, competence in the discipline(s) taught, and mastery of didactic techniques. Indeed, one may well ask whether any *new* insights into teaching have been uncovered during the last two thousand years. The study of educational history tends to confirm that great teachers are born, not made, and also that great teachers are few in number. Must exciting, powerful educational experience always be determined by the chance appearance of the great teacher, or can some way be found to work systematically on improving the quality of educational experience?

If we can come to understand human learning processes better and if we learn to apply this knowledge in the design of new instructional programs, education can be quantitatively and qualitatively much better than it has been. From an improved basic understanding of learning processes can come new insights for the design of improved books, lectures, computer programs, and A-V devices; better teacher education programs can emerge, and more imaginative and functional school facilities can be designed.

Little improvement in agricultural practices occurred in ten millennia of human history despite flashes of human ingenuity, and not until the twentieth century has agricultural productivity surged forward. In a similar way, the history of education has shown a monotonous sameness, a kind of toil by pupils and teachers, adequate for survival but also failing for a substantial number of our students. We have placed men on the moon and returned them safely home, but we have not learned how to apply an almost boundless technological capability to educational problems. To achieve a more than tenfold improvement in our agricultural yields, we needed not only new technology but also an advance in our understanding of biological processes. To achieve a quantum improvement in the quantity and quality of education, we should expect that technology alone will not suffice.

My argument has been that theory development relevant to school learning is possible, that David Ausubel's assimilation theory provides a workable base for new learning research, and that progress in understanding educational processes similar to the progress we have observed in science and associated technologies can be made. In Chapter 2, I argued together with Stephen Toulmin that human understanding is based on the concepts that exist in a society, concepts that change as societies evolve. In Chapter 3 my thesis was that we should apply Ausubel's learning theory, which places focus on the process of concept learning (in contrast with various associationist theories), and that his theoretical constructs have important bearing on instructional planning, which was illustrated in Chapters 5 and 6. I believe the empirical studies to be presented in Chapter 8, which draw data from learning in real school situations, support the value of Ausubel's theory as an explanatory and heuristic model for scientific study of education. In this chapter, I shall show that recent and emerging practices in schools are moving toward goals consistent with the theoretical educational description presented earlier.

Evolving Patterns in Secondary Schools

Systematic studies of facilities and programs on a nationwide basis have become increasingly rare. For a number of years the U.S. Office of Education conducted biennial surveys of school programs and facilities; although publication of survey data was usually delayed for two or more years, trends in school programs and financial support could be observed. Very little data are now gathered on national samples of schools, making it difficult to form a picture of the present—and future—state of our schools. Except for national testing programs that establish norms for various tests, local school personnel have little opportunity to compare their programs and facilities other than through personal contacts and school visits. To me it seems incredible that state and federal education agencies, which supply over sixty billion dollars annually to support schools, have done almost nothing to gather reliable, analytic data from the schools, data that could be used to guide decision making at the local, state, and national levels.

In 1969 the National Science Teachers Association obtained a grant from the National Science Foundation for a study of *exemplary* school science facilities. The purpose of the study, of which I was project director, was to ascertain what appeared to be the best science facilities for present and also for future programs. Our purpose was not to catalogue and give frequencies for the various facilities now in use; instead, we were to make every effort to prepare a report that would be oriented to the future. Our working premise was that some schools are always ten years behind the norm standards while others are ten years ahead. We proceeded on the assumption that if we studied exemplary schools, we could learn what facilities and programs might become the norm, ten years hence, and also we might project the observed trends another ten or fifteen years into the future. Thus we might find it possible to produce a report with recommendations for pratices some twenty-five years ahead of what are now normal in schools. Working with a study team of eight members, we visited over 150 schools one or more times during 1970–1972. Although the study and report (Novak, 1972c) was focused on science facilities and programs, the results of this unique nationwide study have implications for schools in general.

As our school visits proceeded we often found what was an innovation in one school was something another school had tried earlier and then discarded in favor of some other innovation. But the innovations were not cyclic; there was an evident direction. By reanalyzing our earlier reports and revisiting some schools, we found that four evolving patterns could be described. They are:

1. Changes in facilities: from separate lecture-discussion and laboratory rooms, usually for a single subject, to open areas for a wide variety of learning activities.
2. Increased use of technology: from blackboards and overhead projectors and/or closed-circuit television for group teaching to self-paced study guides with 8 mm loop films, filmstrip viewers, and carrel units equipped with various aids for individualized study.
3. Program modifications: from single discipline and group-paced study, norm-grading, lecture-discussion-laboratory programs to individually paced study, criterion-referenced grading, integrated science program with heterogeneous age groups, and some coordination with other studies and career orientation.
4. Varied student-staff relations: from determination of curriculum and performance standards dominated by teachers toward achievement goals planned by student and staff, alternate curriculum paths, and use of resource personnel with varying responsibilities.

Although our study was restricted to science facilities and programs, we found that, in general, those schools outstanding in science were also outstanding in other subject areas. The patterns we described for science could with only minor alteration have equal value in other fields. A more detailed description of the four patterns is shown in Chart 7.1.

In biology, the concept of evolution includes the idea that physiological and anatomical features evolve separately, but that they are not functionally independent. The evolution of an animal's teeth may lead to more effective grazing, but the physiology of an herbivore must also change to allow for optimal utilization of grasses as food. In an analogous way, we found that radical changes in facilities, for example, could lead to increased frustration on the part of students, staff, and parents if appropriate accompanying changes had not occurred in instructional technology, program patterns, and student-staff relationships. A modern open plan school facility, where teacher determination of curriculum decisions and norm-referenced group teaching were practiced, was usually a school where no one was happy. Similarly, an open plan school with much effort to individualize

Chart 7.1. Graphic description of evolving patterns in facilities, technology, program, and student-staff relations. Arrows show general trends from traditional (base) to emerging characteristics, with descriptions ordered in approximately the sequence of development observed by the study team. Adapted from Novak, *Facilities for Secondary School Science Teaching,* NSTA, 1972, with permission.

Facilities	Technology	Program	Student-Staff
Interdisciplinary open space, systems for learning materials ↑	Instructional technology for student-planned individual and small group work ↑	Integrated science; heterogeneous age grouping ↑	Student-staff planning of achievement goals; integration of science study with other student interests ↑
Flexible laboratory-study, space; carrel units; carpeting ↑	Learning resource center with A-V and reference material ↑	Student-planned learning activities ↑	Student-centered learning activities; modules; peer assistance ↑
Lab islands; movable benches ↑	Self-paced study materials; 8 mm loop film; filmstrip viewers ↑	Study units; individually paced; single discipline; single age group *criterion-referenced evaluation* ↑	Differentiated staff, technical support staff ↑
Preparation and storage room for individualized packets ↑	Dail-access TV and audio tape ↑	Alternate experiments; special readings ↑	Team teaching, some student aides ↑
Flexible lab-discussion space; project areas; plant and animal rooms ↑	Computer assistance ↑	Study unit packages group schedule ↑	Text-lab guide but student planning for projects ↑
Integrated lab-lecture-discussion with tables and lab benches ↑	Closed-circuit TV ↑	Extra credit or honors work ↑	Student selection of optional activities ↑
Massive fixed furniture; separate lecture, discussion, and laboratory rooms; wall cabinets equipment storage for group work on common experiments	Overhead projectors ↑ 16 mm films; wall charts; maps; tackboards; chalkboard	Tracking: programs for high and low achievers ↑ Single subject; text-lab program group paced; group exams *norm-referenced evaluation*	Performance standards fixed by the teacher ↑ Teacher determination of curriculum

instruction but without much technological support and without paraprofessional staff was frequently not very successful. Throughout our written report we emphasized the interdependence between elements in the four patterns.

Some other parallels between biological evolution and evolution of school facilities and programs should be noted. Skeletal structures of animals have become adapted to serve new functions, but the basic bone structure has remained the same over 100 million years. The wing of a bird, front leg of a horse, flipper of a whale, and arm of man are all formed from the same basic bone structure. So too in school facilities, a table or blackboard for example will have a long history of usefulness even though student copybooks may be gone and the teacher no longer lectures with chalk in one hand and a hickory switch in the other. But some features do become "extinct"; massive, fixed laboratory benches, although still common in new school buildings, should go the way of the dinosaur. These furnishings continue to find a niche in schools because they are expensive (hence profitable for equipment salesmen who frequently are asked to plan laboratory facilities), and they give the illusion of scientific sophistication. When decision making for school facilities becomes as selective as environmental competitive pressures, massive laboratory furnishings will survive only in some specialized science laboratories.

Throughout this book I have tried to emphasize that all knowledge is "connected," that powerful concepts in one field can be of value in organizing information in another field, that changes occur in concepts but new conceptions are evolutionary products, that there is profit in examining the historical roots of present conceptions, and finally, that education is a human enterprise permeated with the promise and frailties we find in people. Our study of science facilities and programs was a "time slice" through the evolutionary history of schools, and we discerned four evolving patterns. Twenty years from now, we can easily assess whether the patterns and directions we have described were representative and predictive of future changes. We based our projections at the time primarily on the direction of changes that occurred in recent years in the schools studied. Another set of criteria was applied to the analysis of school visitation reports prepared by the study team to determine the extent of the changes that would be supportive of what we know about classroom learning, curriculum theory, and instructional design. Briefly I shall examine the four evolving patterns and show how I believe they suggest changes in directions consonant with the projections based on the theory provided earlier in this book.

Facilities

As indicated in Chart 7.1, preferred facilities have been changing from fixed furniture arranged in classrooms for thirty to thirty-five students to flexible, movable furnishings arranged in large interdisciplinary study areas and smaller individual or discussion group work spaces. In part, the emerging type of facilities reflect the accelerating rate of social change, and also of corresponding changes in school curriculum.

We have passed through roughly a century of secondary school program development with drastic changes, from emphasis on Latin and Greek to the inclusion of "practical" subjects and, most recently, to an emphasis on career education. Possibly we may see accelerated changes in curriculum with the introduction of such subjects as "futurism" (see Toffler, 1974) and courses on human sexuality and emotional development. Flexible facilities will be needed for the special program requirements in the new areas of study.

Technology

Increasingly schools will recognize that a primary difference in student learning is in the rate of learning. As shown before, hereditary factors influence learning rate, but the availability of relevant, well-differentiated subsumers in cognitive structure is an even more important factor. Achievement motivation, which derives from success in new learning tasks, can become an increasingly important form of motivation for learning if flexibility in programs allows for wide variation in student learning rates and/or wider selection of study topics. Most schools still practice lock-step classroom procedures (see Silberman's *Crisis in the*

Classroom, 1970); hence, achievement motivation can rarely be the primary form of motivation. Instead, various forms of aversive or ego enhancement motivation are used. Inflexibility in facilities encourages lock-step programs and discourages application of Ausubel's principle: start with what the learner already knows and teach him accordingly.

To provide for wide variations in learning rates and in school programs, some form of individualized technological support is necessary. Printed study modules combined with inexpensive audiovisual aids can be enormously helpful in providing flexibility to students in the selection of study materials and for varying rates of learning. When appropriate facilities are available, individualized study can be an important source of emotional development, for individualized study does not necessitate study in isolation. I have recommended two-student carrels and space for small group discussions as a vital aspect of individualized study (Novak, 1972c). Expensive isolated cells with closed-circuit audio or TV facilities were neither popular nor successful in schools. Even when expensive investment in capital and technical support provided for somewhat more flexible dial-access audio or TV systems, most students chose to dial in to tapes of popular music; they listened to these as they used the carrel for a study space. Many other technological investments designed for group instructions have been even more disastrous. In all of our visits to exemplary schools, we never found a science classroom where closed-circuit TV monitors were in use, although more than one-third of the schools had such equipment. The tremendously time-consuming task of preparing good TV lessons simply precludes indigenous program development for most schools. Even professionally prepared classroom TV lessons of high quality, have dubious value.

Computer assisted instruction (CAI) shows high promise on theoretical grounds. Highly individualized instruction programs are possible with available CAI technology. However, cost per student-hour has been high (around five dollars), and until fourth-generation computer facilities are much expanded and CAI programming is generally available (at projected costs of fifty cents per student-hour), this form of technological support

will not be important in schools. Because of inertia associated
with school program and facility development, widespread use
of CAI is not likely much before the next century. However,
prospective teachers beginning their college education now will
be only in the middle of their careers when CAI will almost certainly be a major instructional mode. The question is whether
teachers as we train them now will have a viable role in education in the year 2000.

Programs

From what has already been said about facilities and support
technology, it should be evident that the traditional practice of
instruction based on uniform progress through a single textbook
or syllabus flies in the face of almost all the evidence we have
on ways to optimize learning. To present a fixed body of information at a relatively fixed rate is to assure that the majority of
students will be either bored or overburdened. The cumulative
effect of this kind of schooling leads to a range of socially destructive attitudes on both ends of the achievement spectrum.
As was noted earlier, school tasks represent such a small segment of the total range of societal tasks (perhaps not more than
5 percent) that success or failure in school tasks per se is neither assurance of future success nor evidence of inevitable subsequent mediocrity.

The destruction of self-image that occurs for many students
who experience repeated failure is an unjustifiable liability for
them. Clearly, this is not only a waste of human resources but
an outright denial of children's constitutional right for self-
determination. It would not surprise us to see court action in
the future against compulsory education laws which force students to attend schools that destroy their self-image. As courts
increasingly regard children as individuals born with rights that
cannot be abrogated to please their parents, compulsory school
attendance laws will undergo drastic revision or revocation. Traditional school instructional practices will eventually succumb
to the social and economic pressures that will arise when some
portion of the group of teenagers now alienated rise in protest
against what they view as tyranny in the schools. Undoubtedly,

many more children would leave the schools today except that most people are gregarious and school is where friends can be found. Depressing as school can be for every child occasionally and for many children continuously, the ego support obtained from peers and sometimes from a sensitive teacher or counselor continues to be sufficient to keep them coming back. If child labor laws are rewritten—as they surely will be in the future— and if children are offered a choice between class attendance and meaningful work in society, we will find educators eagerly seeking new ways of making major changes in school programs.

Perennial optimism leads me to believe that schools are not doomed. Knowledge continues to be an extremely valuable commodity in our society, and it is likely to be even more valuable in future societies. Granted that much of our school curriculum will be as irrelevant to future citizens as the Latin and Greek of the early nineteenth-century high schools are to today's students, there remains an abundance of knowledge that can and should be the substance of school learning. Appropriate schools can be an efficient means for society to transmit that knowledge. Instructional practices based on the principle of progressive differentiation of cognitive structure through meaningful learning and focused on concepts that are powerful for facilitating new learning should become increasingly prevalent in our schools. At least for the remainder of this century, modified schools can be expected to enjoy increasing success.

Student-Staff Relations

Silberman (1970) and others have pointed out that teaching practices in schools today scarcely reflect the power for transmitting knowledge that was brought about by the printing press, much less the potential of technological advances for information storage and transmission. In my view, the most important single factor limiting advances in schools has been the traditionally narrow role of the teacher as disseminator of knowledge. The teacher's role in the classroom has remained stereotyped for centuries. As Silberman observes:

John I. Goodlad, Dean of the UCLA Graduate School of Education, along with several colleagues, visited some 260 kindergarten-through-first-grade classrooms in 100 schools in thirteen states to determine the extent to which the reform movement had changed the schools. He found what this writer and his colleagues found: that things are much the same as they had been twenty years ago, and in some respects not as good as they were forty years ago, when the last great school reform movement was at its peak. "We were unable to discern much attention to pupil needs, attainments, or problems as a basis for individual opportunities to learn," he reports. "Teaching was predominantly telling and questioning by the teacher, with children responding one by one or occasionally in chorus. In all of this, the textbook was the most highly visible instrument of learning and teaching. . . . Rarely did we find small groups intensely in pursuit of knowledge; rarely did we find individual pupils at work in self-sustaining inquiry . . . we are forced to conclude that much of the so-called educational reform movement has been blunted on the classroom door." [p. 159]

The central problem schools have faced over the past half millennium is our failure to recognize that many kinds of human association can result in learning. The teacher dispensing information from a lectern, facing his class, is a carryover model from the medieval monastery where only the teacher was in possession of the hand-transcribed text. The students were required to record lessons on slates and then to commit this information to memory. Too much school practice is an anachronism perpetuated for centuries. Schools have failed to exploit the varieties of human communication other than the traditional teacher-student form. Many kinds of adult-student and student-student communication are practicable and desirable in schools, but they occur only rarely by design. Even the traditional teacher-pupil communication mode can be substantially enhanced. The humanistic education movement with its emphasis on sensitivity training sessions for teachers has shown that more than knowledge is transmitted when people interact; important cues as to the affective connotations of exchanges can be recognized if we become sensitive to this dimension.

While I applaud this emphasis of the humanistic education movement, I have not seen any careful interpretation of affective and cognitive development as a central core of its philosophy. Although concern with cognitive development is frequently condemned as a reactionary position that signals a failure to recognize the full meaning of positive emotional exchange, such concern does not imply neglect of the affective domain. On the contrary, better cognitive learning is the principal avenue by which schools can enhance affective experience. To the extent that other insights can be brought to bear on improvement of affective experience, we strongly support such work, but we know of no theoretical framework to guide improvement of learning in this area.

A broader range of adult-student and student-student associations is needed. We need many more adults in our schools than those who play the traditional teacher role. Teacher aides have become common in many schools, but their roles frequently are even more limited than are the traditional teacher roles. Regulation by collective bargaining units may have played a significant part in preventing teacher aides from encroaching on the prerogatives of certified teachers. Community leadership to encourage broadened adult-student associations in schools is rare. Leadership from the education profession in this regard has been conspicuous by its absence.

A wider array of learning experience and more allowance for varying rates of learning are necessary if we are to implement what we now know about practices that enhance cognitive growth. To optimize cognitive learning opportunities we must increase the number and variety of adult-student and student-student associations; to enhance significantly the quality of affective exchange, radically modified student-staff associations are an inescapable necessity. I observed some promising practices in my study of secondary schools (Novak, 1972c), and these I would view as only the beginning of a major change that will occur in schools before the end of the twentieth century.

Conclusion

Concepts are what people think with. The human brain has both remarkable potentialities and severe limitations. Unlike modern computers, our brains cannot store millions of detailed items of information for immediate recall. But everything new that we learn influences in at least some minute fashion what we already know, and in turn, what we already know influences new learning. This plasticity of the human mind is at the core of what we mean by being human. Each of us forms a framework of concepts in idiosyncratic ways, even when we attend the same schools and experience similar events. This uniqueness of the individual gives the human race its enormous collective potential. Human beings can generate new knowledge because every individual sees an event in a somewhat different way and can share these experiences through many forms of expression.

We also experience pain and pleasure, joy and sadness, love and hate. These experiences, moreover, are uniquely individual. They may derive from association with other people, but these affective experiences are not transmitted directly in the same way as knowledge is transmitted. There is much to be learned about how we can enrich our own emotional responses and how we can help others enjoy better affective experience. This area is not yet open to the kind of rational analysis that we can apply to cognitive learning studies. Therefore the theory of education presented in this book has placed principal emphasis on cognitive learning and particularly on concept learning.

Insofar as problems are solved—from the daily problems of individuals to the pressing problems of societies—they are solved by humans using concepts. If children were deliberately taught to develop concepts in the disciplines they study, if they were made aware of the explicit role concepts play in their cognitive growth and in problem solving, if they could become convinced of the value and power of concepts in rational human thinking, surely people would begin to demand more rational behavior from those who run their social institutions. They would demand explicit discussion of the concepts their leaders and politicians think with and use to interpret events and to solve problems. Democracy as a form of government has proved to be effective for improvement of societies. The power of democracy derives from open expression of diverse viewpoints and from debate. Debate serves the purpose of testing concepts against one another and of changing people's concepts. It is the source of power of democratic institutions. Schools could become a powerful means to develop a citizenry schooled to seek clarification of concepts through debate and to understand and participate in the political and other social activities that are at the roots of a healthy democratic society.

PART II

EMPIRICAL VALIDATION

The theory of education presented in Part I derives from two decades of my research and teaching involving students at all educational levels. Part II describes the evolution of research programs over these years to illustrate the important interrelationship that has existed between theory and research and also to illustrate the complementary nature of research and involvement in educational practice. This part of the book serves to provide some empirical validation for the theory of education proposed and to offer a model for possible improvement of educational research.

CHAPTER 8

The Evolution of an
Educational Research Program

A Continuing Debate: Should Educational Research Be Based on Theory?

There has been much argument on the question: Is teaching an art or a science? I shall not review issues of this debate, for to do so would require extensive description of not only what is meant by teaching, but also what "learning" means and what criteria determine the selection of worthwhile subject matter. This relationship among subject matter, learners, and teachers has been discussed at length by Gowin (1976). My thesis is that substantial improvement in education can derive from educational research only if the research is based on viable theory. I have assumed that although there are artistic aspects to teaching or the design of learning experiences, research based on appropriate theory can also play a role in the improvement of education. I believe that all teachers, the gifted and less talented (and certainly no one would suggest that all or even a small number of teachers are gifted), can be guided by appropriate research based on theory to improve their practice.

The greatest hope for the improvement of education lies not in selecting more gifted educators, but rather in increasing the effectiveness of the educators we have. Gifted persons are in short supply in every field, and we cannot expect that education, medicine, or any other field can appreciably increase the proportion of truly gifted practitioners. The remarkable progress in health care over the past fifty years did not result from selection of more gifted doctors but rather from advances in research in health sciences, which led to new concepts and materials for health care. A similar parallel could be drawn for agriculture. Chapter 1 argued that any substantial improvement in educational practices must be through improved educational theory. Chapter 2 described how a distorted view of the nature of scientific inquiry has resulted in an emphasis upon methodologies of research, rather than upon the specific conceptual frameworks that necessarily guide the research. Many critics of a science of education (Atkin, 1967; Glass, 1972, Gowin, 1972) have beaten a straw man; the methods of science which they argue are inappropriate for education are not those that scientists have employed for three centuries. We agree with these critics in that much educational nonsense has been generated under the banner of methodologically sophisticated educational research. The problem lies with the poor epistemology of educational researchers (and funding agencies that support them) and not with the concept of a science of education per se.

This chapter will review some of the research done by me and my colleagues since the 1950s. Some of our empirical research studies and the instructional development efforts have convinced me that we now have an adequate and relevant theory for curriculum and instruction (Johnson, 1967) to guide the design of better educational research and instructional practice. This chapter will illustrate that appropriate empirical studies can lead to better educational practices; it is the empirical leg of the educational theory presented in this book. To support the theoretical framework developed in earlier chapters I shall also present a few studies of other research groups, even though some of these were planned to support other theoretical positions (and in certain cases failed).

Problem Solving and College Botany and Biology Students

When I began to look around for an appropriate doctoral research topic in 1954, my reading and graduate studies led me to believe that the most important cognitive activity was problem solving, not only the type of problem solving that characterizes the work of scientists but also the kind that leads to new architectural conceptions, literary plots, or musical scores. The essence of human cognitive functioning appeared to be the capacity to use information to arrive at new formulations. The writings of Wiener (1948), Miller and Frick (1949), Estes (1950), and Ashby (1960) presented a cybernetic model for learning involving information storage and processing, which seemed to place emphasis on problem solving as it occurs in humans, in contrast with writings of the S-R psychologists, whose work dealt mostly with animal experiments. The best learning theory, it seemed to me then, was some adaptation of cybernetic theory, which was developing rapidly with the advent of new computers and experiments in computer simulation of brain functions. I saw human problem solving as a special case of information processing and went on to work with this scheme.

If problem solving were viewed as the most important form of human cognitive functioning, then improvement of education would depend upon enhancement of an individual's ability to solve problems. This view was consistent with writings by such leading educators as William Brownell (1942) and Eugene Smith and Ralph Tyler (1942). These educators were saying that to improve student's ability to solve problems schools needed to provide instruction with extensive opportunity for problem solving, opportunity that is characteristically limited or absent in most school learning. The argument appeared reasonable, so I adopted an experimental approach in teaching college general botany in which students would be given extensive opportunity for problem solving. The study, which formed the basis of my doctoral thesis, compared a conventional laboratory-lecture instructional approach with an experimental approach that allowed six weeks of class time for individual research projects.

Although the experimental section received instruction in the same botanical information as the control section (but in fourteen rather than twenty weeks), no significant differences in achievement were found. This result probably derived in part from the special instructional materials used in the experimental class, and possibly from this group's having had the same instructor for both lecture and laboratory work. In any case, I expected no significant difference in gains in achievement on the botany knowledge tests, but looked for a significant gain in problem solving ability resulting from the extended period of project work by students in the experimental section.

When planning the study, I had great difficulty finding a way to assess problem solving ability. Although some work had been done in measurement of critical thinking (Dunning, 1954) and problem solving ability (Smith and Tyler, 1942), none of the tests used appeared to be satisfactory for my purposes. Therefore, a problem solving test was designed which was thought to be essentially neutral in content and which incorporated the operations suggested by a cybernetic model of problem solving. In this mode, success in problem solving is a function of (1) store of relevant information, and (2) effectiveness in information processing, which required selection from among alternative responses those most likely to succeed. The idea was to provide a statement of a problem and alternative answer choices, all of which would have some plausibility, although one choice would be most consistent with the problem statement and other sequentially selected choices. Analogous to computer functioning, the best successive answer choices would lead to a convergence toward a solution to the problem. In selecting the answer sequence, testees would be required repeatedly to reassess the relevant information in their cognitive stores and to decide how new information supplied in the answer sequence would relate to the problem. (See the section on problem solving in Chapter 4.) The answer choices were not correct or incorrect but rather were either consistent and relevant or inconsistent and or less relevant to the problem. Schematically, a test for problem solving consistent with my interpretation of cybernetic theory and the progressive nature of scientific problem solving would require the following operations:

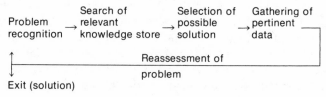

This cycle could be repeated as many times as necessary, or until some acceptable solution of the problem resulted.

The test was constructed with six problems, each presenting two alternative choices in three successive steps. A larger number of problems would have been better for test reliability. This test, as used, required about fifty minutes for completion, a time limit that had to be applied. In any case, the test had significant reliability of about $r = 0.5$. A validation group of scientists and graduate students in science, after being tested, commented favorably on the thinking required to solve the problems. Most of the scientists got five or six problems correct, and errors were distributed over all six problems. When the test was used with the botany students, none got all six problems correct, some missed all six, and most got two or three correct. (Answers were scored wrong unless all three choices were correct.)

The results of the study showed that there were no significant gains in ability to solve problems between the project centered group and the conventionally taught classes; however, the study did produce one interesting result. I had expected that the students scoring highest on the test would tend to make errors in Part III of the problems missed, whereas students who missed all or most problems would make their errors in Part I. Because of my reliance on cybernetic theory, I had anticipated that the successive selection of choices in each of the three parts of a problem would be easier for those who could process information well. Low scoring students, I thought, would not benefit as much from feedback on choices made in Part I or Part II of a given problem, and their errors would tend to occur in Part I. Approximately 80 percent of the errors for all students were in Part I (see Figure 4.2). This result continued to trouble our research group until we turned to an Ausubelian learning model several years later.

Hundreds of studies in education literature compare one teaching approach to another. Most show no significant differences in student achievement under contrasting methods, except when one method is poorly contrived or when testing is strongly biased in favor of content in one approach. One more report of "no significant differences" was added to the educational literature (Novak, 1958). Reviews of many studies on teaching can be found in two summary volumes (Gage, 1963, and Travers, 1973). It is now generally well recognized that educational research studies comparing Method A with Method B almost invariably conclude that no significant differences in student performance were found when the two methods of instruction were compared. Despite these findings, the most common type of doctoral study in education still continues to be a comparison of methods of teaching. The numerous reviews of educational research show that methods comparison studies have little value for advancing our understanding of the teaching-learning processes. I shall try to explain how other types of studies based on Ausubel's theory show more promise.

During the years 1959–1964 at Purdue University, I continued to study problem solving. Several faculty members in the Biology Department were cooperative in modifying instructional procedures and testing so that appropriate data could be gathered. During this period Postlethwait developed his audio-tutorial approach for teaching botany (Postlethwait et al., 1972). This individualized instructional approach provided an opportunity for studying what we now regard as a highly important variable, learning time.

From 1961 to 1963, Darrel Murray was gathering data concerning students in a large general biology course and in Postlethwait's audio-tutorial course. In the course the use of principles of biology for interpreting data in both lectures and laboratories was emphasized; hence, we hoped to see some improvement in student's ability to solve problems as the course progressed.

Murray designed three tests to measure this ability, one for use with the botany students (Problems in Botany Test) and two similar tests to be used with biology students (Problems in Biology Test and Plant Growth Test). These tests are reproduced in Appendixes A and B so that the reader can assess them. The test items used to measure analytic ability were to be classified according to Benjamin Bloom's taxonomy (1956) at levels 2.00 or higher. We expected the biology students to show significant gains in problem solving scores from pretesting to posttesting twelve to sixteen weeks later, but the botany students to show no gains, since problem solving was not emphasized in the instruction they received. Reliabilities of the scores ranged from $r = 0.63$ for the Problems in Biology Test (17 items) to $r = 0.81$ for the Problems in Botany Test (15 items). Table 8.1 shows the results obtained for pretesting and posttesting. No gains in problem solving ability were observed in either the botany or the biology classes.

Table 8.1. Pretest and posttest means and variances for three problem solving tests

Test	n	Pretest mean	Posttest mean	Mean change	Pretest variance	Posttest variance
Problems in Botany [a]	118	7.04	7.20	.16	5.58	5.80
Problems in Biology [b]	51	6.67	6.75	.08	4.11	5.67
Plant Growth	88	7.73	7.73	.00	5.78	4.49

[a] See Appendix A.   [b] See Appendix B.

While awaiting posttest results for the botany and biology classes, Murray thought it might be useful to see whether problem solving scores increased (or decreased) from week to week as the semester progressed. At Purdue students are assigned to laboratory sections by a computer programmed so that assignment is essentially random. Therefore, Murray could test different laboratory sections each week, avoiding "practicing effect" influences and the simple practical limitation that students need laboratory time to work. About six hundred students were registered for the biology course. Murray randomly selected six sections and administered the Plant Growth Test on weeks 1, 3, 4, 5, 6, and 10. The mean scores obtained are shown in Figure 8.1. Except for the period between weeks 3 and 4, the mean scores changed little over the semester. During week 3, students begin a long-term plant growth experiment in the laboratory and received instruction on this. The data in Figure 8.1 show a uniformity one would expect from testing random samples of students (total $n = 276$). The data also show that specific knowledge relevant to plant growth gained during week 3 was

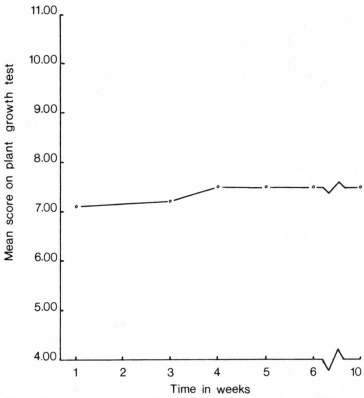

Figure 8.1. Mean scores of six different sample groups (n = 30 ± 5) on plant growth test at weeks 1, 3, 4, 5, 6, and 10.

the most important factor affecting success in problem solving. Although this clearly illustrates Ausubel's theory, we were not working with his theory in 1962 and 1963. We were still hoping that instructional methods using problem solving would produce gains in general problem solving skill. We were still chasing the magic formula sought by enthusiasts of discovery learning and process education described in Chapter 4.

In Postlethwait's audio-tutorial botany course, students recorded time spent in the learning center, and we used this index for comparing differences in study time and achievement.

As noted earlier, the botany course examinations required essentially recall of information, and hence comparative gains in information per unit of study time could have been an indicator of processing efficiency. Students did study outside the botany learning center, but we made the assumption that outside study time was correlated positively with study time in the learning center, an assumption supported by student questionnaire responses at the end of the course. Suddenly, we had some exciting data. Using the Problems in Botany Test as a measure of problem solving, the class was divided into samples of high, middle, and low analysis ability groups. On the average, the group with high problem solving ability spent much less time studying in the learning center than the middle or lower group, although there was wide variation within each group. This line of inquiry looked promising. We subdivided the time groups into three subgroups and examined achievement on the factual botany final exam for the nine subgroups (three levels of analytic ability and three study-time groups). The data are shown in Table 8.2 and plotted in Figure

Table 8.2. Mean scores on information test (final hour exam) for groups classified with respect to problem solving ability and time spent in gaining information

| Problem solving ability [a] | Time spent studying | | |
	(24-16 hrs.)	(15-12 hrs.)	(11-7 hrs.)
High (13-19 pts.)	96.00 (n = 2)	90.64 (n = 14)	86.50 (n = 14)
Middle (8-6 pts.)	86.21 (n = 19)	84.27 (n = 15)	76.63 (n = 8)
Low (5-1 pts.)	81.64 (n = 11)	79.71 (n = 7)	73.00 (n = 9)

[a] Based on Problems in Botany test

8.2. To our surprise, students in the high group were learning more botanical information in seven to eleven hours of study time than students in the middle or low group acquired in sixteen to twenty-four hours of study time. In short, students in the high group appeared to be more than twice as efficient in

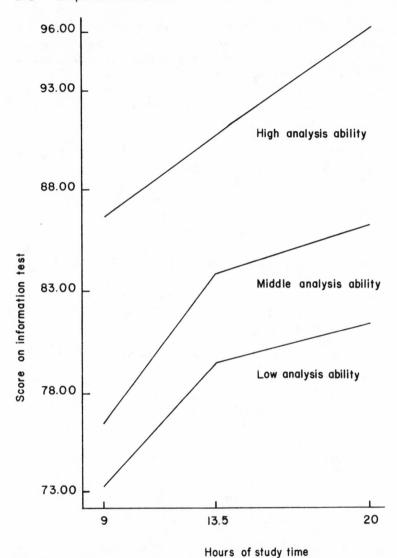

Figure 8.2. The effect of problem solving ability (analysis ability, as measured by scores on Problems in Botany test) and hours spent over five weeks in gaining information on botany achievement test scores.

processing and storing information than those in the other groups. We began to wonder about some of our basic ideas regarding the nature and function of problem solving ability. This ability, whatever it was, appeared to function primarily on the input side of our cybernetic learning model and not on the output side as we had expected. Analysis of variance indicated that both the amount of time spent in study and problem solving ability (analysis ability) were significantly related to achievement, but problem solving ability (as measured) accounted for almost twice as much variance (see Table 8.3). Clearly, the cognitive traits that led to high scores on the problem solving test were also important for learning botanical facts.

Table 8.3. Analysis of variance for the effect of problem solving ability and time spent in gaining information on information test scores (final hour exam)

Source of variation	Degrees of freedom	Variation	Mean square	F	Null hypothesis
Problem solving ability (High-Middle-Low)	2	2091.80	1045.90	15.52[a]	reject
Hours spent (9, 13.5, 20)	2	1090.56	545.28	8.09[a]	reject
Analysis by time spent interaction	4	46.82	11.71	.25	accept
Within	90	6064.65	67.39	–	–

[a] $p < .01$

By 1964 the focus of my research had shifted from the study of problem solving as a generalized ability to concept learning. I had begun to read Ausubel's papers and book (1963) and was persuaded by his work, as well as by my own research results, that problem solving ability was dependent upon the adequacy of specifically relevant concepts in the student's cognitive structure. While I was not prepared to discard the idea of problem solving ability per se, I saw this ability increasingly as a capacity for developing and using concepts. So, the focus of my instructional development activities as well as my research work moved increasingly toward the factors influencing concept learning.

Concept Learning
Studies of Advance Organizers

In Chapter 3, I described Ausubel's concept of meaningful learning in which new information is subsumed by existing relevant concepts and these concepts undergo further development or differentiation. Ausubel suggested that appropriate advance organizers could be used to facilitate meaningful learning in that the advance organizer would increase the probability that new information would be anchored to concepts in cognitive structure. Over several years our research group conducted three studies which included advance organizers as learning variables.

Richard Schulz (1966) worked with thirty-eight sixth-grade classes in Cedar Rapids, Iowa, and divided his sample into two groups, one of which received an advance organizer for the concept "conservation of energy" as well as continued reference to this advance organizer prior to classroom lessons. Schulz also used the Iowa Basic Skills subtest, "Reading Graphs and Tables," to obtain a general measure of problem solving ability. Students were pretested, and after three to six weeks of instruction (classes varied in the amount of time and rate of progress through the lessons), all students were posttested. Somewhat to his disappointment, Schulz found no significant difference between classes that used advance organizers and those that did not. Consistent with other studies we had done, Schulz also found that problem solving ability was a very significant variable in achievement. The data are shown in Table 8.4.

Working with college students majoring in Elementary Education, Kuhn (1967) used an eight-hundred-word advance organizer with one sample of class sections and an eight-hundred-word historical statement (nonorganizer or blank) with another group of students (see Appendix C). He posttested the classes immediately after instruction and three weeks later. The differences in mean scores between the classes with advance organizers and those with the historical passages were significant both after instruction and three weeks later. Kuhn also found highly significant differences in achievement for students ranking high on a "problem solving" test when compared with students ranking average or in the lower third (Kuhn and Novak, 1971).

Another study by our research group involved 288 students in grades 8, 9, and 10. Allan Gubrud (1970) provided one sample of students with an advance organizer for learning concepts of addition and separation of vectors. The advance organizer was a series of photographs illustrating vector concepts. Another sample of students received extra drill problems on vector addition so that learning time for the two groups would be approximately

Table 8.4. Analysis of variance of criterion test A (sixteen sixth-grade classes and 144 subjects) under two methods of study and three levels of analytic ability

Source of variation	SS	df	MS	F
A (methods)	29.51	1	29.51	3.19
B (classes within A)	339.04	14	24.22	2.62[a]
C (analytic ability)	1067.67	2	533.83	57.77[b]
A × C	21.56	2	10.78	1.17
B(A) × C	5.00	28	.18	.02
Within	1140.33	96	11.88	–
Residual—pooled B(A) × C and Within	1145.33	124	9.24	–

[a] p < .005   [b] p < .001

equal. All students received audio-tutorial lessons. Gubrud found no significant differences between the advance organizer groups and the drill problems group. However, in another part of his study, Gubrud found some important differences in achievement between groups, which will be reported below.

The studies done in our research group, together with studies reported by other investigators, led us to recognize that only certain kinds of advance organizers function to facilitate learning and then only under certain conditions. I indicated earlier that advance organizers function only when new materials are inherently meaningful and some rudimentary concept relevant to the new material already exists in the learner's cognitive structure. Under these circumstances, the advance organizer can serve as a cognitive bridge, which links new information to be learned to existing, relevant concepts in cognitive structure and thus facilitates learning. Results of other studies show that superior students do not benefit from advance organizers, and this phenomenon is probably explained by their natural proclivity to learn meaningfully and by their generally superior conceptual frameworks (Ausubel, 1976).

In my view, research studies that focus on the use of various forms of advance organizers with various kinds of groups are not profitable. Far more important and promising are studies that attempt to "ascertain what the learner already knows," and use this as a principal variable in the study of achievement under various instructional treatments.

Toward Emphasis on Concept Learning and Cognitive Structure Variables

Ausubel's first book describing his theory (1963) emphasized the role that subsuming concepts play in the facilitation of meaningful learning. Several research studies done in our group helped us to see what was meant by Ausubel's concept of facilitation of meaningful learning. Most important, and a turning point in our research program, was the work of Murray (1963) cited above, but data from our other studies and our new interpretation of other published studies pointed in the same direction: students inclined to organize experience through developing concepts in cognitive structure were generally better at problem solving and could acquire new facts more rapidly than students who tended to learn by rote.

From 1964 to the present, our research has been directed principally at studies that were designed to assess how students' cognitive structures vary in specific subject matter areas and how concepts function to facilitate learning. In curriculum and instructional development our efforts have been focused on the design of programs directed explicitly toward concept learning. Since we have been bucking the tide of national programs directed mostly toward training in inquiry skills, financial support for our work has been meager. A redeeming feature in this, however, has been that without large federal grants for hiring a corps of postdoctoral research associates and research aides, with the necessary establishment of administrative hierarchies, it has been possible (and necessary) for me to stay close to each aspect of the research and development projects. Moreover, the necessities forced upon our research and development teams have required close cooperation between members with subsequent close personal and intellectual associations. This undoubtedly has been the most satisfying and productive aspect of my efforts since 1964.

Our group has also been forced to enlist cooperation from practicing teachers and professors and to deal with real world situations. In short, we have had to sell our research and development work on the basis of the sense it made to harried educational practitioners; we had no funds to buy them. This acid test approach has done much to give direction and purpose to our work and must be credited for any significant successes that may have accrued.

During a sabbatical leave at Harvard University in 1965–1966, I had the opportunity to initiate an audio-tutorial elementary science program. This experience with young children made evident to me that what children can learn is largely a function of their relevant past experience (resulting in development of rudimentary concepts) and of the quality of the instructional program. This is not to deny the importance of hereditary factors, birth defects or other injuries, as well as severe emotional problems. In some individual cases, these handicaps can be the most significant learning liability for children. By and large, however, children (and adults) appear to have tremendously more learning capability than common school performance would suggest.

However, if the most important factor influencing learning is what the learner already knows, there is a "compound interest" that applies to future learning. If one student has a "5 percent better-than-average" framework of relevant concepts for a new learning task, he will learn more than other students and will have a 5-plus percent better framework of concepts. The converse applies to a student who has a "5 percent poorer-than-average" conceptual framework. We can see that if instructional programs were to allow each student to achieve his potential, the small initial differences in cognitive development could become enormous over a period of twelve or more years of schooling. These conjectures, however, are only theoretical, and many more empirical studies are needed in the real world to see how cognitive structure variables do influence subsequent learning.

Studies of Learning Efficiency

By 1965 two lines of reasoning were guiding our research group's work in the same direction. John Carroll's idea (1963) that school learning could lead to more success if students were given varying amounts of time to learn small segments of material (later expanded in Bloom's concept of mastery learning [1968]), and Ausubel's concern with subsuming concepts and their importance for facilitation of school learning could be seen as complementary ideas. Both Carroll's and Ausubel's writings suggested that to improve school learning we needed to provide varying amounts of time to students. Learning rate would largely depend on adequacy of relevant cognitive structure, and adequate attainment of concepts at one level of schooling would be necessary for success or rapid learning at a higher level of schooling.

When I came to Cornell University in 1967, Ausubelian theory was introduced to the graduate students in Science Education. Two students whose research was already under way were sufficiently attracted to Ausubel's model to try some modification of their planned data analyses. Pinchas Tamir (1968) found that students whose background included "modern" biology programs in high school achieved no better in college freshman biology than students who had taken "traditional" courses. However, when he reanalyzed his data according to specific subject areas of biology, he found that students gained most in those areas in which they had the best pretest (prior to instruction) scores.

Following Tamir's lead, Donald Ring (1969) found similar results with students from modern or traditional high school chemistry courses. However, since Ring was one year behind Tamir in his work, he could plan his pretest to include items that required recall of broad, general concepts of chemistry, and other items that could be answered through application of more specific concepts.

Achievement in the chemistry courses that Ring worked with was measured by combining scores on lab quizzes and lecture examinations. Ring's chemistry pretest included twenty-six items, ten of which required some knowledge of more specific chemistry concepts, while the other sixteen could be answered correctly by students who retained a functional knowledge of more general, more inclusive concepts. In Chapter 1 some of Ring's results were presented to illustrate that prior learning experience does significantly influence achievement in college studies. Figure 1.2 shows the results Ring obtained when achievement in chemistry was plotted as a function of pretest scores on the more specific questions. In Figure 8.3, achievement in chemistry is seen to be almost linearly related to pretest scores on the more general concept items.

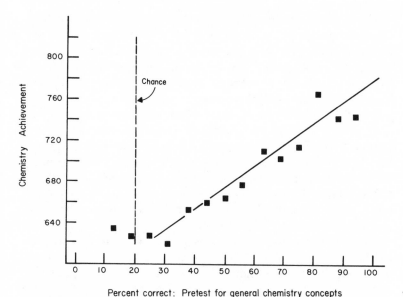

Percent correct: Pretest for general chemistry concepts

Figure 8.3. Effect of general chemistry concepts on subsequent achievement (total laboratory and lecture points earned) in college chemistry.

The studies of Tamir and Ring served to emphasize to our research group that prior concept learning in a specific subject matter area was indeed the most important factor influencing learning. However, the instructional settings in which this work was done did not allow us to obtain reliable data on the time spent by students in learning biology or chemistry. We knew from Murray's work (1963) that students who formed and used general concepts learned more botany in less time. On this basis, we might have expected the results from Ring's study to describe an exponential curve; but this relationship is not likely for two reasons: (1) the total points that students can obtain and the number needed for an A grade are limited, producing a "ceiling" effect, and (2) many able students are satisfied with a C or B grade and do not achieve the level of performance indicated by their pretest scores. This tendency of students, especially of better students, to slack off well before they reach their highest levels of performance constantly frustrates dedicated teachers.

While Ring was completing his thesis in 1969, Gubrud was conducting a study in which learning time was controlled. We have already stated that Gubrud did not find a significant difference in achievement between groups taught with or without advance organizers. The significant part of Gubrud's work, however, was that he showed success in prior learning on the subject of vectors to be much more important than general ability (I.Q. score). Gubrud first gave students audio-tutorial instruction on vector addition (as modified from the Harvard Project Physics program). This initial learning was very much influenced by general ability (I.Q.) as shown in Table 8.5. Gubrud found that only high ability ninth-grade students and most tenth-grade students made significant gains from pretest to posttest; this result is reflected in the important contribution of grade level to variance in test scores. We see that general ability, however, contributed more to posttest score variation than did grade level. This should be expected, since none of the students was previously taught material on vectors, and we should expect the compound interest effect of general ability (I.Q.) differences accumulated over fourteen or fifteen years to be more important than the additional year or two of schooling. Even though I.Q. scores are probably not the best indicators of ability to form hierarchically organized cognitive structure, we should expect them to be a good indicator of ability to form at least lower-order, less inclusive subsuming concepts.

Table 8.5. Relation of grade level and ability on posttest for addition and subtraction of vectors

Source	df	MS	F	P
G (grade level)	2	256.77	17.70	.01
T (time)	2	44.47	3.07	.05
A (ability)	1	689.59	47.55	.01
G × T	4	8.83	.61	n.s.
G × A	2	27.86	1.92	n.s.
T × A	2	14.11	.97	n.s.
G × T × A	4	14.13	.97	n.s.
Error	196	14.50	–	–

The second phase of Gubrud's study was the most interesting. Six weeks after the initial lessons, a sample of students was given an additional audio-tutorial lesson on separation of vectors into components. This material depends highly upon the degree

Table 8.6. Relation of grade level and ability on posttest on separation of vectors

Source	df	MS	F	p
Grade (G)	2	41.10	12.61	.01
Ability (A)	1	4.01	1.23	n.s.
G × A	2	6.51	2.00	n.s.
Error	66	3.25	–	–

of mastery of the previous lessons and upon understanding of certain concepts from algebra, which most of the tenth-grade students had already studied. On a posttest for knowledge of separation of vectors, Gubrud found no significant variations in scores due to ability differences, but grade level was a significant factor with tenth-grade students performing best (see Table 8.6). The first set of self-paced, audio-tutorial lessons apparently allowed students of high ability to make gains on the test used, but only tenth-grade students developed concepts sufficiently or had the supporting algebra concepts to make significant gains six weeks later on the separation of vectors lesson.

Here once again is evidence for Ausubel's dictum that the most important factors influencing learning are the relevant concepts the learner already has. In contrast to the claims of Arthur Jensen (1969) and others, success in learning about separation of vectors is not primarily dependent on genic (I.Q.) differences but rather on the adequacy of relevant concepts students bring with them (reflected in part in lower I.Q. scores). Poor school practices subsequently compound this purported genic limitation Jensen describes for American Negroes. In my view, Jensen and other opponents of the environmental influence school of thinkers have a case only because most research they cite has not been conducted within a framework based on sound learning theory; hence the research masks the overriding importance of environmental factors in school success. I do not wish to suggest that genic factors are unimportant in school achievement. Schools using the most psychologically and sociologically sound practices would doubtlessly increase achievement differences, if we were to set no limits on the levels to which schools might push children. Ultimate intellectual equality is ruled out by the limitations of biological realities, but social egalitarianism is more likely to be achieved if schools are improved. Too many people now fail to acquire from our schools even the minimum intellectual and personal competence necessary for contributing to democracy and their own personal welfare.

I was eager to continue studies that would enable me to monitor learning time more accurately than was possible with conventional lecture-laboratory science courses. The chairman of the Physics Department at Cornell was kind enough to offer me some laboratory space, and in 1969 I began a series of curriculum development and research projects in physics. Over several years, an audio-tutorial course in introductory physics was developed which proved to be very popular with the students and participating faculty members of the Physics Department.

Martin Thorsland was the first doctoral student to take advantage of the research potential developed in Physics 101–102.

The new audio-tutorial course was pilot tested and compared with the traditional lecture-laboratory course. The results were predictable: no significant differences in student achievement were observed. However, there was a significant difference in the students' enthusiasm for physics, with approximately twice as many favorable reactions reported by students in the A-T sections than by those in conventional sections. The A-T approach was subsequently adopted for the Physics 101-102 course.

Students recorded the time upon entering and leaving the A-T learning center, so Thorsland had a good measure of learning time. Using this as a variable, Thorsland found, as expected, that students who studied more hours tended to receive higher scores on course examinations. We were interested in other issues, however. Thorsland had devised an interview test using four simple physics problems. On the basis of this test, he ranked each student in the sample studied on a scale of 0 to 5 for each problem, with a separate ranking for *intuitive* ability and *analytic* ability as defined below:

Analytic: Student proceeds a step at a time; steps are reasonably explicit; student often uses mathematics, equations, or logic and an explicit plan of attack.

Intuitive: In this approach to the solution of problems individuals possess an implicit feel of the subject matter and often arrives at an answer with little awareness of the steps taken; they may not be able to provide an adequate account of how an answer was obtained.

The evaluation approach was designed to present the problems to students on a one-to-one basis and to have them describe what they were thinking about as they were solving the problems. The dialogue during these sessions was tape-recorded for subsequent analysis. The objective was to analyze each individual's responses and to assign an intuitive and an analytic ability ranking. These rankings were not considered to be on the same continuum, from analytic to intuitive, but rather on two separate continua. Also this evaluation was not measuring the same thing we called problem solving ability in our earlier research, for the latter was based on success in solving written problems and probably involved use of *both* intuitive and analytic abilities. In effect, Thorsland had refined our old definition and separated what we were measuring into two abilities. A detailed report on Thorsland's approach has been published (Thorsland and Novak, 1974).

With a good measure of learning time available for students in the A-T Physics 101–102 course, we could compute what we have come to call *learning efficiency*, an index of the amount learned per minute or hour of study time. One approach to obtaining a value of learning efficiency is to divide the score on some measure of learning achievement by the number of minutes or hours of study time. Thorsland used minutes in the A-T center as a measure of study time, and achievement on preliminary and final examinations in the Physics 101–102 course as measures. Using these values, he could compute learning efficiencies for students in various analytic ability or intuitive ability categories.

As Thorsland's work progressed, it became evident that students with high rankings on intuitive and/or analytic ability were doing significantly better on course examinations than students with low rankings on these ability estimates. In pursuing a line of reasoning that had become fundamental to the thinking of our research group, we began to ask again how intuitive and analytic thinking could be related to an Ausubelian model of learning. We discussed this issue in conferences and seminars and a consensus emerged that intuitive thinking might best be considered as problem solving in which initial solutions were suggested by higher level concepts, and subsequent interpretation proceeded to lower level concepts for the specific problem solution. In contrast, analytic thinking could be viewed as problem solving in which an individual proceeded from specific low level concepts relevant to the specific problem and applied these to solution of the problem. The analytic approach, for example, would begin by recognizing that a problem relating to a pendulum would involve the formula for the period (time) of a pendulum or:

$$p = 2\pi \sqrt{\frac{l}{g}}$$

The student could then proceed from this *formula* to explain how the period of a pendulum would vary. Schematically, an intuitive problem solver would move from the superordinate concepts relevant to the problem to possible alternative subordinate concepts specifically involved with the problem, whereas an analytic problem solver would begin with the specifically relevant subordinate concepts in approaching the problem solution. These two patterns are schematized in Figure 8.4. After refer-

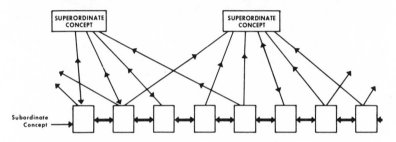

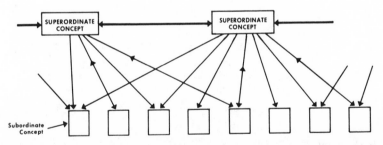

Figure 8.4. The conceptual organization in cognitive structure of the high analytic individual and the relationship to cognitive functioning as compared with the high intuitive individual. *Upper figure:* High analytic individual moves primarily *within* subordinate concepts and *to* superordinate concepts, with referral back to subordinate concepts, thus expanding the superordinate concepts. (There is very little, if any, exchange between superordinate concepts.) *Lower figure:* High intuitive individual moves freely from one superordinate concept to another with frequent referral primarily *to* (and less frequently *from*) subordinate examplars. From Thorsland and Novak (1974) in *Science Education, 58* (2), 247–248. Reproduced by permission of John Wiley & Sons.

ring back to Chapter 4, one can see that intuitive patterns of problem solving could be associated with creativity, and hence to some extent this proclivity may be genetically determined. In fact, Thorsland's research results provided the major insights that led to the view of creative ability I have described in Chapter 4.

Thorsland carefully analyzed the recorded sessions in problem solving and assigned intuitive ability and analytic ability rankings for each student on each of the four problems. The students were relatively consistent in their problem solving for

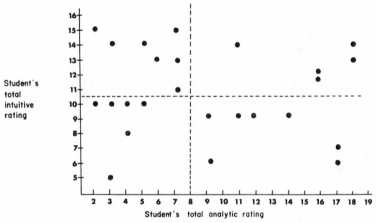

Figure 8.5.   Intuitive-analytic rankings for subjects in Thorsland's study.

the four problems; therefore, the rankings were totaled and overall scores for intuitive ability and analytic ability were obtained. These totals ranged from 5 to 15 on the intuitive dimension and 2 to 18 on the analytic dimension. The values for each of the twenty-five students are shown in Figure 8.5. There was considerable variability among students on these dimensions, and analytic ability was judged more variable than intuitive ability. This variability may reflect the greater difficulty found in assigning intuitive rankings. In any event, there was sufficient variability in scores, and we had enough confidence in these values to proceed with further analysis.

The higher, significant intercorrelations for analytic ability ratings on the four problems used suggested a greater consistency with which students apply this ability and/or a higher reliability in ranking students on this dimension. The nonsignificant correlations between intuitive and analytic rankings show that these are probably separate abilities, as we have hypothesized. Correlations between I (intuitive) and A (analytic) rankings and Scholastic Aptitude Test (SAT) scores were negative for intuitive ability but positive for analytic ability (see Table 8.7). Since the significance of correlation coefficients is strictly dependent upon the sample size, the consistently negative correlations for I and SAT scores suggest that intuitive ability is at best uncorrelated with traditional measures of school achievement, and similar results have been obtained in a more recent study.

Table 8.7. Correlations between intuitive and analytic rankings and scholastic aptitude test scores (verbal and math); n = 25

	Intuitive rankings	Analytic rankings
SATV	−.21	.46
SATM	−.23	.46

These data tend to support the descriptions of I.Q. and creative abilities given in Chapter 4 and also attest to the independence of these abilities. Unfortunately, most selection machinery in schools and industry tend to consider only the analytic type of ability (low-level concept differentiation). We will show that higher-order concept differentiation, characteristic of intuitive individuals, is very important in physics achievement, as it was in Ring's study of chemistry achievement. One reason why the SAT and similar tests are not better predictors of subsequent academic achievement (these measures account only for about 25 percent of subsequent variance in course performance) is that they do not assess all of the cognitive attributes associated with facilitation of learning. This kind of result would be expected on the basis of Jay Paul Guilford's model of intellect (1959), but the 120 factors he identifies are so abstruse as to render the model useless for instructional design.

Thorsland computed analysis of variance tables to assess the relative effects of intuitive and analytic ability on achievement. We see from Table 8.8 that both abilities are significantly re-

Table 8.8. ANOVA: Intuitive-anlaytic rankings with Physics Exam One as dependent variable

Source of Variance	df	MS	F	p<	p'<[a]
Intuitive Rating (I)	1	1442.663	4.427	.048	.022
Analytic Rating (A)	1	1808.355	5.550	.028	.225
IA	1	364.653	1.119	.302	.524

[a] From analysis of covariance where SATM and SATV scores are held constant.

lated to achievement in physics. Also notice that when adjustment is made for individual differences on SAT scores, the significance values show higher significance for the intuitive component but lower significance for the analytic component. These data again suggest that high intuitive ability is selected against in usual measures of academic aptitudes but that this ability is very helpful in learning.

In some ways, Thorsland's data became more interesting when the effects of intuitive and analytic ability differences were measured in terms of *learning efficiency.* Figure 8.6 shows that, on the average, high analytic ability students spent much *more* time in the learning center than did those with low analytic ability. Of course, high analytic ability students did earn higher grades in the physics course, but when learning efficiencies were compared, we found that the high intuitive, high analytic group was the most efficient in learning (see Figure 8.7). Further discussion of this issue has been presented elsewhere (Thorsland and Novak, 1974).

To summarize, Thorsland's work helped to advance our thinking in several ways. First, his technique for assessing intuitive and analytic abilities showed sufficient reliability and practicability to warrant further use of the approach. Second, that intuitive ability was uncorrelated or negatively correlated with

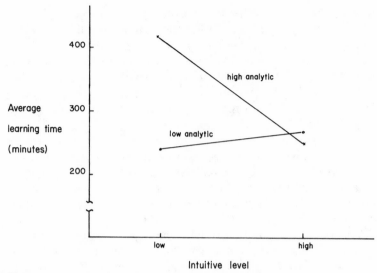

Figure 8.6. Interaction of intuitive and analytic rankings on average A-T learning time.

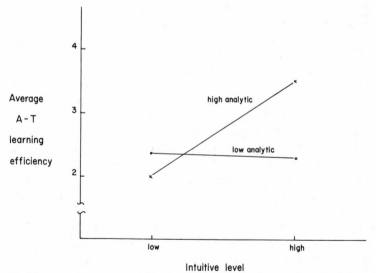

Figure 8.7. Interaction of intuitive and analytic rankings on A-T learning efficiency.

SAT scores indicates that these scores do not measure this ability or are biased against it. Third, the significant influence of intuitive ability on achievement in physics suggests that hierarchical cognitive differentiation with a proclivity to develop and utilize higher-order concepts in problem solving may be particularly helpful for the learning of physics. Some aspects of Thorsland's work have been repeated and with similar results (Peter Castaldi, 1975).

When Thorsland's work was completed and his results showed positive student response to the audio-tutorial format, the Physics Department remodeled some old laboratories to provide a learning center for Physics 101–102. All students enrolled in the course received audio-tutorial instruction, which provided a large sample of students for other research studies.

We were interested in studying more specifically than Ring and Tamir had done how entry cognitive structure influenced success in Physics 101–102. Joseph Wesney devised a pretest for basic mathematics needed in physics and also used the Dunning-Abeles physics test as a pretest. Wesney's results (1977) showed that students with better preparation in math and physics performed better on all seven instructional units in Physics 101.

From the work of Wesney, we knew that correlations between pretest scores and achievement on unit exams could be expected to vary. Carl Naegele's research (1974) was designed to study this variation further and to relate differences in the students' study time on each unit to achievement on those units.

One significant change made in the time between Wesney's and Naegele's studies was that evaluation in Physics 101–102 was modified from norm-referenced, group testing to criterion-referenced, individual testing (see the section on evaluation in Chapter 6). This meant that varying amounts of study time were provided for students to achieve at least a minimum of 80 percent required on each unit exam. In this way, we could expect some degree of mastery of concepts in early units and some positive influence on achievement in later units. Table 8.9 shows a comparison of correlation coefficients between pretest scores and achievement in Physics 101. The data show that the physics pretest had a positive $(r = 0.40)$ correlation with achievement under the norm-referenced evaluation but the correlation fell to zero under the criterion-referenced evaluation. We see that when both flexibility in study time and criterion-referenced evaluation are used, mastery learning is possible. Thus, variation in prior knowledge of physics is remediated through the instructional program. The correlation for the math pretest and physics achievement dropped somewhat but remained positive and significant. The latter result is what we should expect, because math was taught only incidentally in the program.

Table 8.9.   Correlation of prior knowledge with final grade in mastery vs. norm-referenced system

Prior knowledge	Mastery (fall 1972) n = 700	Norm-referenced (fall 1971) n = 498
SATM	.160	.500 [b]
SATV	.243 [a]	.335 [b]
Math pretest (Total)	.246 [a]	.528 [b]
Physics Pretest (Total)	−.003	.400 [b]

[a] p. < .05   [b] p. < .01

From a practical standpoint, the combined results from the studies of Wesney and Naegele show that good multimedia learning programs and self-paced instruction designed to enhance learning for the majority of students must include criterion-referenced evaluation.[1] Students cannot or will not gauge their study time and direct their study efforts to reach minimum levels of concept mastery for all basic materials unless testing and retesting is a required part of the instructional program.

A very interesting product of Naegele's research from a theoretical as well as a practical standpoint was his findings on learning efficiency for each of the units in Physics 101–102. He defined learning efficiency as:

[1] More recently, domain reference evaluation has been described, wherein test items are samples from a pool of items that test specified knowledge or skills. This form of evaluation is used now in Physics 101–102 at Cornell.

$$\text{Efficiency} = \frac{\text{Score on unit test}}{\text{Study time needed to complete unit}}$$

Because a minimum score was needed to pass a unit, most variation in efficiency scores was due to variation in hours of study time used to pass the unit. Naegele found that for the course as a whole, students who ranked in the upper half of the class on both mathematics and physics pretests were the most efficient learners, and the converse was true for students who ranked in the lower half on both pretests. This result was expected, but we were surprised at the data obtained when learning efficiency was compared for high and low scoring groups on the physics pretest on a unit-by-unit basis. Figure 8.8 shows the results obtained. We see that on several units, the students with low physics pretest scores were actually more efficient than the students with high pretest scores. Moreover, units 1–3 were closely related, with unit 3 requiring the use of concepts taught in units 1–2b. Similarly, units 6 and 4 were related. The time invested in mastery of physics concepts in early units of a sequence paid off for students who initially were poorly prepared in physics. As the course progressed, these students continued to show an advantage in later units, and even on the final retention (R) unit that involved materials from all other units.

Two points are illustrated by Naegele's results. First, the mastery mode of instruction used in Physics 101–102 allowed students to compensate for initial deficiencies in concepts of physics. These data strongly support arguments for mastery teaching (see Block, 1971). Second, in conceptually related sequences of learning, adequacy of early concept development (even at the expense of more study time) results in facilitation of subsequent, related concept learning. Study times, as well as pretest scores in physics, significantly influence the subsequent facilitation of learning; this fact strongly supports Carroll's model of school learning (1963) and Ausubel's thesis that the adequacy of prior *relevant* learning most importantly influences subsequent learning.

We have repeated Naegele's study and found similar results.

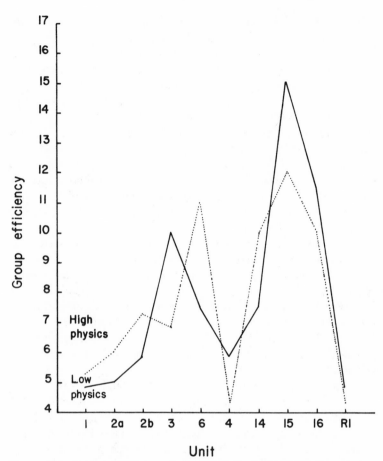

Figure 8.8. Group efficiency on each unit for two pretest groups; low math—low physics vs. low math—high physics.

We have a growing body of data for Physics 101–102 that shows that enriching the learning environment and providing adequate time for mastery of concepts can serve to reduce or eliminate much of the disadvantages of poor prior preparation in physics. We recognize that there is an important value issue at stake. If all students can now get A's in Physics 101–102, who will judge which students should be admitted into medical or other graduate schools? If we provide a rich instructional program and reduce or eliminate advantages conferred by the adequacy of prior schooling, we move toward egalitarianism in education. Many teachers, parents, students, and administrators, however, do not desire egalitarian educational practices.

Concept Learning in Elementary School Science

The data I had collected at Purdue in my studies of problem solving and concept learning of college students clearly showed that Ausubel's general theoretical framework could be applied to explain the importance of relevant entry cognitive structure for facilitation of learning. Although continued study of cognitive learning with college students seemed necessary in 1965, my growing conviction was that we needed to examine concept learning in young children who did not already possess relatively elaborate cognitive structures, and who would respond to instruction with fewer of the motivation variables that significantly influence learning in older students. A sabbatical leave from Purdue University during 1965–1966, and support from the Learning Research and Development Center at Harvard University, provided the opportunity to commence a research program based on audio-tutorial science lessons for elementary school children.

Other than the manifold problems associated with the development of A-T lessons, our first clash with the hard realities of cognitive learning research with six year olds was the problem of measurement of learning. The work of Jean Piaget and his followers offered a precedent, but it involved individual interviews, which are time-consuming for both the researcher and the classroom teacher who must free students for interviews. We hoped to devise forms of paper-and-pencil tests that would have validity and reliability. Our first efforts involved the use of sketches. For example, students were shown sketches of corn seedlings at various stages of growth and were asked to identify the oldest or the youngest seedling. When we began to ask students why they chose one drawing over another, we found that some errors resulted from misinterpretation of the drawings and others from difficulties in language. First graders do not have uniform concepts of older and younger. Older usually means bigger, and since all the seedlings were drawn the same size, those children who had not focused on morphological differences tended to make arbitrary selection of answers. Of course, the objective of the lessons partly was to have children recognize and interpret morphological changes in the seedlings. We eventually found that carefully structured interviews were the only reliable form of evaluation of children's concepts. Our procedures have been published elsewhere (Postlethwait, Novak, and Murray, 1972; Novak, 1972a).

During 1966-1969, most effort devoted to elementary school studies went into the development of audio-tutorial lessons. Each lesson required about one hundred hours of staff time to develop, test, revise, and polish. A completed lesson went through considerable formative evaluation before it was used in a sequence of lessons in a classroom, at which time no direct involvement of teachers or aides was required. Eventually some sixty functional lessons were developed, but the high costs of manufacturing and distributing these lessons, combined with heavy competition from well-funded NSF programs, have blocked publication of the program. This is another instance in which federal dollars primarily are used to direct innovations toward support of the prevailing biases in the funding agencies. Federal dollars can negatively influence the ecosystem of ideas and more concern for this is needed from Washington bureaucracies.

Our first systematic research work using structured interviews was done with second-grade students who received five approximately twenty-minute lessons on energy and energy transformation. The lessons were developed by Gerald McClelland, who also contributed to our work in Physics 101-102.

On the basis of interview responses, McClelland classified all students according to their responses on questions dealing with four forms of energy. His criteria for a satisfactory classification required that the student recognize the form of energy in novel contexts and for several different kinds of examples. The performance required was roughly that expected for nonquantitative answers from high school students. Table 8.10 shows the number of students whose answers were classified into satisfactory, dubious, and unsatisfactory categories for the four forms of energy. The lessons contained the most examples of kinetic and potential energy and the fewest of elastic energy. The pattern of satisfactory responses roughly followed the frequency of examples offered in the lessons, but the large number of unsatisfactory answers for elastic energy was probably due to relatively fewer experiences with this form of energy in everyday activities. In any case, the second-grade students who were interviewed showed a very substantial grasp of energy concepts, and one-half of the group (sixteen students) gave completely satisfactory answers in all instances.

Table 8.10. Numbers of interviewed subjects according to response category

Energy form	Satisfactory	Dubious	Unsatisfactory
Kinetic	28	2	2
Potential	18	6	8
Elastic	20	2	10
Heat	25	3	4

McClelland's work (1970) confirmed our more subjective experience that students were learning substantial science concepts through the rather limited study exposure of the A-T lessons with essentially no teacher supplementation. Moreover, it was evident that many of the students were not simply repeating answers given in the lessons but were using concepts of energy and energy transformation in novel problem solving situations. At least 25 percent of these eight-year-old children were capable of formal reasoning, according to Piagetian criteria. This was our first hard evidence that Ausubel's model was more appropriate than Piaget's for describing children's development of concepts.

Michael Hibbard had joined our group in January 1968. Hibbard's research work focused on achievement of first-grade students who received twenty-six, fifteen-to-twenty-minute A-T lessons in science. His evaluation materials dealt with lessons seventeen through twenty-six in this sequence, a lesson series which presented the following concepts:

17. Air is a substance; we can feel air and see it move things.
18. Open containers are full of air; air has weight; air weighs less than sand or cement; air is a gas; plaster is a solid.
19. Study of solids, liquids and air—all are made of particles called molecules.
20. Molecules of solids are held tightly, liquids and air have molecules that can be moved about.
21. Further demonstrations of solids, liquids and air, relating molecular properties.
22. Extension of lesson 21.
23. Demonstrations showing that molecules must be very small; molecules are constantly moving.
24. Smells come from substances; molecules of the substances diffuse through air. Heat makes molecules move faster.
25. Extension of lesson 24.
26. Macroscopic changes result from molecular changes.

From the abbreviated lesson descriptions we clearly see that the lesson content was substantially more sophisticated than what is usually presented in first-grade science instruction. Some reasons for this were included in Chapter 5. An obvious question, therefore, was whether children were learning these concepts meaningfully, and to what extent.

Lessons were administered to eighty-four children in two Ithaca elementary schools from October 1969 to February 1970. Test development was also proceeding during this interval, so it was not possible to pretest children. Some maturation and incidental learning could be expected, however, so we compared the test performance of instructed children with performance of a comparable group of uninstructed first-grade children. In our experience virtually no formal science teaching occurs in the primary grades, although children do occasionally grow seeds in the spring or comment on the weather. Hence, those students who received no A-T science lessons could be considered uninstructed, especially in the area of molecular structure and behavior of matter. The samples included eighty-four instructed and thirty-eight uninstructed children. In April 1970, twenty-five instructed children and ten uninstructed children were interviewed.

In the interview sessions, students were asked to describe

phenomena. For example, coffee was poured into a U tube and children were asked to explain why they could smell the coffee (see Figure 4.4). Responses to this question were categorized as shown in Chart 8.1. The results Hibbard obtained for the smell question are shown in Figure 8.9. Over 90 percent of the instructed children gave good descriptions of how a smell emanated from the U tube, whereas only 20 percent of the uninstructed children were ranked in the two best explanation categories. The responses of the instructed children to this and

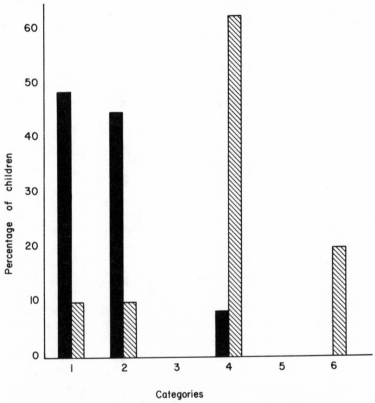

Figure 8.9. Percentage of instructed and uninstructed children responding in the categories. Interviewer asked the child to explain a smell.

Chart 8.1. Categories used to classify children's verbal description of a smell.

Categories 1–4—mechanism suggested in the responses.
Categories 1 and 2 represent responses where there is a clear indication that the child considers the smell to have physically originated from the source of the smell—in this case the coffee in the tube.)
Category 1: The molecules of the liquid coffee or from the liquid coffee come up out of the tube.
Category 2: The smell from the coffee or the coffee air comes up out of the tube.
(Categories 2 and 3 represent responses where there is a clear indication that the child does not consider the smell to have physically originated from the source.)
Category 3: The molecules of air come up. These molecules of air are not physically the same as the coffee and never were. In Category 2 the coffee air was once liquid coffee but is now air or airlike.
Category 4: The air comes up. The air was never part of the coffee. The child may suggest that the air (from outside the tube) went into the tube and then came back out smelling like coffee.
No mechanisms suggested
Category 5: The coffee smells—it just smells that way.
Other
Category 6: I don't know.

other interview questions dealing with smells were significantly more accurate than for the uninstructed group.

Hibbard's work (1971) contributed importantly to the improvement of the evaluation of concept learning in children. Quite unequivocally, our A-T science lessons were shown to be teaching science concepts to elementary school children.

Our program of studies with elementary school children using the tool of audio-tutorial instruction has continued. Reports by Joseph Nussbaum (1972), Sheri Wagner (1971), Hibbard (1971), Hibbard and Novak (1976), Janet Whitman (1975), and Richard Rowell (1975) establish conclusively, in my view, that from 20 to 90 percent of children in grades one and two can acquire and use basic science concepts. In many instances the use of these concepts in novel problem solving situations requires cognitive functioning that would be classified in Piaget's framework as formal operations (see above Chapter 4). We do not claim that all or even the majority of students can acquire these concepts with the limited instruction offered in our audio-tutorial science program. What we have shown is that children's capability for acquiring and using science concepts is very substantially greater than many educators have proclaimed. We will subsequently show that the use of formal thinking by children as well as adults can best be explained by Ausubel's model for progressive differentiation of content-specific concepts as individuals mature. Currently, we are engaged in a long-term study of concept development in which children receiving audio-tutorial lessons in grades one to three are interviewed several times to map their science concepts, according to the technique developed by Rowell (1975). We expect to continue interviewing these children until they leave the Ithaca public schools. Our hypothesis is that we will see in our sample groups evidence for progressive differentiation and integrative reconciliation of science concepts with wide individual variation and little correspondence to Piagetian cognitive developmental norms.

Related Empirical Studies

A long tradition in the sciences requires verification of theories by work in two or more independent laboratories. This tradition is admirable, for the variations in the endemic population of concepts from laboratory group to laboratory group as well as those in instrumentation or research techniques serve to test the generalizability of new theories. With few exceptions, this practice has not been common in education. As a matter of fact, not only is parallel investigation in different research settings lacking, but doctoral students, who do most of the research as theses studies, usually work in isolation at the same institution. In contrast to research in the sciences, the research group in education is a rarity. A major contention of this book has been that we have had mostly disjointed, nonprogressive research in education because we have lacked an adequate theoretical foundation upon which to base conceptually and methodologically systematic research programs. The learning theory of David Ausubel provides a theoretical basis for a major reorganization of our research and the subsequent attack on practical educational problems.

Ideally, a series of studies done by other research groups which bear on the issues discussed earlier in the chapter would now be presented. However, Ausubel's theory has been far from a popular theoretical framework for educational research; hence, research studies that parallel our work are very hard to find. We have been delinquent in our own way, for little of our research effort over the years has been directed at confirming findings of other researchers. On those occasions when some preliminary work in replicating selected research studies has been done, the results showed no more promise than those found in reports by the other groups; hence, the work was dropped or not reported in the literature. The major exception has been our investigations of the role of advance organizers in the facilitation of learning, and even here we have been skeptical about the value of this line of inquiry. For these reasons, the studies summarized in this section represent a variety of research issues, and the data reported do not always address the specific issues we have highlighted in our own work. The studies do however represent a sample of work done by other researchers which supports the theoretical framework developed in this book.

Studies Related to Piaget's Work

Recently, I reviewed over four hundred education research studies reported in 1972 (Novak, 1974). This experience once again confirmed what other reviewers have lamented, that the overall quality of research in education is poor, that studies lack theoretical foundation, and that research methodology is often inexcusably inadequate. Of these four hundred studies, only five made specific reference to learning theory, and three of these dealt with Ausubel's advance organizer idea. A large group of the studies (about fifty) dealt directly or indirectly with the work of Piaget. While I do not regard Piaget's developmental psychology as a general learning theory, his framework for the design of research and for collection and interpretation of data does provide a much-welcomed basis for coherence between independent research studies. As I shall try to show in this section, much of the research using Piaget's methodology has produced results that are more parsimoniously interpreted by Ausubel's theory than by Piaget's stages of cognitive development.

The careful research of Kenneth Lovell, working in England, showed that young children do exhibit cognitive characteristics described by Piaget. In an early study, Lovell and Ogilvie (1960) showed that not every youngster between seven and eleven years could conserve substance (clay rolled into a ball or a sausage), and confirmed Piaget's findings that students in this age range were conservers, nonconservers, or in a transitional stage, where they vacillated between responses that showed conservation or nonconservation. Their research results only confirmed the obvious, for all subjects must fall into one of these categories. In Table 8.11 we see that first-year elementary school youngsters conserve less frequently than second-, third-, or fourth-year students. On the surface, such data support Piaget's

Table 8.11. Children in grades 1–4 at various cognitive stages

	Average Age Yr.	Mo.	Conservation	Transition	Nonconservation	Total
1st year	7	8	30	27	26	83
2nd year	8	10	44	8	13	65
3rd year	9	9	73	15	11	99
4th year	10	8	64	7	4	75

Source: Lovell and Ogilvie, "A Study of the Conservation of Substance in the Junior School Child," *British Journal of Educational Psychology,* 30 (1960), 112.

notion that children do not conserve substance until they are about eight or nine years old, because they have not reached the general developmental stage of concrete operations necessary for this task. I shall describe later more recent studies that have shown that many college students fail to conserve also. Lovell and Ogilvie (1960) performed other studies with young children and concluded:

Thus, it seems that children who are conservers of continuous quantities in one situation were not inevitably conservers in another. On this point the more recent findings seem to lead to conclusions at variance with those of Piaget. Our interpretation of his view is that once the concept of the conservation of substance has been attained, it holds in all situations involving conservation of substance. If we have understood him correctly, then our evidence . . . does not support his viewpoint, which seems to hide the *particularities* of child thinking. It seems rather that *the concept is applicable only to highly specific situations at first and that it increases in depth and complexity with experience and maturation.* [p. 117; emphasis added]

As early as 1960, then, we had a nicely stated argument for what Ausubel has referred to as progressive differentiation of concepts in cognitive structure—a lifelong development, rather than the Piagetian fixed stages of cognitive growth. Lovell and Ogilvie continued their argument:

Piaget's view that the child arrives at the concept because he is able to argue logically in concrete situations may or may not be correct. A careful scrutiny of all our evidence does not enable us to prove or disprove his viewpoint. *It is equally likely that the concept of conservation of substance—or indeed, any concept—grows out of interlocking of several organisations of past impressions that normally remain outside consciousness (schemata) which in turn grow out of many and varied experiences.* The child may then invoke logical arguments to justify the concept which was obtained on other grounds. Or it may be that experience and the ability to use logical thought aid one another and bring about certainty. [p. 117; emphasis added]

The observation here sounds very much like Ausubel's process of integrative reconciliation, which continues throughout life together with progressive differentiation of concepts.

Inhelder and Piaget (1958) describe children's interpretations of the pendulum problem to illustrate growth in logical thinking. After children observe pendulum swings with different string lengths, weights of bobs, and shorter and longer swings, they are asked to explain the changes in the period (time) for the swings. Robert Lengel and Robert Buell (1972) used the pendulum problem with students in grades seven, nine, and twelve, recording discussions with the students as they explained what they observed. Lengel and Buell used a six-point scale to rank individuals' responses as follows:

Score   Description

1   The subject does not arrive at any conclusions regarding the four variables. Indifferentiation between subject actions and pendulum motion.

2   Subject can recognize some variables but cannot differentiate. Serial ordering not accurate.

3   Subject can separate variables. Serial ordering accurate.

4   Subject can exclude, can identify crucial factor with minimal questioning. Can separate factors when given combinations in which only one factor varies.

5   Subject, by own insight, eliminates all but crucial factor, has achieved exclusion of inoperant links.

6   Subject can quantify answers.

The data obtained by Lengel and Buell are shown in Tables 8.12 and 8.13. We see that there is an improvement in children's ability to separate variables and to arrive at better explanations as they progress through the grades. However, even at

Table 8.12. Sample means for three grades

	Grade 7 n = 20	Grade 9 n = 20	Grade 12 n = 20
Age	12:10	14:8	17:5
I.Q.	105	108	116
Conservation score	3:35	4:05	4:65

Source: Adopted from Lengel and Buell in *Science Education,* 56, 1 (1972), 68. Reprinted with permission of John Wiley & Sons.

Table 8.13. Percentage of children in grades 7, 9, and 12 receiving each conservation score

Conservation score	Grade 7 n = 20	Grade 9 n = 20	Grade 12 n = 20
5	10	35	80
4	35	45	5
3	35	10	15
2	20	10	0

Source: Adopted from Lengel and Buell in *Science Education,* 56, 1(1972), 69. Reprinted with permission of John Wiley & Sons.

grade twelve, with a mean age of 17.5 years, none of the subjects was able to quantify his answers and only 80 percent could exclude irrelevant variables in the pendulum problem. Yet Piaget holds that the logical operations necessary to solve this problem are available to a child who has reached the stage of formal operations, normally by age fourteen or fifteen. While Piaget recognizes that not all children achieve formal operations by this age, the data of Lengel and Buell indicate that most children at age fourteen years, eight months are still having difficulty with the pendulum problem as are some seventeen- and eighteen-year-old students. What the data suggest more parsimoniously is that the *specific* concepts necessary for separation of relevant and irrelevant variables in this problem develop gradually with age and experience and that none of the twelfth graders in this sample knew or could recall the highly specific concept (formula) for computing the period of a pendulum swing. These data, in our view, support the need for differentiation of relevant concepts in cognitive structure for solution of a specific problem, as Ausubel would contend, much more than they support Piaget's doctrine of cognitive developmental stages.

I turn now to work with college students. Anton Lawson, Floyd Nordlund, and Alfred De Vito (1974) used five different formal operational tasks with college freshmen and sophomores (median age 18.5 years). The five Piagetian tasks were (1) conservation of volume using clay, (2) conservation of volume using metal cylinders, (3) pendulum problem, (4) separation of variables using metal rods, and (5) equilibrium in the balance. The primary purpose of this study was to determine the possible effect of retesting on achievement, because some earlier studies suggested that significant improvement occurred from pretesting to posttesting when no intervening experience was programmed. If children's cognitive growth is dependent on gradual differentiation (equilibration, to use Piaget's term) of general cognitive stages, such pronounced test-retest effect should not be observed. Lawson and his colleagues interviewed all subjects and rated them as follows:

1. Early concrete operational—1 point
2. Fully concrete operational—2 points
3. Early formal operational—3 points
4. Fully formal operational—4 points

A total interview score for each subject was obtained by summing the scores on each of the five Piagetian tasks. The data obtained are shown in Table 8.14. We see that Lawson and his associates rated most of these college students in the concrete operational stage on all five Piagetian tasks. There were significant gains from pretests to posttests on three of the tasks, an effect the researchers attributed to relative ease of recall of correct responses. But even on the posttests for these tasks, the majority of the students did not offer fully formal operational answers.

Table 8.14. College-student scores on pretests and posttests with five Piagetian tasks

Task	Pretest		Posttest		F	Test-retest reliability
	Mean	S D	Mean	S D		
Conservation volume clay	1.69	.467	1.94	.232	11.57	.239
Conservation volume cylinders	2.33	.756	2.75	.554	12.96	.481
Exclusion	2.78	.989	3.00	.894	.1.99	.487
Separation of variables	2.83	.910	2.97	.878	1.96	.785
Equilibrium	2.53	.774	3.00	.756	[b]17.25	.571
Total interview score	12.17	2.90	13.67	2.392	[b]24.11	.763

[a] $p < .01$ [b] $p < .001$

Source: Lawson, Nordlund, and DeVito in *Science Education, 58,* 4(1974), 572. Reproduced with permission of John Wiley & Sons.

Once again we have to ask if the age-related developmental stage is the primary determinant of students' problem or puzzle solving ability, or if it is more parsimonious to suggest that the students' lack of adequately differentiated concepts that are *specifically relevant* to the problems principally determines the adequacy of their answers.

Continuing this line of questioning, we turn now to a study by Elizabeth and Robert Karplus (1970) dealing with the Island Puzzle shown in Figure 8.10. For all groups studied, a map of

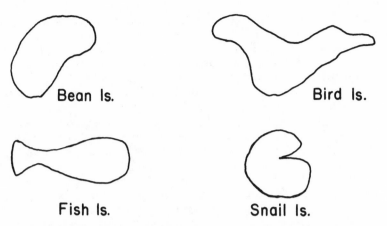

Bean Is.   Bird Is.

Fish Is.   Snail Is.

Introduction: The puzzle is about four islands in the ocean. People have been travel-ing among these islands by boat for many years, but recently an airline started in business. Listen carefully to the clues I give you about possible plane trips. The trips may be direct or they may include stops on one of the islands. When I say a trip is possible, it can be made in both directions between the islands.

This is a map with the four islands, called Bean Island, Bird Island, Fish Island, and Snail Island. You may make notes or marks on your map to help you remember the clues. Raise your hand if you have questions about the clues.

First clue: People can go by plane between Bean and Fish Island.

Second clue: People cannot go by plane between Bird and Snail Islands. Use these two clues to answer question 1.

Question 1: Can people go by plane between Bean and Bird Islands?

Yes _____ No _____ Can't tell from the two clues. _____

Explain your answer.

Third clue: People can go by plane between Bean and Bird Islands. Use all three clues to answer questions 2 and 3. Don't change your answer to question 1.

Question 2: Can people go by plane between Fish and Bird Islands?

Yes _____ No _____ Can't tell from the three clues. _____

Explain your answer.

Question 3: Can people go by plane between Fish and Snail Islands?

Yes _____ No _____ Can't tell from the three clues. _____

Explain your answer.

Figure 8.10. Karplus Islands Puzzle. Reprinted from Karplus and Karplus in *School Science and Mathematics, 70* (May 1970), 398. Reference cited in Bibliography.

the four islands was shown, instructions were given, and it was emphasized that all plane routes operate in both directions. Four categories of responses were established:

Category N: no explanation or statement "I can't explain."

Category I (prelogical): an explanation which makes no reference to the clues and/or introduces new information. Subcategories are the mere repetition of the answer to be explained, appeal to the diagram itself, and fanciful stories.

Category IIa (transition to concrete models): direct appeal to or repetition of clues. Since all three questions require inferences, a direct appeal to the clues does not provide a logical justification.

Category IIb (concrete models): the clues are used to construct models which are then used to make the predictions. This model-based approach, when correctly used, leads to correct answers to all three questions in the problem. It assumes information not given in the clues, however, and cannot be generalized to solve similar puzzles with different data.

Category IIIa (transition to abstract logic): logical explanation to question 2, that Bird Island can certainly be reached from Fish Island by way of a stop at Bean Island. Since the logical inference from the two positive statements (clues 1 and 3) needed for question 2 is easier, in our view, than the use of the negative statement (clue 2), question 2 does not make maximum demand on the subject's reasoning ability. We have therefore classified the logical answer here as being transitional to the abstract stage, rather than representing attainment of the abstract stage.

Category IIIb (abstract logic): logical explanations to questions 1 and 3.

The data obtained by the Karpluses is shown in Table 8.15.

We see in the Karplus data that success with the Island Puzzle improved with age up to grade twelve, but adults at the NSTA meetings did somewhat poorer than twelfth graders. On the other hand, physics teachers at the AAPT meeting did much better than twelfth graders or adults (teachers) at the NSTA meetings. Clearly, we need some explanation for these data other than that afforded by Piaget's notion of developmental stages. We should expect that college-educated adults would be at least as cognitively mature as seniors in high school, and we cannot reasonably assume that AAPT teachers are inordinately more advanced in the development of their general cognitive structure. We can assume that physicists have concepts related to vector problems, similar to those used by Gubrud and reported earlier, and hence that they would have differentiated concepts that could be specifically relevant to the Island Puzzle. Karplus and Karplus have inadvertently demonstrated that the

Table 8.15.   Subjects and categories of response on Karplus Islands test

Subject group and designation	Number
Suburban fifth and sixth graders (5–6)	55
Suburban seventh, eighth, and ninth graders enrolled in a science class (7–9)	78
Suburban tenth, eleventh, and twelfth graders in several college preparatory classes (10–12)	98
Suburban twelfth graders in physics classes (12P)	66
NSTA Convention participants at Piaget symposium (NSTA)	83
Participants at American Association of Physics Teachers meeting (AAPT)	69
Total subjects	449

Categories of responses (percentage) by subject group

Response category	5–6	7–9	10–12	12P	NSTA	AAPT
N	24	3	1	9	10	0
I	40	39	9	15	4	3
IIa	11	26	13	6	18	6
IIb	18	18	62	47	54	51
IIIa	7	15	11	15	8	27
IIIb	0	0	3	8	6	13

Source: Adapted from Karplus and Karplus in *School Science and Mathematics, 70* (May 1970), 398–406; also reference cited in Bibliography.

most important factor in new learning or in problem solving is the adequacy of relevant concepts in cognitive structure.

Once again I should like to emphasize that Piaget's developmental psychology is based on a psychological preformationist philosophy which assumes that cognitive development unfolds in fixed sequences up to maturity. Although not as rigid as Greek preformationist notions of the human homunculus in the sperm cell enlarging to form the adult, Piagetian psychology is rooted in the same kind of absolutist philosophy.

In *Psychology and Epistemology* (1972), Piaget rightly criticizes the simplistic notions that all knowledge is acquired from sensorial impressions; but if I understand him correctly, we need to explain new learning by the sequence of developmental stages that arrive in fixed order. From an Ausubelian interpretation we conclude that an individual's capacity for new learning or problem solving is a function of the adequacy of relevant concepts, and while well-differentiated, broadly relevant concepts tend to develop with age, thus giving the illusion of general stages of cognitive development, the more parsimonious explanation is that cognitive differentiation is experience-dependent (and hence, somewhat culture-dependent) in a highly specific way. All the data we have seen consistent with Piaget's developmental stages are also consistent with Ausubel's theory of progressive differentiation of subsuming concepts in cognitive structure. Hundreds of studies, including the few cited above, cannot be parsimoniously explained by Piaget's developmental psychology.

Studies of Intelligence and Creativity

Systematic study of gifted students has gone on for almost a century. Francis Galton (1892), who was instrumental in establishing the science of statistics, investigated the hereditary backgrounds of gifted individuals and showed that genius tends to run in families. He was able to show that children of gifted individuals also were gifted, but there was a regression toward the mean, that is, a tendency for progeny to be more normal. This phenomenon is characteristic of genically determined traits, and hence it was later concluded that the giftedness was a genically rather than an environmentally controlled human trait.

Perhaps most outstanding in the history of giftedness have been Lewis Terman's studies of 1500 intellectually superior individuals. Terman's sample was drawn from students nominated by teachers and subsequently tested for I.Q. He found that not all students recommended by teachers met his criterion of I.Q. = 140 or more. Terman's study began in 1921 and continued, with new data gathered on individuals up to mid-career. To Terman, giftedness was essentially synonymous with high I.Q. (most testing utilized the Stanford-Binet), although he recognized that some able students did not achieve high I.Q.

scores. Terman's work did much to popularize I.Q. testing and the dogma that genetic fate determines I.Q. and that I.Q. determines chances for excellence. This unfortunate dogma continues to predominate in the thinking of many lay people and educators today. It has been under attack by such books as those by Alan Gartner, Colin Greer, and Frank Riessman (1974) and Keddie (1973).

On the positive side, Terman also gathered data on physical characteristics and on such factors as suicide rates. He could show that on any characteristic studied, the gifted individuals rated as well or better than their age group as a whole. They were taller, healthier, happier, and more stable than "normal" subjects. Thus, Terman's work did much to dispel a popular myth that had grown in the last half of the nineteenth century that intellectually superior individuals were sickly and neurotic.

The equivalence of I.Q. with intelligence held sway for much of the first half of the twentieth century. There were, to be sure, some striking examples of students who tested low in early years and much higher in later years, or of outstanding achievement by individuals with average or below average I.Q.'s. These cases were often regarded as anomalies, rather than as indicators that I.Q. measures were not adequate measures of intellectual potential. The unwarranted faith in I.Q. tests perhaps began to crumble first with the manpower shortages during World War II, when persons were drafted into jobs or schooling for which they otherwise would have been rejected, and many did strikingly well. Moreover, correlation studies became popular, and it became evident that correlation of early I.Q. scores with later academic achievement dropped to low or nonsignificant levels and that almost no correlation was found with subsequent job performance. Thus, while Terman's highly selected "gifted" individuals continued to show group superiority, by the 1950s it became increasingly evident that I.Q. tests were not all they had been alleged to be. Psychometrists and educators began to look for new ways to measure and predict human potential.

Under the leadership of Calvin Taylor at the University of Utah, several symposium sessions and seminars were held on the subject of creativity. The reports (Taylor, 1956, 1958, 1959) of three national conferences did much to gather ideas of scholars from various disciplines, thus substantially broadening perspectives as to the nature of the creative process and to the possible associations between creativity and other cognitive and affective traits.

A significant impetus for the systematic study of creative ability, as distinct from I.Q., came from Guilford's presidential address to the American Psychological Association in 1950. Guilford had been using different mental measurement instruments to study intellectual abilities and had concluded that I.Q. tests measure only a small part of the variety of abilities he and his associates were identifying. Guilford (1952, and later) eventually developed a structure of intellect model that predicted at least 120 individual mental abilities, and I.Q. measurements were found to be associated with only some of these.

Perhaps the first bombshell that hit the cult of I.Q. was Getzels' and Jackson's *Creativity and Intelligence* (1962). Using a variety of creativity tests, questionnaires, I.Q. tests, and other measures with 292 boys and 241 girls in a private school, they found that creativity was not highly correlated with I.Q. tests. Although this low correlation between measures of creativity and I.Q. had been noted before, Getzels' and Jackson's work was significant because of the technique used for apportioning the sample and for noting the effect of I.Q. and creativity on school achievement. Two groups were formed: one composed of students in the top 20 percent on I.Q. but below the top 20 percent on combined scores for creativity tests (the high I.Q. group), and a second group composed of students in the top 20 percent on creativity tests but below the top 20 percent on I.Q. tests (the high creative group). Means and standard deviations for I.Q. and school achievement for the two groups are shown in Table 8.16. We see that both the high I.Q. and the high creatives did significantly better in school achievement (as measured by standardized achievement tests normally administered in the school) than did the total student population. Moreover, the high creative group did at least as well as the high I.Q. group. Questionnaire data from teachers indicated that the high

I.Q. students were better liked by their teachers than the high creatives, and presumably, this may have been a mediating factor in favor of the high I.Q. group. In Chapter 4, I discussed the tendency of I.Q. scores to correlate with standard achievement measures, in contrast with measures suggesting high-order conceptual development or intuitive thinking. These two factors make the comparative success of the high creative group even more impressive.

Table 8.16. Means and standard deviations of I.Q. and school achievement for total student population and experimental groups

		Total population [a] (n = 449)	High I.Q. (n = 28)	High creative (n = 24)
I.Q.	$\overline{X}$	132.00	150.00 [b]	127.00
	s	15.07	6.64	10.58
School	$\overline{X}$	49.91	55.00 [b]	56.27 [b]
achievement	s	7.36	5.95	7.90

[a] For purposes of comparison, the scores of each experimental group were extracted from the total population before "t" tests were computed.
[b] Differs significantly from the total population at the .001 level.
Source: Getzels and Jackson (1962), p. 24. Reproduced with permission from Creativity and Intelligence (New York: John Wiley & Sons).

The studies by Getzels and Jackson have been criticized for several reasons. For one, they used a relatively select student body that was not representative of school children in general. Their high creative group was also comparatively high in I.Q., averaging about two standard deviations above the mean for "normal" students. In other words, most of the high creative group would also rank in the top 10 percent of their age group on I.Q. scores. There also were questionable research methodology practices in the sampling and data processing procedure. Nevertheless, the work of Getzels and Jackson had to be and was taken seriously by cognitive psychologists and educators.

Strong support for the major findings in Getzels and Jackson's studies was reported soon after by Torrance (1962). His samples were drawn from more representative public and private schools, and also from university classes. Torrance used a technique similar to that employed by Getzels and Jackson for identifying high intelligence and high creative groups. He found that, although the difference in mean scores on intelligence measures for the samples studied was significant at the .001 level, high creatives did as well as high I.Q. groups on

Table 8.17. Means or critical measures of achievement of highly intelligent and highly creative individuals in eight learning situations and tests of significance

Group and date	Number each group	Achievement measure	Means Intelligence	Creatives	F-ratio	Probability
Elementary School A, 1959	21	Iowa Basic Skills Battery	141.2	139.1	0.16	Not significant
Elementary School A, 1960	10	Iowa Basic Skills Battery	137.8	136.6	0.01	Not significant
Elementary School B, 1959	18	Iowa Basic Skills Battery	139.2	121.7	8.84	<.01
Elementary School C, 1960	36	Iowa Basic Skills Battery	113.4	103.8	23.61	<.01
Elementary School D, 1960	13	Iowa Basic Skills Battery	119.2	110.4	3.18	Not significant
High School A (Grades 0–12)	26	Iowa Tests of Education Development	26.0	22.9	1.37	Not significant
Counseling Institute (University of Minn.), 1959	10	Pre-post test Gain, Achievement Test	13.4	16.4	0.23	Not significant
Educational Psychology 159 (University of Minn.), 1960	13	Total Score on Course Achievement	340.8	332.2	0.38	Not significant

Source: Torrance, *Guiding Creative Talent* (Englewood Cliffs, N.J.: Prentice-Hall, 1964), p. 64. Reproduced with permission of the author.

school achievement measures in six out of eight cases. The data are shown in Table 8.17. The results appeared in general to confirm the findings of Getzels and Jackson that creative ability can contribute to scholastic achievement to an extent similar to I.Q. type of ability. Again, we should note that this was true although achievement tests such as the Iowa Basic Skills Battery measure cognitive competencies that are much more similar to those measured by I.Q. tests than by creativity tests.

Torrance also identified other personality and sociological traits of "creatives." By the time his book was published (1964), research and training programs in creativity had become very widespread in educational circles, management training, and employee improvement programs. Concern for and interest in creativity seemed to reach a peak of interest in the mid-1960s.

The heavy demands for scientific talent resulting from booming industry and a much-expanded space program led to an interest in talent identification criteria, especially with respect to identification of creative talent. Studies such as Lindsey Harmon's (1963) were showing that correlations between undergraduate grade point averages and supervisors' ratings of creative value of scientific personnel were negative or near zero. Similarly, standardized achievement tests also showed little or no correlation with supervisors' ratings of individuals' creative output. Calvin Taylor, William R. Smith, and Brewster Ghiselin (1963) found that in a sample of 239 successful scientists, those rated by their supervisors in the first third in research competence had about the same college grade point averages as those rated in the lower third. In all three rating categories, a broad distribution of the undergraduate grade point averages was found. The data are shown in Table 8.18. These data would not have been available, of course, if the manpower demands during World War II had not led to employment of trained scientists with low GPA's, who previously would have been almost automatically excluded from many industries and government laboratories. Here again we have evidence that the abilities needed to be successful in a job assignment (and a rather specialized, intellectually demanding one at that) are not related to the abilities and/or motivation that result in high grade point averages.

Toulmin (1972) describes the evolutionary character of disciplines and subdisciplines. We see in the case of creativity research that the number and influence of research workers increased substantially in the 1960s and the inevitable professional mutation occurred. The *Journal of Creative Behavior* was launched in 1967 to serve as a publication for creativity research. An examination of the nine volumes published to date

Table 8.18. Relation of scientists' grade point averages to research performance

Grade point average	Merit rating of performance on research duties			Total subjects
	Top	*Second*	*Third*	
3.80–3.99	1	–	–	1
3.60–3.79	2	2	2	6
3.40–3.59	8	4	2	14
3.20–3.39	7	9	4	20
3.00–3.19	5	9	4	18
2.80–2.99	13	13	5	31
2.60–2.79	4	26	5	35
2.40–2.59	13	20	8	41
2.20–2.39	8	16	5	29
2.00–2.19	11	9	3	23
1.80–1.99	4	5	3	12
1.60–1.79	–	5	1	6
1.40–1.59	–	3	–	3
Total	76	121	42	239
Mean	2.73	2.60	2.69	2.66

Triserial correlation = 0.06

Source: Taylor, Smith, and Ghiselin, in Taylor and Barron, eds., *Scientific Creativity, Its Recognition and Development* (New York: John Wiley & Sons, 1963), p. 74. Reproduced with permission.

shows that many issues raised in the early 1960s continue to be issues today. Guilford's structure of intellect model continues to be the dominant theoretical framework, although some other theoretical views of creative ability and general cognitive functioning have been advanced. No research reported in this journal has drawn on the work of Ausubel.

The continuing issue of possible relationships between intelligence and creative ability has been examined. Guilford and Christensen (1973), working with 435 children in grades four, five, and six, found that Divergent Productions (DP) tests correlated $r = 0.25$ with I.Q. scores. Their principal concern, however, was with the pattern of scores for DP and I.Q.: are scores scattered over a broad ellipse when values for DP and I.Q. are plotted, or do they form a triangular shape with both high and low DP's for high I.Q.'s but only low DP's for low I.Q.'s? Guilford and Christensen found that semantic DP tests tended to show triangular plots whereas figural DP tests showed elliptical plots. They concluded that no threshold value exists for correlation between DP tests and I.Q. tests but rather that only some correlation exists and the higher the I.Q. of an individual, the more likely higher creativity (DP) may be evidenced. In a related earlier study, Martha Mednick and Frank Andrews (1967) also found evidence that SAT math and SAT verbal scores showed low correlations with a creativity test at five different levels of the SAT score groups. Together these two studies suggest at best a weak positive relationship between I.Q. or standardized achievement scores and measures of creativity.

The interpretation of creativity, presented in Chapter 4, is consistent with the data provided above. However, if creative ability is primarily a function of the degree of higher-order (more inclusive) conceptual organization and an emotional predisposition to use or develop higher-order concepts in cognitive structure, considerable extension of past research is indicated.

Progressive differentiation of higher-order concepts would be facilitated by the development of many relevant lower-order concepts, primarily the kind of development measured by I.Q. or standardized achievement tests. Therefore, we should expect that high creative potential in a broad variety of instances would be much enhanced by moderate or higher levels of I.Q. Furthermore, since differentiated higher-order concepts can serve as relevant subsumers for a broad range of new low-order concept or knowledge acquisition, high creative ability should almost necessarily result in moderate or above-average I.Q. and/or achievement scores, provided that the learning environment has not been unduly disadvantaged.

We see, then, that according to views on the nature of creativity presented in this book, we should expect an *interaction* between creative production and low-order concept or knowledge acquisition, and this interaction should become greater at higher levels of creativity and/or achievement score ranges. This expectation is precisely what we found in the study by Thorsland reported earlier (see Figure 8.7) and is also suggested in the data given above. Our views on creativity support Ausubel's contention that the truly creative individual appears to be qualitatively different from others, for when high levels of creative ability, high levels of I.Q. or achievement abilities, and a rich environment are combined, the nonlinear, synergistic interaction of both high-level and lower-level concept differentiation gives the appearance of unique cognitive functioning. It is more parsimonious to see ordinary learning capability and creativity as dependent on the same set of cognitive factors, that is, the number and degree of differentiated concepts in cognitive structure and the degree of hierarchical integration between concepts. The latter factor is primarily characterized as creative ability and the former is characterized as I.Q. or standardized achievement test indicators of ability.

A study relevant to the above hypothesis was reported by M. A. Wallach and N. Kogan (1965). This research was based on the hypothesis that highly creative students differed from students low in creativity primarily in the uniqueness of associations they could make, given adequate time to respond. An examination of the literature suggested to Wallach and Kogan that simply determining the number of associations a student can make with a stimulus word, picture, or story does not take into account *qualitative* differences in responses unless unlimited time for response is offered, a factor that is usually not present in creativity testing. Therefore, production of a large number of stereotyped responses could rank a subject as more creative than one who produces stereotyped responses less readily but, given sufficient time, is capable of producing numerous unique associations. Working with 151 elementary school children, Wallach and Kogan found some empirical support for their hypothesis. Creative ability appeared to contribute to the frequency of unique associations, whereas high I.Q. was associated more with the *quantity* of associations.

To illustrate the hypothesis we are suggesting for the relationship of I.Q. and creativity to associations or suggestions made by students, some assessment of the comparative inclusiveness of conceptual categories is necessary. Because we cannot talk about low-order or higher-order conceptualizations except with respect to a specific content area, we would require that testing be done in reference to specific subject matter and not in the general areas usually employed in creativity testing. If we assess both the number and degree of inclusiveness of concepts students exhibit, we should see that both low creatives and low I.Q. students tend to produce less inclusive concept associations only, whereas high I.Q. and high creatives can produce both less inclusive and more inclusive conceptualizations but with strikingly different frequencies. Since we regard abilities of the I.Q. type as at least somewhat independent of creative abilities, an individual can be both high I.Q. and high creative, hence coming forth with numerous and qualitatively more inclusive conceptual associations. The synergistic effect of high I.Q. and high creativity would result in the unique performance Ausubel associates with the "truly creative" person. In discussions on this issue, Ausubel and I have agreed that our views differ.

We have found paper and pencil testing methods to be unreliable for determining the extent to which a student forms higher-order concepts. Some of our current research deals with this issue, and we are utilizing clinical interview techniques described earlier. We are only beginning to obtain data on the extent of concept differentiation and the degree of integration between lower-order and higher-order concepts. So far, our data appear to be consistent with the theoretical views presented here, but much more work remains to be done.

Summary of Related Empirical Studies

If we were to follow the philosophy of Karl Popper (1959), we would have to show that Ausubel's theory is valid by the criterion of falsifiability: competing theories are falsified by empirical studies and that Ausubel's theory has survived efforts at falsification. However, Popper's views derive from an epistemology which I believe is invalid, not only for science but for educational research especially. In Chapter 2, I have argued that logical proof, as embodied in Popper's concept of falsifiability, is not the only or the most relevant avenue to rational discourse. I agreed with Toulmin (1972) that rational thought is not synonymous with logical thought and that "a man demonstrates his rationality, not by a commitment to fixed ideas, stereotyped procedures, or immutable concepts, but by the manner in which, and the occasions on which, he changes those ideas, procedures, and concepts" (p. x).

In this chapter I have tried to show not that other theories are falsified by empirical data, but rather that Ausubel's theory is most consistent with the current status of evolving concepts pertinent to classroom learning. Referring back to the criteria for judging the adequacy of learning theories presented in Chapter 3, I have shown how rational interpretation of data from a variety of learning contexts is facilitated by Ausubel's theory and by our extensions in the areas of hierarchical concept differentiation and relationships to creativity. My contention is that the validity of Ausubel's theory cannot be established by empirical refutation of other theories (albeit, some data presented are not consistent with or relevant to other theoretical views) but rather by the power his theory has for making decisions on the design of research and/or classroom instruction that produce results consistent with our expectations. The history of science has shown that the value of theories comes from their power to focus attention on salient variables and to predict relationships between variables—not from their unfalsifiability. In the end, all theories are falsified in whole or in part, and their value derives from the extent of conceptual evolution they have brought about and not from their ultimate veracity. I am convinced that Ausubel's theory can help to advance our concepts of cognitive learning processes and related educational practices. I trust that the data presented in this chapter support this contention.

APPENDIXES TO CHAPTER 8

A. Murray's Problems in Biology Test

Questions 1–17 are concerned with some problems in biology. Prior knowledge of these problems is NOT necessary to answer them. Read them carefully and *think*.

Questions 1–6

Miss O wished to study the effect of light on oat growth. Below are the results she obtained from an experiment. The dotted line (.....) represents plants grown in the light; the solid line (_____) represents plants grown in the dark.

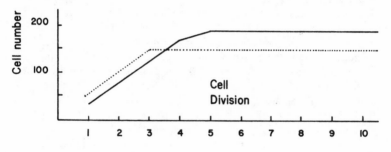

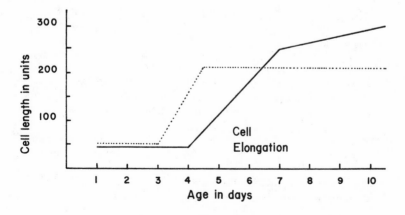

1. Cell division occurs by 1 cell giving rise to 2; 2 cells giving rise to 4; etc. What is the *minimum* number of cell divisions that can occur in plants grown in the dark between days 1 and 2? A. 1. B. 2. C. 3. D. 4. E. 5.

2. What assumption(s) must be made in order to calculate the above? A. The time for 1 cell division is constant. B. Each original cell must have divided. C. Each product of cell division must be the same size. D. A and B. E. None of the above.

3. On the basis of the data you can conclude: A. Cell division occurs at a constant rate until it stops. B. Cell division occurs at varying rate. C. Cell division results in an increase in cell length. D. Cell division must have terminated before cell elongation can occur. E. None of the above.

4. Under what conditions would you expect to find both cell division and cell elongation occurring? A. Light, under 3 days age. B. Light, over 6 days age. C. Dark, under 3 days age. D. Dark, over 6 days age. E. Never.

5. What generalizations can be made about the effect of light conditions on plant growth? A. Light accelerates cell division, but does not affect cell elongation. B. Light inhibits cell division, but does not affect cell elongation. C. Light accelerates cell elongation, but does not affect cell division. D. Light inhibits cell elongation, but does not affect cell division. E. Light has no effect on either cell division or cell elongation.

6. 1. 3-day plant—light   3. 7-day plant—light
   2. 3-day plant—dark   4. 7-day plant—dark
   Order the above with respect to total stem length (shortest to tallest).
   A. 1-2-3-4. B. 1-3-2-4. C. 2-1-3-4. D. 2-1-4-3. E. None of the above.

Questions 7–11

Potato plants were sprayed with various concentrations of two substances (auxins). These auxins influenced plant growth as is shown below. Plus (+) represents a speeding up of growth; minus (−) represents a slowing of growth; 0 represents normal growth.

Experimental conditions	Root growth	Stem growth
1. water	0	0
2. low concentration of *auxin A* + water	+	0
3. low concentration of *auxin B* + water	0	0

4. medium concentration of *auxin A* + water	0	+
5. medium concentration of *auxin B* + water	0	–
6. high concentration of *auxin A* + water	–	+
7. high concentration of *auxin B* + water	0	–

Choose from the following:

A. *True* for *auxin A* but *not* for *auxin B*.
B. *True* for *auxin B* but *not* for *auxin A*.
C. *True* for *both auxin A and B*.
D. *False* for *both auxin A and B*.
E. Data insufficient to determine.

Statements:

7. At any concentration the effect of the auxin is dependent of the organ (root or stem).
8. The effect of an auxin on growth stimulation or inhibition is dependent on the kind of plant studied.
9. A low concentration of auxin does NOT inhibit potato growth.
10. It is possible to conclude that the effect of an auxin on potato plant growth is directly proportional to the concentration of that auxin.
11. It is possible to grow taller potato plants by spraying plants with auxin.

Questions 12–17

The following information may be helpful in answering the questions below: (1) enzymes "speed up" chemical reactions that are otherwise slow; (2) enzyme activity refers to the degree to which the reaction is "speeded up"; (3) an enzyme in action—$2H_2O_2 \xrightarrow{\text{enzyme}} 2H_2O + O_2$. The 7 mixtures shown below were incubated for 15 minutes. A sample of each mixture was then subjected to tests for compounds A, B, and C. Positive and negative results are indicated below.

Incubation mixture	A Test	B Test	C Test
1. unknown + water	–	+	–
2. enzyme + water	–	–	+
3. unknown + enzyme + water	+	+	+
4. unknown + enzyme + 0.2% base	+	–	+
5. unknown + enzyme + 0.2% acid	–	+	+
6. unknown + water (both boiled)	+	+	–
7. unknown + enzyme + water (all boiled)	+	+	+

12. Which of the above compounds is the enzyme? A. (A).
B. (B).   C. (C).   D. Two of the above.   E. None of the above.
13. The data indicates that the enzyme acts in the conversion of compound A. A to B.   B. A to C.   C. B to C.   D. B to A.   E. None of the
above.
14. If   you   were   to   do   the   following   experiment-
—unknown + water + 0.2% acid (all boiled)—you would expect the results to resemble experiment A. 1.   B. 3.   C. 4.   D. 6.   E. None of
the above.
15. Which experiment(s) demonstrate(s) that enzyme activity can be
destroyed? A. 3.   B. 4.   C. 5.   D. 7.   E. None of the above.
16. Order the rate of enzyme activity for experiments 3, 4, and 5 (slow-
est to fastest). A. 3-4-5.   B. 3-5-4.   C. 4-3-5.   D. 4-5-3.   E. None of
the above.
17. Order the rate of enzyme activity for experiments 1, 3, and 7 (slow-
est to fastest). A. 1-3-7.   B. 1-7-3.   C. 3-1-7.   D. 3-7-1.   E. None of
the above.

B. Problems in Botany Test

The following questions are concerned with some problems in
botany. Prior knowledge of these problems is NOT necessary to answer them. Read them carefully and *think*.

Below are the results of a study on oat growth. The dotted line (.....)
represents plants grown in the light; the solid line (_____) represents
plants grown in the dark.

1. The greatest difference in cell length between plants grown in the
   light and those grown in the dark is observed on what day?
   A. 2.   B. 3.   C. 4.   D. 5.   E. 6.

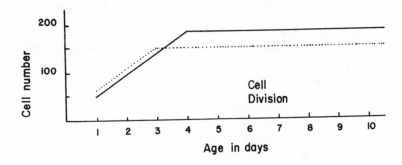

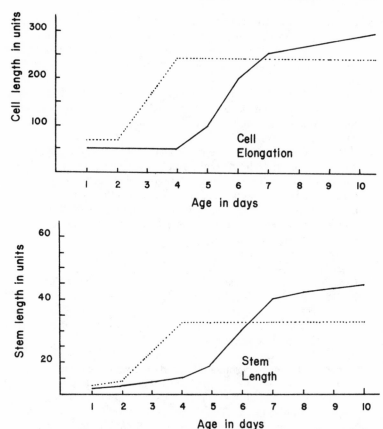

2. Under what conditions do you find a doubling of cell length? A. Between days 2–3 in light. B. Between days 3–4 in light. C. Between days 4–5 in dark. D. Between days 5–6 in dark. E. Between days 6–7 in dark.

3. Cell division occurs by 1 cell giving rise to 2; 2 cells giving rise to 4; etc. What is the *minimum* number of cell divisions that can occur in plants grown in the dark between days 1 and 2? A. 1. B. 2. C. 3. D. 4. E. 5.

4. What assumption(s) must be made in order to calculate the above? A. The time for 1 cell division is constant. B. Each original cell must have divided. C. Each product of cell division must be the same size. D. Two of the above. E. None of the above.

5. On the basis of the data you can conclude that A. cell division occurs at a constant rate until it stops. B. cell division occurs at a varying rate. C. cell division results in an increase in cell length. D. cell division can *not* occur while cell elongation is occurring. E. none of the above.

6. Under what conditions might you expect to find both cell division and cell elongation occurring? A. Light, under 3 days age. B. Light, over 6 days age. C. Dark, under 3 days age. D. Dark, over 6 days age. E. Never.

7. What generalizations can be made about the effect of light conditions on stem growth? A. Light accelerates cell division, but does *not* accelerate cell elongation. B. Light delays cell division, but does *not* delay cell elongation. C. Light accelerates cell elongation, but does *not* accelerate cell division. D. Light delays cell elongation, but does *not* delay cell division. E. Light has no affect on either cell division or cell elongation.

8. 1. 3-day plant—light   3. 7-day plant—light
   2. 3-day plant—dark   4. 7-day plant—dark
   Order the above with respect to stem length (shortest to tallest).
   A. 1-2-3-4.   B. 1-3-2-4.   C. 2-1-3-4.   D. 2-1-4-3.   E. None of these.

9. How many times larger are the units of stem measurement than the units of cell measurement?
   A. 1.   B. 10.   C. 100.   D. 1,000.   E. 10,000.

10. Which of the following generalizations is *true* on the basis of the data? A. Most of the cells in the oat stem normally divide more than once. B. Most of the growth in stem length occurs as a direct result of cell division. C. The length of the stem is directly proportional to the number of cells present. D. Stem length is a product of cell number times cell length. E. None of the above.

Potato plants were sprayed with various concentrations of two substances (auxins). These auxins influenced plant growth as is shown below. Plus (+) represents a speeding up of growth; minus (−) represents a slowing of growth; 0 represents normal growth.

Experimental conditions	Root growth	Stem growth
1. water	0	0
2. low concentration of *auxin A* + water	+	0
3. low concentration of *auxin B* + water	0	0

4. medium concentration of *auxin A* + water   0   +
5. medium concentration of *auxin B* + water   0   −
6. high concentration of *auxin A* + water   −   +
7. high concentration of *auxin B* + water   0   −

Choose from the following:

A. *True* for *auxin A* but *not* for *auxin B*.
B. *True* for *auxin B* but *not* for *auxin A*.
C. *True* for both *auxin A* and *B*.
D. *False* for *both auxin A* and *B*.
E. Data insufficient to determine.

Statements:

11. At all concentrations the effect of the auxin is dependent on the organ (root or stem).
12. The effect of an auxin on growth stimulation or inhibition is dependent on the kind of plant studied.
13. A low concentration of auxin does NOT inhibit potato growth.
14. It is possible to conclude that the effect of an auxin on potato plant growth is directly proportional to the concentration of that auxin.
15. It is possible to grow taller potato plants by spraying plants with auxin.

C. Advanced Organizer and "Blank" Organizer from Kuhn's Homeostasis Study
Advanced Organizer–Homeostasis (Dynamic Equilibrium)

The ability to maintain relatively stabilized internal conditions, even when under stress, is called homeostatic regulation, or more simply homeostasis. The stabilized or steady state conditions that are maintained through homeostatic regulation are key factors in the ability of living organisms to survive.

A fundamental trait of homeostatic regulation is that it is self-regulating, that is, it possesses the ability to make corrections for deviations from normal conditions. Sometimes the self-regulatory mechanisms which accomplish homeostasis are obvious. If the dog becomes too warm, it will probably awaken and move to a more comfortable spot in the shade. This movement is obviously a form of regulation, involving activity of the brain.

Homeostatic regulation is present on all levels of life from the molecular to the community levels. The regulatory mechanism functions in much the same manner at all the levels with the degrees of complexity being different.

Picture in your mind the image of a ten-year-old boy attempting to walk along the top of a fence. This may help you understand homeostasis better. As the boy slowly moves along the fence, his brain (this regulator which receives messages and sends them is known as a *modulator*) is continually receiving messages (feedback) from his eyes, ears, etc. The information sent through this system keeps the body informed of the position of his body in relation to the fence. Any tilting or swaying by the boy results in feedback information that the brain analyzes in order to issue messages to the parts of the body that carry out activities (the muscle or glands). After continued practice, he may eventually become quite skillful and be able to walk the entire fence with very little swaying; then it can be said that he has achieved a homeostatic relationship. Therefore, the concept of homeostasis is based on the ability of an organism for self-regulation by making corrections for deviations from normal conditions.

The principle of dynamic equilibrium (balance) can be illustrated by a single analogy. If one compares the organism and the cells that compose it to the flow tank in Figure 1, certain similarities to the dynamic balance of the living system may be noted in the workings of the tanks.

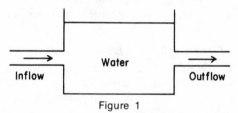

Figure 1

If the amount of water entering the tank is just equal to the amount of water leaving it, the water level will not change and such a system is said to be actively balanced. The circus juggler who maintains an active balance as he juggles several objects keeps them in dynamic equilibrium. Our body processes are regulated so that many such dynamic equilibria are maintained.

Remember that the flow tank is an dynamic equilibrium only when the inflow is equal to the outflow. To arrange a system in dynamic equilibrium, you must regulate either the inflow or the outflow, or both.

Figure 2 illustrates a simple mechanical model that could be used to regulate the outflow. The outflow would increase when the amount of water entering is increased. If this regulation device operated fast and effectively enough, it would keep the level of water in the tank nearly constant.

In the living organism both the inflow and outflow of the blood glucose (sugar) must vary a great deal from time to time depending on the activity of the body cells, the chemical composition of the food, and many other factors.

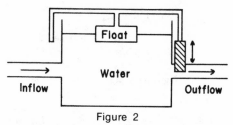

Figure 2

The regulating devices that maintain constant concentration in the blood are very complicated. The regulation of a body function such as glucose regulation is much more complicated than the single flow system illustrated by the diagram. Yet, like the flow system, all the mechanisms that regulate the glucose concentration are likely to depend on the glucose concentration itself.

The simplest type of homeostatic regulation is through thermostat-like action. A thermostat-like regulator is one which causes any variation from an acceptable range to trigger a corrective measure and bring the activity back into the range. A physical model for the thermostat-like regulator may be found in the heat-controlling device in our homes. The action of the home thermostat causes the completing or breaking of an electrical circuit. When the circuit is completed, the furnace goes on and the temperature rises. When the circuit is broken, the furnace turns off and the temperature falls. Can you think of an activity in the human body that functions in a somewhat similar manner?

The second type of homeostatic regulation is through the use of feedback action. A feedback regulator is one in which the accumulation of an end product of the system inhibits (slows) the initial reaction; e.g.

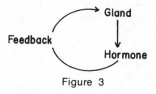

Figure 3

the accumulation of a hormone in the blood would eventually slow up its production by affecting the glands that produce it.

In more complex systems, it is also possible that feedback action may have a stimulating effect (positive effect) e.g. an increase in hormone A production by Gland I may influence Gland II to produce more of hormone B.

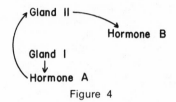

Figure 4

"Blank" Organizer–Homeostasis (Dynamic Equilibrium)

To seek the origin of an idea is a fascinating pastime. It is also terribly imprecise. Perhaps that is one of the reasons why an idea cannot be patented; the use of it can, but not the idea itself.

A tireless and imaginative medical historian could no doubt go back into Egyptian literature, or that of the Middle East, and find the seed that ultimately flowered into the idea of homeostasis. It would be easier to attribute it to Hippocrates. Hippocrates believed that disease is cured by natural powers. This concept embraces the idea that there are, within the living organism, mechanisms (natural powers) which tend to right things when they have gone astray, to return the state of health to normal, even to oppose the change toward abnormality as soon as the change begins.

The great American physiologist Walter B. Cannon, who is generally credited with first using the term homeostasis in this connotation, paid homage to the German physiologist Pfluger and the Belgian physiologist Fredericq, as well as to Hippocrates for the generation of the concept. In 1877, Pfluger stated, "The cause of every need of a living being is also the cause of the satisfaction of the need." Fredericq, in 1885, declared, "The living being is an agency of such sort that each disturbing influence induces by itself the calling forth of compensatory activity to neutralize or repair the disturbance. The higher in the scale of living beings, the more perfect and the more complicated do these regulatory agencies become. They tend to free the organism completely from the unfavorable influences and changes occurring in the environment." Cannon also quotes the French physiologist Charles Richet, who said: "The living being is stable. It must be so in order not to be destroyed, dissolved, or disintegrated by the colossal forces, often adverse, which surround it. By an apparent contradiction it maintains its stability only if it is excitable and capable of modifying itself according to external stimuli and adjusting its response to the stimulation. In a sense it is stable because it is modifiable—the slight instability is the necessary condition for the true stability of the organism."

Oddly enough, it is only in the French translation of his book *The Wisdom of the Body* that Cannon pays tribute to the renowned French scientist Claude Bernard. There Cannon states: "The central idea of this book, 'the stability of the inner medium of the organism in higher vertebrates,' is directly inspired by the precise views and deep understanding of the eminent French physiologist Claude Bernard. This book can even be considered a tribute to his memory." In the French edition, Cannon makes it clear that Bernard deserves priority for emphasizing the role of the inner environment in the establishment and maintenance of steady states in the body.

Claude Bernard was born in 1813. Interestingly, he studied French, Latin, history, and elementary mathematics. In this preparatory period, which would correspond to our high school, he had no contact with science. At that point, Bernard had little idea what he wanted to do. To make a living he took a job in a pharmacy. The experience may have helped his technical skills, but it did nothing to further his scientific development. In fact, he fancied himself an author—a playwright—and enjoyed limited success in this endeavor. Flushed with success in a small town, he went to Paris to win fame and fortune, but there the best thing he won was the sound advice to abandon any thought of making a career in the theater.

Claude Bernard gave up the theater and began the study of medicine, but before he could qualify for the practice of medicine, he came under the influence of the leading French physiologist François Magendie. This influence was so compelling that the future course of the young Claude Bernard was set. In 1843, he won his degree and then quickly made his name in physiology.

Bernard's contributions to physiology are well known. It is not germane to discuss his findings here. We are interested in the birth of the concept of homeostasis, and for that purpose we must turn to the major writings of Claude Bernard. In those happy days, one could write at length, one could insert his own personality into those writings, one could create literature rather than a mere tabulation of data and a laconic statement of conclusions. And he did. If any of you are even remotely considering a career in science, or even if you have a hunger to experience a creative mind at work, read the *Introduction to the Study of Experimental Medicine* by Claude Bernard. Read it, study it, savor it. Remarkably enough, it was even appreciated in his own day. It was published in 1865.

There is enough meat in the *Introduction to the Study of Experimental Medicine* to take us far afield. It would be delightful to wander, but our purpose is to trace the origins of the concept of homeostasis and in the *Introduction* we find it. Herein Bernard uses the expression *milieu vital,* living environment, which, of course, flows logically into the germ cell we are seeking, namely the *milieu interieur,* internal environment. It is this internal environment that concerns us for as Claude Bernard states so significantly, "The constancy of the internal environment is the condition of the living thing."

The work of Claude Bernard fills volumes, and additional volumes have been written about him, his research, his contributions, his philosophy. But if he did no more than to plant the seed that flowered into the concept of homeostasis his place would be secure.

Walter B. Cannon was of a different age. He was born in 1871, just 7 years before Bernard died. He was an American, educated both in the United States and abroad. He obtained the M.D and Sc.D. degrees and was the recipient of many honorary degrees. He was the long-time Professor of Physiology at the Harvard Medical School. He was one of the giants of his time, brilliantly responsible for the great strides that physiology experienced at the beginning of this century. Walter Cannon died in 1945.

In 1929, Cannon published an article entitled "Organization for Physiological Homeostasis." In other words, he suddenly was struck by the remarkable constancy of the internal environment. He enjoyed this revelation as though Bernard had never existed!

But, as has already been noted, at long last he paid homage to his predecessor, at least in the French edition of his brilliant monograph *The Wisdom of the Body.* It was the idea of the constancy of the internal environment that he adopted, developed, and then neatly packaged under the label of homeostasis.

Bibliography

Alpert, D., and D. L. Bitzer. 1970. "Advances in Computer-Based Education."
Science, 167(3925), 1582–1590.
American Association for the Advancement of Science, Commission on Science
Education. 1968. *Science: A Process Approach.* Washington: American Asso-
ciation for the Advancement of Science.
Anderson, John R., Gordon H. Bower. 1973. *Human Associative Memory.*
Washington: Winston.
Anderson, Ronald D. 1965. "Children's Ability to Formulate Mental Models to
Explain Natural Phenomena." *Journal of Research in Science Teaching, 3,*
326–332.
Ashby, William R. 1960. *Design for a Brain.* 2d ed. New York: Wiley.
Atkin, J. Myron. 1967. "Research Styles in Science Education." *Journal of Re-
search in Science Teaching,* 5:338–345.
———. 1968. "Behavioral Objectives in Curriculum Design: A Cautionary Note."
The Science Teacher, 35(5), 27–30.
Ausubel, David P. 1960. "The Use of Advance Organizers in the Learning and
Retention of Meaningful Verbal Material." *Journal of Educational Psychology,
51,* 267–272.
———. 1963. *The Psychology of Meaningful Verbal Learning.* New York: Grune
and Stratton.
———. 1965. "An Evaluation of the 'Conceptual Schemes' Approach to Science
Curriculum Development." *Journal of Research in Science Teaching, 3,*
255–264.
———. 1966. "Evaluation of the BSCS Approach to High School Biology." *American Biology Teacher, 28,* 176–186.
———. 1968. *Educational Psychology: A Cognitive View.* New York: Holt, Rinehart and Winston.
———. 1976. "The Facilitation of Meaningful Verbal Learning in the Classroom."
Washington: Paper presented at the American Psychological Association.
———. and Floyd G. Robinson. 1969. *School Learning: An Introduction to Educational Psychology.* New York: Holt, Rinehart and Winston.
Bacon, Sir Francis. 1952. *Advancement of Learning, Novum Organum, and The
New Atlantis.* Chicago, London, Toronto: Encyclopaedia Britannica.
Barbizet, Jacques. 1970. *Human Memory and Its Pathology.* San Francisco:
W. H. Freeman.
Beauchamp, George A. 1961, 1968. *Curriculum Theory.* Wilmette, Ill.: Kagy
Press.

Bethune, Paul. 1966. "The Nova Plan for Individualized Learning." *The Science Teacher*, 33(8), 55–57.

Bjerstedt, Åka. 1972. *Educational Technology: Instructional Programming and Didakometry*. New York: Wiley-Interscience.

Block, James H., ed. 1971. *Mastery Learning: Theory and Practice*. With selected papers by Peter W. Airasiah, Benjamin Bloom, and John Carroll. New York: Holt, Rinehart and Winston.

Bloom, Benjamin S. 1968. "Learning for Mastery." *UCLA Evaluation Comment*, 1(2), 1.

——, ed. 1956. *Taxonomy of Educational Objectives—The Classification of Educational Goals, Handbook 1: Cognitive Domain*. New York: David McKay.

——. 1976. *Human Characteristics and School Learning*. New York: McGraw-Hill.

Bowen, Barbara L. 1972. "A Proposed Theoretical Model Using the Work of Thomas Kuhn, David Ausubel and Mauritz Johnson as a Basis for Curriculum and Instruction Decisions in Science Education." Ph.D. thesis, Cornell University.

Brandwein, Paul F. 1962. "Elements in a Strategy for Teaching Science in the Elementary School." In Joseph J. Schwab and Paul F. Brandwein, *The Teaching of Science*. Cambridge: Harvard University Press.

——. 1966. *Concepts in Science*. New York: Harcourt, Brace and World.

Bremer, Ann, and John Bremer. 1972. *Open Education: A Beginning*. New York: Holt, Rinehart and Winston.

Breukelman, John, Ted F. Andrews, and Joseph D. Novak. 1959. "A Study of Problems Involved in Teaching Large Classes in College General Biology." *Transactions of the Kansas Academy of Science*, 62(4), 245–251.

Bridgeman, P. W. 1959. *The Way Things Are*. Cambridge: Harvard University Press.

Brownell, William A. 1942. "Problem Solving." In the National Society for the Study of Education Forty-first Yearbook, pt. 2, *The Psychology of Learning*. Chicago: University of Chicago Press. Pp. 415–443.

Bruner, Jerome S. 1960. *The Process of Education*. New York: Vintage Books, Random House.

——. 1966. *Toward a Theory of Instruction*. Cambridge: Harvard University Press.

——, Jacqueline Goodnow, and George Austin. 1956. *A Study of Thinking*. New York: Wiley.

Brush, Stephen G. 1974. "Should the History of Science Be Rated X?" *Science*, 183(4130), 1164–1172.

Burks, Barbara S., Dortha W. Jensen, and Lewis M. Terman. 1930. The Promise of Youth. Genetic Studies of Genius, Vol. 3. Stanford: Stanford University Press.

Busch, Karen. 1973. "Gaming Techniques for Concept Learning: A Case Study." M.S. thesis, Cornell University.

Carroll, John B. 1963. "A Model of School Learning." *Teachers College Record*, 64, 723–733.

—— and Roy O. Freedle, eds. 1972. *Language Comprehension and the Acquisition of Knowledge*. Washington: Winston.

Castaldi, Peter. 1975. "A Summary of Cognitive Educational Research Done in Introductory Science Courses at Cornell University, and a Study of the Effects of Tutoring Made and Learner's Conceptual Abilities on Learning

Efficiency in Introductory College Physics." Ph.D. thesis, Cornell University.

Chiappetta, Eugene L. 1976. "A Review of Piagetian Studies Relevant to Science Instruction at the Secondary and College Level." *Science Education*, 60(2), 253–261.

Chomsky, Noam. 1972. *Language and Mind*. New York: Harcourt, Brace and Jovanovich.

Collingwood, Robin G. 1940. *An Essay on Metaphysics*. Oxford: Oxford University Press.

Commoner, Barry. 1971. *The Closing Circle: Nature, Man, and Technology*. London, Toronto, New York: Bantam Books.

Conant, James B. 1947. *On Understanding Science*. New Haven: Yale University Press.

Cox, Catherine M., et al. 1926. *The Early Mental Traits of Three Hundred Geniuses*. Genetic Studies of Genius, Vol. 2. Stanford: Stanford University Press.

Creager, Joan G., and Darrel L. Murray. 1972. *The Use of Modules in College Biology Teaching*. Washington: Commission on Undergraduate Education in the Biological Sciences.

Cunningham, Harry A. 1946. "Lecture-Demonstration vs. Individual Laboratory Methods in Science Teaching." *Science Education*, 30, 70–82.

Darwin, Francis. 1897. *The Life and Letters of Charles Darwin*. New York: Appleton.

Dewey, John. 1910. *How We Think*. Boston: Heath.

Duetsche, Jean M. 1937. *The Development of Children's Concepts of Causal Relations*. Minnesota: University of Minnesota Press.

Dunning, Gordon M. 1954. "Evaluation of Critical Thinking." *Science Education*, 38, 191–211.

Ebbinghaus, Hermann. 1913. *Memory: A Contribution to Experimental Psychology*. Trans. Henry A. Ruger. New York: Teachers College Press.

Ehrlich, Paul R. 1968. *The Population Bomb*. New York: Ballantine.

Elkana, Yehuda. 1970. "Science, Philosophy of Science and Science Teaching." *Educational Philosophy and Theory*, 2, 15–35.

———. 1971. "The Problem of Knowledge." *Studium Generale*, 24, 1426–1439. Berlin, Heidelberg: Springer-Verlag.

———. 1972. *The Theory and Practice of Cross-Cultural Contacts in Science: Queries and Presuppositions*. The Hebrew University of Jerusalem, Van Leer Jerusalem Foundation.

Ellson, Douglas G. 1976. "Tutoring." In Nathaniel L. Gage, *The Psychology of Teaching Methods*. Chicago: University of Chicago Press.

Estes, William K. 1950. "Toward a Statistical Theory of Learning." *Psychological Review*, 57, 94–107.

Farnham-Diggory, Sylvia. 1972. *Cognitive Processes in Education: A Psychological Preparation for Teaching and Curriculum Development*. New York: Harper and Row.

Festinger, Leon. 1957. *A Theory of Cognitive Dissonance*. New York: Harper and Row.

Flanders, Ned A. 1960. *Interaction Analysis in the Classroom: A Manual for Observers*. First edition, Minneapolis: University of Minnesota.

Flavell, John H. 1963. *The Developmental Psychology of Jean Piaget*. Princeton: Van Nostrand.

Fleishman, E. A. 1969. "Motor Abilities." In R. L. Ebel, ed., *Encyclopedia of Educational Research*. New York: Macmillan. Pp. 888–895.

Fromm, Erich. 1956. *The Art of Loving*. New York: A Bantam Book, Harper and Row.

Gage, Nathaniel L. 1963. *Handbook of Research on Teaching*. Chicago: Rand McNally.

Gagné, Robert M. 1965, 1970, 1977. *The Conditions of Learning*. New York: Holt, Rinehart, and Winston.

Galton, Francis. 1892. *Hereditary Genius*. 2d. ed. London: Macmillan.

Gartner, Alan, Colin Greer, and Frank Riessman. 1974. *The New Assault on Equality: I.Q. and Social Stratification*. New York: Perennial Library, Harper and Row.

Gerard, Ralph W., ed. 1958. "Concepts of Biology." *Behavioral Science*, 3(2), 89–215.

Getzels, Jacob W., and Philip W. Jackson. 1962. *Creativity and Intelligence: Explorations with Gifted Students*. New York: Wiley.

Ghiselin, Brewster, ed. 1952. *The Creative Process*. Berkeley: University of California Press.

Ginsberg, Herbert and Sylvia Opper. 1969. *Piaget's Theory of Intellectual Development: An Introduction*. Englewood Cliffs, N.J.: Prentice-Hall.

Glass, Bentley. 1965. "Theory into Action—A Critique." *Science Teaching*, 32(5), 29–30, 82–83.

Glass, Gene V. 1972. "The Wisdom of Scientific Inquiry on Education." *Journal of Research in Science Teaching*, 9(1):3–18.

Gowin, D. Bob. 1970. "The Structure of Knowledge." *Educational Theory*, 20, No. 4.

——. 1972. "Is Educational Research Distinctive?" In *Philosophical Redirection of Educational Research*, ed. L. G. Thomas and H. G. Richey. Chicago: University of Chicago Press. Chap. 1.

——. 1976. "The Domain of Education." Unpublished paper, Cornell University.

Gubrud, Allan. 1970. "The Effect of an Advance Organizer and Concrete Experience on Learning of the Concept of Vectors in Junior and Senior High School." Ph.D. thesis, Cornell University.

—— and Joseph D. Novak. 1973. "Learning Achievement and the Efficiency of Learning the Concept of Vector Addition at Three Different Grade Levels." *Science Education*, 57(2), 179–191.

Guilford, Jay Paul. 1957. "A Revised Structure of Intellect." *Reports from the Psychology Laboratory*. Los Angeles: University of Southern California, 19, 6–7, 9.

——. 1959. "Three Faces of Intellect." *American Psychologist*, 14, 469–479.

——. 1967. *The Nature of Human Intelligence*. New York: McGraw-Hill.

—— and Paul R. Christensen. 1973. "The One-Way Relation between Creative Potential and I.Q." *Journal of Creative Behavior*, 7(4), 247–252.

—— et al. 1952. "A Factor-Analytic Study of Creative Thinking II: Administration of Tests and Analysis of Results." *Reports from the Psychology Laboratory*, 8 Los Angeles: University of Southern California.

—— et al. 1954. "A Factor-Analytic Study across the Domains of Reasoning, Creativity, and Evaluation I: Hypotheses and Description of Tests." *Reports from the Psychology Laboratory*, 11 Los Angeles: University of Southern California.

Hagerman, Howard. 1966. "An Analysis of Learning and Retention in College Students and the Common Goldfish (*Carassius auratus*, Lin)." Ph.D. thesis, Purdue University.

Haggerty, Patrick. 1973. "Research and Development, Educational Productivity and the American Economy." *Educational Researcher*, 2(9), 6.

Hamilton, Sir William. 1853. *Discussions on Philosophy*. 2d ed. London: Longmans, Brown, Green.

Harlow, Harry F. 1958. "The Development of Affectional Responses in Infant Monkeys." *Proceedings of the American Philosophical Society*, 102, 501–509.

Harmon, Lindsey R. 1961. "High School Backgrounds of Science Doctorates." *Science*, 133(3454), 679.

——. 1963. "The Development of a Criterion of Scientific Competence." In Calvin W. Taylor and Frank Barron, eds., *Scientific Creativity: Its Recognition and Development*. New York: Wiley. Pp. 44–52.

Harris, Thomas A. 1967. *I'm OK—You're OK*. Evanston, Ill.: Harper and Row.

Hebb, Donald O. 1949. *The Organization of Behavior*. New York: Wiley.

Hedges, William D. 1966. *Testing and Evaluation for the Sciences in the Secondary School*. Belmont, Calif.: Wadsworth.

Herrick, Virgil E., and Ralph W. Tyler. 1950. "Toward Improved Curriculum Theory." *Supplementary Educational Monograph No. 71*. Chicago: University of Chicago Press.

Herrigel, Eugen. 1973. *Zen in the Art of Archery*, New York: Vintage Books.

Hibbard, K. Michael. 1971. "An Approach to the Development of Instruction in Science at the First Grade Level: The Concept of a Particulate Model for Matter." Ph.D. thesis, Cornell University.

—— and Joseph D. Novak. 1975. "Audio-Tutorial Elementary School Science Instruction as a Method for Study of Children's Concept Learning: Particulate Nature of Matter." *Science Education*, 59(4), 559–570.

Hibbard, Marybeth K. 1971. "An Approach to the Evaluation of Science Concepts Held by Third Graders from Ithaca and Lansing Public Schools." M.S. thesis, Cornell University.

Hilgard, Ernest R., and Gordon H. Bower. 1975. *Theories of Learning*. 4th ed. Englewood Cliffs, N.J.: Prentice-Hall.

Hoffman, Banesh. 1962. *The Tyranny of Testing*. New York: Crowell-Collier.

—— with Helen Dukas. 1972. *Albert Einstein: Creator and Rebel*. New York: Viking.

Holt, John. 1964, 1968. *How Children Fail*. New York, Toronto, London: Pitman.

——. 1967. *How Children Learn*. New York: Pitman.

Hunt, Earl B. 1962. *Concept Learning*. New York: Wiley.

Illich, Ivan. 1970. *Deschooling Society*. New York, Evanston, San Francisco, London: Harrow Books, Harper & Row.

Inbody, Donald. 1963. "Children's Understanding of Natural Phenomena." *Science Education*, 47(3), 271, 274–277.

Inhelder, Barbel, and Jean Piaget. 1958. *The Growth of Logical Thinking from Childhood to Adolescence*. New York: Basic Books.

—— and Jean Piaget. 1964. *The Early Growth of Logic in the Child*. New York: Norton.

Jensen, Arthur R. 1969. "How Much Can We Boost IQ and Scholastic Achievement?" *Harvard Educational Review*, 39, 1–123.

Jerkins, Kenneth F. 1964. "An Exploratory Study of Learning and Retention in General Science Classes Utilizing the MPATI Telecast Course Investigating the World of Science." Ph.D. thesis, Purdue University.

—— and Joseph D. Novak. 1971. "The Study of Concept Improvement of Junior High School Students Viewing MPATI Telecasts with and without Supplementary Aids." *Science Education*, 55(1), 21–30.

Johnson, Mauritz, Jr. 1967. "Defintions and Models in Curriculum Theory." *Educational Theory*, 17(2), 127–140.

Jones, M. G., and H. B. English. 1926. "Notational vs. Rote Memory." *American Journal of Psychology*, 37, 602–603.

Karplus, Elizabeth F., and Robert Karplus. 1970. "Intellectual Development beyond Elementary School." *School Science and Mathematics*, 70(5), 398–406.

Karplus, Robert, and Herbert D. Thier. 1968. *A New Look at Elementary School Science*. Chicago: Rand McNally.

Kavanagh, James F., and Ignatius Mattingly. 1972. *Language by Ear and Eye: The Relationship between Speech and Reading*. Cambridge: MIT Press.

Keddie, Nell, ed. 1973. *The Myth of Cultural Deprivation*. Baltimore: Penguin Books.

Keller, F. S. 1968. "Goodbye Teacher . . ." *Journal of Applied Behavioral Analysis*, 1, 79–89.

Kendall, Maurice. 1955. *Rank Correlation Method*. London: Charles Griffin.

King, Arthur R., and John A. Brownell, Jr. 1966. *The Curriculum and the Discipline of Knowledge*. New York: Wiley.

King, W. H. 1965. "The Development of Scientific Concepts in Children." In Ira F. Gordon, ed., *Human Development (Readings in Research)*. Chicago: Scott, Foresman.

Klausmeier, Herbert J., and Chester W. Harris. 1966. *Analysis of Concept Learning*. New York: Academic Press.

——, Elizabeth S. Ghatala, and Dorothy A. Frayer. 1974. *Conceptual Learning and Development: A Cognitive View*. New York: Academic Press.

Kozol, Jonathan. 1967. *Death at an Early Age*. Boston: Houghton Mifflin.

——. 1972. *Free Schools*. Boston: Houghton Mifflin.

Krathwohl, David R., Benjamin S. Bloom, and Bertram B. Masia. 1956. *Taxonomy of Educational Objectives—The Classification of Educational Goals, Handbook II: Affective Domain*. New York: David McKay.

Kuhn, David J. 1967. "A Study of Varying Modes of Topical Presentation in Elementary College Biology to Determine the Effect of Advance Organizers in Knowledge." Ph.D. thesis, Purdue University.

—— and Joseph D. Novak. 1971. "A Study of Cognitive Subsumption in the Life Sciences." *Science Education*, 55(3):309–320.

Kuhn, Thomas S. 1962, 1970. *The Structure of Scientific Revolutions*. International Encyclopedia of Unified Sciences, 2d ed. enlarged Vols. 1 and 2: Foundations of the Unity of Science, Vol. 2, No. 2. Chicago: University of Chicago Press.

Lashley, Karl S. 1963. *Brain Mechanisms and Intelligence: A Quantitative Study of Injuries to the Brain*. New York: Dover.

Lawson, Anton E., Floyd H. Nordlund, and Alfred DeVito. 1974. "Piagetian Formal Operational Tasks: A Crossover Study of Learning Effect and Reliability." *Science Education*, 58(4): 569–575.

Lengel, Robert A., and Robert R. Buell. 1972. "Exclusion of Irrelevant Factors (The Pendulum Problem)." *Science Education,* 56(1), 65–70.

Lovell, Kenneth, and E. Ogilvie. 1960. "A Study of the Conservation of Substance in the Junior School Child." *British Journal of Educational Psychology, 30,* 109–118.

Lyon, D. O. 1914. "The Relation of Length of Material to Time Taken for Learning and Optimum Distribution of Time." *Journal of Educational Psychology,* 5, 1–9, 85–91, 155–163.

McClelland, J. A. G. 1970. "An Approach to the Development and Assessment of Instruction in Science at Second Grade Level: The Concept of Energy." Ph.D. thesis, Cornell University.

McNeil, John D., and Evan R. Keislar. 1962. "An Experiment in Validating Objectives for Curriculum in Elementary School Science." *Science Education,* 46, 153.

Mager, Robert F. 1962. *Preparing Objectives for Programmed Instruction.* San Francisco: Fearon.

Mayeroff, Milton. 1971. *On Caring.* New York: Perennial Library, Harper & Row.

Meadows, Donella H., Dennis L. Meadows, Jorgan Randers, and William W. Behrens, III. 1972. *The Limits to Growth.* A Report for the Club of Rome's Project on the Predicament of Mankind. New York: Universe Books.

Mednick, Martha T., and Frank M. Andrews. 1967. "Creative Thinking and Level of Intelligence." *Journal of Creative Behavior,* 1(4), 428–431.

Melton, Arthur W., and Edwin Martin, eds. 1972. *Coding in Human Memory.* Washington: Winston.

Miller, George A. 1956. "The Magical Number Seven, Plus or Minus Two: Some Limits on Our Capacity for Processing Information." *Psychological Review,* 63, 81–97.

—— and F. C. Frick. 1949. "Statistical Behavior and Sequence of Responses." *Psychological Review,* 56, 311–324.

Murray, Darrel L. 1963. "The Testing of a Model for the Interpretation of Concept Formation Using College Biology Students." Ph.D. thesis, Purdue University.

Naegele, C. J. 1974. "An Evaluation of Student Attitudes, Achievement, and Learning Efficiency in Various Modes of an Individualized, Self-Paced Learning Program in Introductory College Physics." Ph.D. thesis, Cornell University.

National Science Teachers Association. 1964. *Theory into Action.* Washington: NSTA.

——. 1971. *Evolving Patterns for School Science Facilities* (filmstrip). Washington: NSTA.

Nedelsky, Leo. 1965. *Science Teaching and Testing.* New York: Harcourt, Brace and World.

Neurath, Otto, Rudolf Carnap, and Charles Morris. 1938. *International Encyclopedia of Unified Science.* Chicago: University of Chicago Press.

Novak, Joseph D. 1957. "A Comparison of Two Methods of Teaching a College General Botany Course." Ph.D. thesis, University of Minnesota.

——. 1958. "An Experimental Comparison of a Conventional and a Project Centered Method of Teaching a College General Botany Course." *Journal of Experimental Education,* 26, 217–230.

——. 1961. "An Approach to the Interpretation and Measurement of Problem Solving Ability." *Science Education, 45*(2), 122–131.

——. 1963. "A Preliminary Statement on Research in Science Education." *Journal of Research in Science Teaching, 1,* 3–9.

——. 1964. "Importance of Conceptual Schemes for Science Teaching." *The Science Teacher, 31*(6), 10.

——. 1965. "A Model for the Interpretation and Analysis of Concept Formation." *Journal of Research in Science Teaching, 3,* 72–83.

——. 1966. "The Role of Concepts in Science Teaching." In H. J. Klausmeier and C. W. Harris, *Analysis of Concept Learning.* New York: Academic Press.

——. 1969. "A Case Study of Curriculum Change—Science since PSSC." *School Science and Mathematics, 69,* 374–384.

——. 1970a. *The Improvement of Biology Teaching.* Indianapolis, New York: Bobbs-Merrill.

——. 1970b. "Relevant Research on Audio-Tutorial Methods." *School Science and Mathematics,* 777–784.

——. 1972a. "Audio-Tutorial Techniques for Individualized Science Instruction in the Elementary School." In H. J. Triezenberg, ed., *Individualized Science: Like It Is.* Washington, D.C.: NSTA.

——. 1972b. "The Use of Audio-Tutorial Methods in Elementary School Instruction." In Samuel N. Postlethwait, Joseph D. Novak, and Hal Murray, *The Audio-Tutorial Approach to Learning.* Minneapolis: Burgess.

——. 1972c. *Facilities for Secondary School Science Teaching: Evolving Patterns in Facilities and Programs.* Washington: NSTA.

——. 1974. *A Summary of Research in Science Education—1972.* Columbus, Ohio: ERIC Science, Mathematics, and Environmental Education Information Analysis Center.

——. Donald G. Ring, and Pinchas Tamir. 1971. "Interpretation of Research Findings in Terms of Ausubel's Theory and Implications for Science Education." *Science Education, 55*(4), 483–526.

Nunnaly, Jum C., Jr. 1967. *Psychometric Theory.* New York: McGraw-Hill.

Nussbaum, Joseph. 1972. "An Approach to Teaching and Assessment: The Earth Concept at the Second Grade Level." Ph.D. thesis, Cornell University.

Oakes, Merwin E. 1947. *Children's Explanations of Natural Phenomena.* Contributions to Education No. 926. New York: Teachers College, Columbia University.

O'Neill, George, and Nena O'Neill. 1973. *Open Marriage.* New York: Avon Books.

Pavlov, I. P. 1960. *Conditioned Reflexes: An Investigation of the Psyiological Activity of the Cerebral Cortex.* Trans. and ed. G. U. Anrep. Oxford: Oxford University Press, 1927. New York: Dover.

Pearson, Karl. 1900. *The Grammar of Science.* 2d ed. London: Adam and Charles Black.

Pella, Milton O., and Ronald E. Ziegler. 1967. "The Use of Static and Dynamic Mechanical Models in Teaching Aspects of the Theoretical Concept: The Particulate Nature of Matter." Technical Report no. 20. Madison, Wis.: Research and Development Center for Cognitive Learning.

Piaget, Jean. 1926. *The Language and Thought of the Child.* New York: Harcourt, Brace.

——. 1965. *The Child's Conception of Number.* New York: Norton.

———. 1952. "Autobiography." In E. G. Boring et al., *History of Psychology in Autobiography, Vol. 4.* Worcester, Mass.: Clark University Press.

———. 1957. *Logic and Psychology.* New York: Basic Books.

———. 1962. *Play, Dreams and Imitation in Childhood.* New York: Norton.

———. 1972. *Psychology and Epistemology.* New York: Viking.

———. Barbel Inhelder. 1967. *The Child's Conception of Space.* New York: Norton.

Polanyi, Michael. 1956. "Passion and Controversy in Science." *The Lancet, 270,* 921–925.

Popper, Karl R. 1934, 1959. *The Logic of Scientific Discovery.* New York: Basic Books.

Postlethwait, Samuel N. 1962. "The Use of Audio-Tape for a Multi-Faceted Approach to Teaching Botany." *American Journal of Botany, 49,* 681.

———. 1976. *Audio Tutorial Modules for College Biology.* New York: Wm. B. Saunders.

———, Joseph D. Novak, and Hal Murray. 1972. *The Audio-Tutorial Approach to Learning through Independent Study and Integrated Experience.* 3d ed. Minneapolis: Burgess.

Powers, William T. 1973. *The Control of Perception.* Chicago: Aldine.

Psychobiology: The Biological Basis of Behavior. 1967. Readings from *Scientific American* with introductions by James L. McGaugh, Norman M. Weinberger, and Richard E. Whalen. San Francisco and London: W. H. Freeman.

Reed, H. B. 1938. "Meaning as a Factor in Learning." *Journal of Educational Psychology, 29,* 419–443.

Reich, Charles A. 1970. *The Greening of America.* New York: A Bantam Book, Harper and Row.

Reimer, Everett. 1971. *School Is Dead: Alternatives in Education.* Garden City, N.Y.: Doubleday.

Ring, Donald G. 1969. "An Analysis of the Cognitive Influence of High School Chemistry Instruction on College Chemistry Achievement." Ph.D. thesis, Cornell University.

——— and Joseph D. Novak. 1971. "The Effects of Cognitive Structure Variables on Achievement in College Chemistry." *Journal of Research in Science Teaching, 8*(4), 325–333.

Rogers, Carl R. 1969. *Freedom to Learn.* Columbus, Ohio: Charles E. Merrill.

Roszak, Theodore. 1968, 1969. *The Making of a Counter Culture: Reflections on the Technocratic Society and Its Youthful Opposition.* Garden City, N.Y.: Doubleday.

———. 1972. *Where the Wasteland Ends: Politics and Transcendence in Postindustrial Society.* Garden City, N.Y.: Doubleday.

Rowell, Richard M. 1975. "Children's Concept of Natural Phenomena: Use of a Cognitive Mapping Approach to Describe These Concepts." Los Angeles: Paper presented at NARST Annual Convention, Session IX-D, March 19.

Schulz, Richard W. 1966. "The Role of Cognitive Organizers in the Facilitation of Concept Learning in Elementary School Science." Ph.D. thesis, Purdue University.

Schwab, Joseph J., and Paul F. Brandwein. 1962. *The Teaching of Science.* Cambridge, Harvard University Press.

Scriven, Michael. 1967. "The Methodology of Evaluation." In *Perspectives of*

Curriculum Evaluation, AERA Monograph Series on Curriculum and Evaluation, no. 1, pp. 39–84. Chicago: Rand McNally.

Senesh, Lawrence. 1973. *Our Working World*. Chicago: Science Research Associates.

Shulman, Lee S., and Evan R. Keislar, eds. 1966. *Learning by Discovery: A Critical Appraisal*. Chicago: Rand McNally.

Silberman, Charles E. 1970. *Crisis in the Classroom: The Remaking of American Education*. New York: Random House.

Simon, Herbert A. 1974. "How Big Is a Chunk?" *Science, 183*, 482–488.

Skinner, B. F. 1938. *The Behavior of Organisms: An Experimental Analysis*. New York and London: Appleton-Century.

———. 1968. *The Technology of Teaching*. New York: Appleton-Century-Crofts.

———. 1971. *Beyond Freedom and Dignity*. New York: A Bantam / Vintage Book, Knopf.

Smith, Eugene R., and Ralph W. Tyler. 1942. *Appraising and Recording Student Progress*. New York: Harper.

Smith, Karl U., and Margaret F. Smith. 1966. *Cybernetic Principles of Learning and Educational Design*. New York: Holt.

Smith, Mary H., ed. 1961. *Using Television in the Classroom*. Midwest Program on Airborne Television Instruction. New York, Toronto, London: McGraw-Hill.

Strike, Kenneth A. 1974. "On the Expressive Potential of Behavioral Language." *American Educational Research Journal, 11*(3), 103–120.

Strong, E. K. 1913. "The Effect of Time Interval upon Recognition Memory." *Psychology Review, 20*, 339–372.

Taba, Hilda. 1962. *Curriculum Development: Theory and Practice*. New York: Harcourt, Brace and World.

Talisayon, Vivian M. 1972. "Some Cognitive Variables in Meaningful Learning and Energy: A Study of Ausubelian Learning Model." Ph.D. thesis, Cornell University.

Tamir, Pinchas. 1968. "An Analysis of Certain Achievements and Attitudes of Cornell Students Enrolled in Introductory Biology with Special Reference to Their High School Preparation." Ph.D. thesis, Cornell University.

Taylor, Calvin W., ed. 1956. *The 1955 University of Utah Research Conference on Identification of Creative Scientific Talent*. Salt Lake City: University of Utah Press.

———, ed. 1958. *The Second (1957) University of Utah Research Conference on the Identification of Creative Scientific Talent*. Salt Lake City: University of Utah Press.

———, ed. 1959. *The Third (1959) University of Utah Research Conference on the Identification of Creative Scientific Talent*. Salt Lake City: University of Utah Press.

——— and Frank Barron, eds. 1963. *Scientific Creativity, Its Recognition and Development*. New York: Wiley. See especially Calvin W. Taylor, William R. Smith, and Brewster Ghiselin. "The Creative and Other Contributions of One Sample of Research Scientists." Pp. 53–76.

Taylor, Morris. 1966. "The Use of a Model for the Interpretation of Concept Formation in College Chemistry." Ph.D. thesis, Purdue University.

Teaching by Television. 1959. A Report from the Ford Foundation and the Fund for the Advancement of Education.

Terman, Lewis M., et al. 1925. *Mental and Physical Traits of a Thousand Gifted Children*. Genetic Studies of Genius, Vol. 1. Stanford: Stanford University Press.
—— and Melita Oden. 1947. *The Gifted Child Grows Up*. Genetic Studies of Genius, Vol. 4. Stanford: Stanford University Press.
—— and Melita Oden. 1959. *The Gifted Group at Mid-Life*. Genetic Studies of Genius, Vol. 5. Stanford: Stanford University Press.
Thatcher, David A. 1973. *Teaching, Loving, and Self-Directed Learning*. Pacific Palisades, Calif.: Goodyear.
Thier, Herbert D. 1965. "A Look at a First Grader's Understanding of Matter." *Journal of Research in Science Teaching, 3*, 84–89.
Thomas, Lawrence G., ed., and Herman G. Richey (editor for the Society). 1972. *Philosophical Redirection of Educational Research*. The Seventy-First Yearbook of the National Society for the Study of Education, pt. 1. Chicago: University of Chicago Press.
Thorsland, Martin N. 1971. "Formative Evaluation in an Audio-Tutorial Course with Emphasis on Intuitive and Analytic Problem Solving Approaches." Ph.D. thesis, Cornell University.
—— and Joseph D. Novak. 1974. "The Identification and Significance of Intuitive and Analytic Problem Solving Approaches among College Physics Students." *Science Education, 58*(2), 245–265.
Toffler, Alvin. 1970, 1971. *Future Shock*. New York: A Bantam Book, Random House.
——, ed. 1974. *Learning for Tomorrow: The Role of the Future in Education*. New York: Random House.
Torrance, E. Paul. 1962. *Guiding Creative Talent*. Englewood Cliffs, N.J.: Prentice-Hall.
——. 1972a. "Can We Teach Children to Think Creatively?" *Journal of Creative Behavior, 6*(2), 114–143.
——. 1972b. "Predictive Validity of the Torrance Tests of Creativity." *Journal of Creative Behavior, 6*(4), 236–252.
—— and W. R. Nash. 1974. "Creative Reading and the Questioning Abilities of Young Children." *Journal of Creative Behavior, 8*(1), 15–19.
Toulmin, Stephen. 1972. *Human Understanding, Vol. 1: The Collective Use and Evolution of Concepts*. Princeton: Princeton University Press.
—— and June Goodfield. 1963. *The Architecture of Matter*. London: Hutchinson.
—— and June Goodfield. 1965. *The Discovery of Time*. London: Hutchinson.
Travers, Robert N. W., ed. 1973. *Second Handbook of Research on Teaching*, Chicago: Rand McNally.
Triezenberg, Henry J., ed. 1972. *Individualized Science: Like It Is*. Washington: NSTA.
Tulving, Endel, and Wayne Donaldson, eds., 1972. *Organization of Memory*. New York: Academic Press.
Tunstall, Jeremy. 1974. "Open Road Scholars." *The Guardian*. Leeds, England. January 1.
Tyler, Ralph W. 1930. "What High School Pupils Forget." *Education Research Bulletin, 9*, 490–492.
——. 1949 (1969, 29th impression). *Basic Principles of Curriculum and Instruction*. Chicago and London: University of Chicago Press.

Uznadze, D. 1966. *The Psychology of Set.* New York: Consultants Bureau.

Vygotsky, Lev S. 1962. *Thought and Language.* Trans. and ed. E. Hanfmann and G. Vakar. Cambridge: MIT Press.

Wagner, Sharon K. 1971. "A Study of Second Grade Children's Responses on Picture and Interview Questions Dealing with Concepts of Solids, Liquids and Gases." M.S. thesis, Cornell University.

Wallach, Michael A., and Nathan Kogan. 1965. *Modes of Thinking in Young Children.* New York: Holt, Rinehart and Winston.

Walters, Louis. 1965. "Ninth vs. Tenth Grade Biology—A Follow-Up Study." *Journal of Research in Science Teaching, 3,* 230–234.

Watson, James D. 1968. *The Double Helix.* New York: A Signet Book, The New American Library.

Wesney, Joseph. 1977. "An Analysis of Factors Influencing Achievement in Elementary College Physics." Ph.D. thesis, Cornell University.

Whitman, Janet C. 1975. "An Approach to the Evaluation of Selected Spontaneous and Scientific Concepts and Misconceptions of Second Grade Children." M.S. thesis, Cornell University.

Whorf, Benjamin Lee. 1956. *Language, Thought and Reality: Selected Writings of Benjamin Lee Whorf.* Ed. with an introduction by John B. Carroll. Cambridge: MIT Press.

Wiener, Norbert. 1948. *Cybernetics.* New York: Wiley.

———. 1954. *The Human Use of Human Beings.* 2d ed. Garden City, N.Y.: Doubleday.

Winer, B. J. 1962. *Statistical Principles in Experimental Design.* New York· McGraw-Hill.

Wittrock, M. C. 1963. "Response Mode in the Programming of Kinetic Molecular Theory Concepts." *Journal of Educational Psychology, 54(2),* 89.

Index

Library of Congress Cataloging in Publication Data
(For library cataloging purposes only)

Novak, Joseph Donald.
  A theory of education.

  Bibliography: p.
  Includes index.
  1. Learning, Psychology of. 2. Education—Philosophy. I. Title.
LB1051.N68   370.1   77-3123
ISBN 0-8014-1104-1